Psych. Monograph

Suppl. Guide for W-B
Form 1

Kitzinger
Blumberg

'75¢

THE MEASUREMENT

of

ADULT INTELLIGENCE

BY

DAVID WECHSLER

*Chief Psychologist, Bellevue Psychiatric Hospital. Assistant
Clinical Professor of Medical Psychology, New York
University College of Medicine. Lecturer, School
of Education, New York University.*

THIRD EDITION

BALTIMORE

THE WILLIAMS & WILKINS COMPANY

1944

First Edition, April, 1939
Second Edition, October, 1941
Reprinted, February, 1943
Third Edition, April, 1944
Reprinted, April, 1945
Reprinted, July, 1946
Reprinted, November, 1946
Reprinted, October, 1947
Reprinted, September, 1948
Reset and Reprinted, July, 1949
Reprinted, February, 1950
Reprinted, December, 1950
Reprinted, January, 1952

COMPOSED AND PRINTED AT THE
WAVERLY PRESS, INC.
FOR
THE WILLIAMS & WILKINS COMPANY
BALTIMORE, MD., U. S. A.

TO
FREDA

PREFACE TO THIRD EDITION

In preparing this third, "war" edition of the Measurement of Adult Intelligence my primary aim has been to increase the book's usefulness to those engaged in the field of applied psychometrics. I have borne in mind particularly the military applications of the Wechsler-Bellevue Scale, as it is now being used by some of the armed services of our own country as well as of Great Britain. Accordingly, most of the changes made will be found in the chapters dealing with *Clinical applications* and the *Problem of mental deterioration*. These chapters have been somewhat extended and in part rewritten. The table of 'signs' for different clinical entities has been completely revised and a new quantitative method for determining mental deterioration elaborated. Both of these presentations should be of value not only in the field of neuropsychiatric diagnosis but also in questions connected with rehabilitation.

In addition to the above, some changes have been made in the scoring of certain subtests of the Scale. The effect of these changes will be to increase the I.Q. range at the upper end of the Scale, without however altering significantly the norms for the population as a whole. In the case of one or two tests (noticeably, the Arithmetic) the change has necessitated slight alteration in the scoring of some of the subtest items. Little alteration has otherwise been made in the substance of the text. One table and two figures which were not particularly useful have been omitted and two new tables which should be of immediate and practical value added. Also added is a bibliography of most of the important studies with the Weschsler-Bellevue Scale, published up to March 1944. For editorial perusal of the text I am indebted to Miss Ventura Smith, psychologist to the Westport, Conn., public schools, who not only read the page proofs but was also kind enough to prepare a new index.

DAVID WECHSLER.

April, 1944

CONTENTS

CONTENTS

PART I

THE NATURE AND CLASSIFICATION OF INTELLIGENCE

CHAPTER 1

THE NATURE OF INTELLIGENCE

Some years ago when interest in intelligence tests was at its height, a prominent psychologist is reported to have answered an inquiry as to what he meant by intelligence by saying that it is what intelligence tests measure. A similar attitude would not be maintained today by any considerable number of psychologists. But the continued failure of authors of intelligence tests to declare explicitly what they understand by general intelligence would almost compel one to assume that they still maintain this circular position. The lay person is entirely justified in asking, as he does, "How do you know that your test measures intelligence?", and every author of a test should be ready to answer the question, however imperfectly. Obviously, the more data the psychologist has, the easier his task will be. But he will be able to make no answer at all unless there is some provisional agreement between him and his challenger as to what they are willing to call intelligence, or at least intelligent behavior. We shall, therefore, begin by giving our own definition of intelligence and then consider its relation to the more important current theories on the subject.

Intelligence is the aggregate or global capacity of the individual to act purposefully, to think rationally and to deal effectively with his environment. It is global[1] because it characterizes the individual's behavior as a whole; it is an aggregate because it is composed of elements or abilities which, though not entirely independent, are qualitatively differentiable. By measurement of these abilities, we ultimately evaluate intelligence. But intelligence is not identical with the mere sum of these abilities, however inclusive. There are three important reasons for this: (1) The ultimate products of intelligent behavior are not only a function of the number of abilities or their quality but also of the way in which they are combined, that is, upon their configuration. (2) Factors other than intellectual ability, for example, those of drive and incentive, enter into intelligent behavior. (3) Finally, while different orders of intelligent behavior may require varying degrees of intellectual ability, an excess of any given ability may add relatively little to the effectiveness

[1] In the adopted French sense of the term, "pertaining to or embracing the totality of a group of items or categories." Cf. Oxford Dictionary.

3

of the behavior as a whole. It would seem that, so far as general intelligence is concerned, intellectual ability as such merely enters as a necessary minimum. Thus, to act intelligently, one must be able to recall numerous items—i.e., have a retentive memory. But beyond a certain point this ability will not help much in coping with life situations successfully. This is true of even more important capacities, such as the ability to reason, particularly when specialized. The unusual reasoning abilities of the mathematician are more highly correlated with the thing that we ultimately measure as intelligence than sheer memory is, but possession of this ability is no surety that behavior as a whole will be very intelligent in the sense above defined. Every reader will be able to recall persons of high intellectual ability in some particular field, whom they would unhesitatingly characterize as below average in general intelligence.

Although intelligence is no mere sum of intellectual abilities, the only way we can evaluate it quantitatively is by the measurement of the various aspects of these abilities. There is no contradiction here unless we insist upon the identity of general intelligence and intellectual ability. We do not, for example, identify electricity with our modes of measuring it. Our measurements of electricity consist of quantitative records of its chemical, thermal and magnetic effects. But these effects are not identical with the "stuff" which produced them. General intelligence, like electricity, may be regarded as a kind of energy. We do not know what the ultimate nature of this energy is, but as in the case of electricity, we know it by the things it does or, better, by the things it enables us to do—such as making appropriate associations between events, drawing correct inferences from propositions, understanding the meaning of words, solving mathematical problems or building bridges. These are the effects of intelligence in the same sense as chemical dissociation, heat, and magnetic fields are the effects of electricity, but psychologists prefer the term *mental products*. We know intelligence by what it enables us to do.

Professor Thorndike was the first to develop clearly the idea that the measurement of intelligence consists essentially of some qualitative and quantitative evaluation of mental productions in terms of their number, and the excellence or speed with which they are effected. That is the only function which any measure of intelligence can possibly have. Abilities are merely these mental products sorted into different classes or types of operation. Thus, the class of operations which consists of effectually associating one fact with another and recalling either or both at an appropriate time is called learning; that of drawing inferences or educing relations between them, reasoning ability; that of merely retaining them, memory. The older psychologists were inclined to use a relatively small number of such classes based primarily on the type of mental process supposedly involved. More recently psychologists have begun to emphasize not only the processes but the content as well. They speak not only of memory but of auditory memory; not only of reasoning but of abstract, verbal or arithmetical reasoning. In a like manner some psychologists have begun to distinguish various kinds of intelligence. Thorndike, for example, has suggested subdividing intelligence into three main types: (1) abstract or verbal intelligence, involving facility in the use of symbols; (2) practical intelligence, involving facility in manipulating objects; (3) social intelligence, involving facility in dealing with human beings. The significant thing about this classification is that it emphasizes *what* a person can do as well as *how* he can do it. This distinction between function and content is fully justified by experimental evidence. The rating which an individual attains on an intelligence examination depends to a considerable degree on the type of test used. His score on a test made up largely of verbal items may differ significantly from that obtained on a test involving questions of social comprehension and still more from another test made up of items involving predominantly psychomotor reactions and the perception of spatial relationships.

Though test results show that the rating which an individual attains will frequently depend upon the type of intelligence test used, they also show a contrary tendency. When large numbers of individuals are examined with a variety of intelligence tests, those who make high scores on any one of them tend to make high scores on the remaining ones; and the same holds for those who make low and intermediate scores. This dual characteristic of human abilities—their specificity on the one hand and interdependence on the other—has long been appreciated by psychologists. But unfortunately, the reaction to this observation was not to accept it as a fact, but rather as a logical dilemma from which one had to escape. The older writers tried to escape it by accepting the scholastic formulated faculties; the modern ones, by their theory of independent unit or group traits. But more than 30 years ago Professor Carl Spearman put an end to the dilemma by showing, through rigorous mathematical proof, that all intellectual abilities could be expressed as functions of two factors, one a *general* or intellectual factor common to every ability, and another a *specific* factor, specific to any particular ability and "in every case different from that of all others". This proof first appeared as a brief article in the American Journal of Psychology (1904). It has since been subjected to a great amount of discussion, criticism and experimental investigation. We cannot enter into all this here, but can only indicate our own position by saying that Professor Spearman's generalized proof of the two-factor theory of human abilities constitutes one of the great discoveries of psychology.

As has often been the case in the history of science, the proof of the two-factor theory, in addition to being a discovery, was also an explicit formulation of an hypothesis which workers in the field had unknowingly been assuming for some time. The fact is, that from the day psychologists began to use a series of tests for measuring intelligence, they necessarily assumed the existence of a general or common factor. This becomes immediately apparent if one recalls what the actual contents of intelligence tests are. They consist of various intellectual tasks which we call tests that require the subject to do such things as to define words, reproduce facts from memory, solve problems in arithmetic and recognize likenesses and differences. The variety of tasks used, their difficulty and manner of presentation varies with the type of scale employed. But so far as measuring intelligence is concerned, these specific tasks are only a means to an end. Their object is not to test a person's memory, judgment or reasoning ability, but to measure something which it is hoped will emerge from the sum total of the subject's performance, namely, his general intelligence. One of the greatest contributions of Binet was his intuitive assumption that in the selection of tests, it made little difference what sort of tasks you used, provided that in some way it was a measure of the child's general intelligence. This explains in part the large variety of tasks employed in the original Binet scale. It also accounts for the fact why certain types of items which were found useful at one age level, were not necessarily employed at other age levels. More important than either of these details is the fact that for all practical purposes, the combining of a variety of tests into a single measure of intelligence, *ipso facto*, presupposes a certain functional unity or equivalence between them.

The functional equivalence of the test items, an assumption implicit not only in the Binet Scale but in any scale which is composed of a variety or pool of intellectual tasks, is absolutely necessary for the validation of the arithmetic employed in arriving at a final measure of intelligence. This arithmetic consists, first, of assigning some numerical value to every correct response; secondly, of adding the partial credits so obtained into a simple sum; and, thirdly, of treating equal sums as equivalent, irrespective of the nature of the test items which contribute to the total. For example, every test passed on the Stanford-Binet (between ages 3 and 10) contributes two months to the mental age (M.A.) score of the subject, irrespective as to whether the test passed calls for a repetition of a series of digits, the copying of a square, the definition of a word, or the correct reply to a common sense question. To all intents and purposes, therefore, the simple addition of these groups necessarily assumes an arithmetical equivalence of the test items so combined. If the different tests were taken to represent generically different entities, one could no more add the values assigned to them in order to obtain an M.A. total than one could add 2 dogs, 3 cats and 4 elephants, and expect the unqualified answer of 9. That, of course, does not mean that their addition is impossible. If instead of being concerned with the characteristics of the dog, the cat and the elephant, which differentiate them from one another, we restrict our interest to those which they all have in common, we can say that 2 dogs, 3 cats and 4 elephants make 9 animals. The reason we can get an answer of 9 here is because dogs, cats and elephants are in fact all animals. The addition would no longer be possible if for cats we were to substitute turnips.

The same principle is involved when we attempt to add up the number of tests correctly passed on an intelligence scale into a simple sum. The reason we can add together scores obtained from tests requiring such seemingly different abilities as those involved in solving arithmetic problems, repeating digits and defining words, is because they are in fact alike in certain ways. They are alike in that they are all measures of general intelligence. This means that all must have a common characteristic, or to use the current psychological term, a common factor. Professor Spearman has shown that such a common factor not only has to be assumed in any attempt to measure general intelligence by means of tests, but has demonstrated that its presence can always be revealed through appropriate statistical procedures. The common factor turns out to be a recurrent mathematical quantity which can be "extricated" from the tests by special correlational methods,—a quantity which he has called "g". Just what "g" is psychologically and to what extent it may be identified with general intelligence, are still matters of speculation and dispute. As will be seen shortly, the present writer is far from being in full agreement either with Professor Spearman's concept of general intelligence or even with his views regarding the best mode of measuring it, but as regards the demonstration of the existence of "g" as a common factor, there seems to be no possibility of doubt. Psychometrics, without it, loses its basic prop.

A few words as to the nature of "g". First and foremost, it is a purely mathematical quantity, "originally intended to explain correlations that exist between the most diverse sorts of cognitive performance", which recurs in all data obtainable from measures of intellectual ability. In this respect it may be said to be similar, or at least comparable, to some of the constants met with in physical and more particularly atomic measurements. But "g" is also more specific than that. It is evidently a kind of something that must be posited to explain the effects of mental work or the operations of the mind. It is, therefore, a kind of energy, or more correctly, a measure of the same. This is the second and more general interpretation of "g". Combining these two conceptions, we may say that "g" is a psychomathematical quantity which measures the mind's capacity to do intellectual work.

Everybody will agree that the capacity to do intellectual work is a necessary and important sign of general intelligence. The question is whether it is the only important or paramount factor. In this writer's opinion it is not. Professor Spearman seemingly thinks it is, although on this point he has failed to declare himself unequivocally. On the one hand, he states, "Such a factor as this ["g"] can scarcely be given the title of intelligence at all." But after having said this, he devotes several chapters[2] in an attempt to prove that the best tests of intelligence are precisely those which contain the largest amounts of "g". If this is so, then for all practical purposes, "g" and general intelligence may be said to be equivalent. This equivalence, indeed, is implied by the mathematical relationship of the "g" and "s" factors in the two-factor theory. According to this relationship an intelligence scale made up of a large number of tests especially rich in "g" would in the end be a measure of "g" exclusively.[3] In the writer's opinion, such a scale would not be a very good measure of general intelligence because it would eliminate a number of abilities essential for effective behavior.

The view that other salient factors besides "g" enter into measures of intelligence is based on several sources of evidence. The first is clinical. We know from experience that individuals attaining identical scores on intelligence tests cannot always be classified in the same way. This is perhaps most obvious in cases where test results call for practical action, as for example when they are used as a basis for deciding

[2] Spearman, C.: *The Abilities of Man.* New York, 1927.
[3] For, by pooling such tests, the "g" factor (being common) becomes cumulative, whereas the specific factors (being incidental) tend to cancel each other.

whether or not a subject should be committed to an institution for mental defectives. In such cases the test results, e.g., a Binet I.Q., cannot be used as the sole criterion. One child with an I.Q. of 75 may be definitely defective while another with an identical I.Q., or indeed one 5 or 10 points less, be far from so classifiable. Of course, the objection may be made that the classification of mental deficiency is in part a social diagnosis. But is not the capacity for social adaptation also a sign of intelligence? Should not the capacity to avoid mischief and the ability to work persistently at a task, enter into one's definition of general intelligence just as well as the ability to define words, and perceive analogies? The clinician's answer has always been "yes", and by so saying, he has implicitly assumed that there are other factors besides the intellective "g" which enter into intelligent behavior. Hitherto he has been unable to demonstrate their existence experimentally. In recent years, however, thanks to new correlational techniques, especially the method of factorial analysis as developed by Professor Thurstone in this country, a beginning has been made. Of particular importance has been the work of W. P. Alexander whose monograph on *Intelligence, Concrete and Abstract*[4] is in many ways fundamental.

Alexander set himself the problem of testing experimentally the evidence for and against the main theories now currently favored in psychological circles. The first of these is Professor Spearman's *two-factor theory* which we have already referred to. The other is the *unique traits theory*, according to which intelligence involves several abilities or factors, each *independent* of one another. More specifically, his investigation took the form of an experimental study to determine whether test results supported the view that "practical" and "verbal" intelligence were each distinct and independent capacities, or the view of Spearman according to which both were essentially the same in that they were not independent capacities but only differed with respect to their non-intellective or specific factors.

Alexander's findings were extremely interesting. They confirmed Spearman's main contention that there was one and only one common factor in all measures of intelligence and, at the same time, showed that this factor alone is not sufficient to explain the total correlational variance which existed between the tests used to measure intelligence. In addition to the common factor there are seemingly other broad factors which, while not showing the same generality, are nevertheless recurrent in a significant number of abilities which form subgroups or "com-

[4] *Brit. J. Pyschol.*, 1935.

munal clusters". The individual tests by which these abilities are measured contain a common factor of their own with respect to which they function in much the same way. Alexander has termed abilities involved in tests showing such similarity of function *functional unities*. Thus, verbal ability is one functional unity, practical ability another, and so on. But while each of these functional unities requires a separate factor to take care of its respective contribution to any global measure of intelligence, they are nevertheless "definitely related", that is, correlated with one another.[5] This means that they cannot be unitary traits in the sense implied by the unique traits theory. On the other hand, neither can they be considered as specific factors in the sense required by Spearman's two-factor theory. For, these factors, unlike the "s" factors, actually contribute a considerable amount to the correlation variance of the test composites of which they form a part.

Another important conclusion suggested by Alexander's investigation was that in order to account for the complete intercorrelation variance found among any large battery of intelligence tests one has to posit other factors in addition to the purely intellectual ones. After eliminating the general factor ("g"), and such other factors[6] as were contributed by the above described "functional unities", Alexander found that a considerable amount of his total intercorrelational variance was still unaccounted for. In addition to these factors there were apparently certain other supplementary global ones which, though not directly measurable, nevertheless contributed significant amounts to the total variance of the observed data. These latter factors he has provisionally labeled "X" and "Z". They cover such items as the subject's interest in doing the tasks set, his persistence in attacking them and his zest and desire to succeed,—items which might more familiarly be described as temperamental or personality factors, but which nevertheless must be recognized as important in all actual measures of intelligence. For this reason, one might appropriately refer to them as the non intellective-factors or, more specifically, as the *non-intellective factors in* general intelligence.[7]

---

[5] Thus verbal ability correlates with practical ability to the extent of .50.

[6] These were primarily the factors "v", common to tests involving verbal ability, and "f" common to tests purporting to measure practical ability.

[7] For further evidence as to the existence of these factors, see D. Wechsler: The non-intellective factors in general intelligence. *J. Abnorm. and Soc. Psychol.*, 1943, **38**: 100–104.

It thus appears that the entity or quantity which we are able to measure by intelligence tests is not a simple quantity. Certainly it is not something which can be expressed by one single factor alone, say "g", whether you define it in its most general terms as mental energy, the ability to educe relations or merely as the intellective factor. Intelligence is all this and yet something more. It is the ability to utilize this energy or to exercise this ability in contextual situations,—situations that have content and purpose as well as form and meaning. To concede as much is to admit that any practical definition of intelligence must be fundamentally a biological one in the widest sense of the term. That has been the hypothesis assumed in the construction of the intelligence scales that are to be described in the ensuing pages. We think that they measure general intelligence in the sense defined above. We shall not, however, claim that they measure all that goes to make up general intelligence, because no tests at present are capable of doing it. The only thing we can ask of an intelligence scale is that it measures sufficient portions of intelligence to enable us to use it as a fairly reliable index of the individual's global capacity.

It is important to realize that intelligence tests do not and cannot be expected to measure all of intelligence, but it is of equal importance to emphasize that they measure a great deal more than the delimited capacities to which contemporaneous theory seems desirous of restricting them. Intelligence tests measure more than mere learning ability or reasoning ability or even general intellectual ability; in addition, they inevitably measure a number of other capacities which cannot be defined as either purely cognitive or intellective,—abilities heavily loaded with factors like "X" and "Z", the non-intellective factors mentioned above. Hitherto, authors of intelligence scales when recognizing this situation, looked upon these factors as disturbing elements and tried as far as possible to eliminate them. Unfortunately, experience has shown that the more successful one is in excluding these factors, the less effective are the resulting tests as measures of general intelligence. What are needed are not tests from which the non-intellective factors have been eliminated (even if that were possible), but, on the contrary, tests in which these factors are clearly present and objectively appraisable. The performance tests described in Part II of this volume are an attempt in this direction. They are only a beginning; but the results already obtained show that tests of verbal ability, abstract reasoning and the like when used alone in a general intelligence examination give only an incomplete picture of the individual's capacity for effective adjustment and achievement.

We have concluded above that intelligence tests cannot measure all of intelligence. We must further qualify this conclusion by the statement that at different ages they measure different portions of it. In general it might be stated that as the individual grows older our tests become less and less an effective measure of his global intelligence. The failure to realize this has led to a great deal of confusion in interpreting test results, particularly when used for the evaluation of adult intelligence. The difficulty is most acutely apparent when intelligence levels are given in the now almost universal notation of mental age. Most psychologists are aware of the fact that when an adult of 30 scores a mental age of 12, and a child of 12 scores a mental age of 12, their intelligence is not identical, yet there does not seem to be any general understanding as to why they are not identical. If what we have said above is correct, the answer is not far to find. The basic reason a mental age of 12 at 12 does not mean the same thing as a mental age of 12 at 30, is that the measured abilities and hence the M.A. scores represent different portions of the subjects' respective total intelligence. At age 12 the tests are capable of tapping far more of the individual's capacities than at 30.[8] How much more we cannot say without further investigation. But even if the differences were small it would challenge our entire present method of defining at least adult intelligence in terms of M.A. levels. The same observation may be made as regards intelligence quotients with even greater force, because as we shall have occasion to see, the I.Q. concept as a mental age score divided by a chronological age score, presupposes a constancy of relationship between the two, which in point of fact does not exist.

Sufficient has been said to show that the definition of general intelligence, far from being a mere theoretical question, is one which enters immediately into any practical attempt at measurement. It is particularly important when we come to measuring adult intelligence, because we are at once confronted with a wider range of criteria against which our definition may be checked. But before this checking can be done, the tests themselves must of course have been available. The scales presented in the following pages are an attempt to supply this. The extent of the present need for them will form the content of our next chapter.

[8] It should be added that the same might be said of age 6 as compared to age 12.

CHAPTER 2

NEED FOR AN ADULT INTELLIGENCE TEST

Although the earliest investigations in the field of psychometrics were made largely with adult subjects, the great bulk of the test data which now forms the basis of intelligence scales, has been derived from the examination of school children. The reasons for this are several. Perhaps the most important is the relative ease with which one may obtain young subjects; children are nearly always available through the schools. Another is the fact that it is generally much easier to devise children's tests than adults' tests, both from the point of view of the definition of ability measured, as well as the likelihood of interest and appeal. Finally, there is the fact that the results obtained by the testing of children lend themselves more readily to concrete applications.

Demonstration of the value of intelligence tests for children has come from two important fields. The first of these is the school. From the very beginning it was apparent that intelligence tests, particularly of the Binet type, correlated very highly with scholastic achievement. A well trained psychologist after an hour of standardized testing could often more accurately differentiate between the superior, the average, and the dull than the teacher who may have had the children under daily observation for a period of several months. Here, then, was an instrument that could be of great value in the matter of proper grading of school children, particularly at the outset of their training. Naturally psychologists and educators who were at all interested in tests, devoted a large part of their energies to the development of these important possibilities.

The other field in which intelligence tests early demonstrated their usefulness was in the diagnosis of mental deficiency. Tests supplied for the first time a quantitative measure of the degree of mental defect. And here the tests seemed not only applicable to the diagnosis of retardation among children, but for the classification of defective adults as well. The fact that the tests were originally standardized on children, was looked upon by those who applied them as no great limitation upon their usefulness. Indeed, because the tests made possible a comparison of adult functioning with that of children, they offered the clinician a new basis for classifying degrees of deficiency. We refer, of course, to the definition of degrees of deficiency in terms of mental age levels.

For the first ten years after their publication, the Binet tests and those of their type, were primarily used in the examination of children or defectives. Binet, himself, seemingly intended them to be used only with children since the scale was originally standardized only through the age of 15. The possibility of using intelligence tests with adults, however, was immediately apparent, and a number of efforts were made in this direction. The earliest of these confined themselves largely to the testing of special groups of adults, such as inmates of prisons or mental hospitals. But it was really not until 1917 when the U. S. Army enlisted the help of psychologists for the purpose of classifying the soldier draft, that the intelligence tests were tried out on a large scale on normal adults. In the meantime, Terman had brought out the Stanford Revision of the Binet Tests, the extension of which included tests at adult levels. Unfortunately, the urgency of examining large numbers of individuals in a relatively short time made it impossible to use this scale to any considerable degree. To meet the practical need for group examinations, the psychologists assigned to the task devised the now justly famous Army Alpha and Beta group tests. Given as they were to more than a million men, they constituted the most thoroughly standardized group-tests yet devised. The Alpha test, in the opinion of the writer, still remains the best instrument of this type. But its merit is primarily to enable the examiner to make a rapid examination and subsequent classification of a large number of subjects in a short time. It does not furnish means for an individual diagnosis.[1]

Following World War I a number of new adult group tests, mostly modeled after the Army Alpha, were devised. Little was done, however, to restandardize the individual intelligence examinations although one of the most outstanding results of the army experience with those available was their general inadequacy for use with adults. In the case of the Stanford-Binet, a special study on some 400 unselected subjects revealed that the mental age adult norm was some three years lower than that given by Terman in his book. Thus the average mental age of the adults[2] examined in the army turn out to be 13.08 years instead of 16 years as originally claimed. Approximately the same results were obtained with performance tests on the same group of individuals.

[1] Diagnosis of individual cases—such as of soldiers who were referred for discharge or to development battalions—was nearly always made on the basis of one or another of the individual examinations then available, namely, the Stanford-Binet, Yerkes Point Scale, Army Performance, etc.

[2] Males ages 21 to 30.

In view of the fact that the army data were derived from a much better statistical sample of adult population than that of the original Stanford-Binet standardization, one might have supposed that the new norms made available by them would have replaced the old ones; but this was not the case. Psychologists have from time to time protested against using the old norms. In some instances they have gone to the extent of discarding 16 years and substituting 14 or 15 years, as the denominator for calculating adult I.Q.'s. In other instances, they have reinterpreted the significance of the I.Q. when calculated on the original basis, as for example, by considering an I.Q. of 88 rather than 100 as average for the adult population. But such has been the wide acceptance of the Stanford-Binet norms, that in spite of the cumulative evidence as regards their inaccuracy when applied to the measurement of adult intelligence, their use for this purpose has continued without much abatement. It is true that within the last year Terman and Merrill[3] have published a thorough revision of the Stanford-Binet in which 15 years is used as the average adult mental age. Unfortunately, these tests were again not standardized on adults, that is, on individuals over 18 years. The new Terman-Merrill like the old Stanford-Binet still leaves unanswered the question of the "true" mental age of the average adult.

If we inquire why the Binet and other children's scales have continued to be used for the testing of adults, in spite of the criticism that has been leveled against this practice, the answer is not far to find. No better instruments were on hand. Up to very recently there has been no suitable individual adult examination available. Moreover the children's tests did meet a need, however imperfectly. Finally, and this is of peculiar interest, the continued employment of these tests instead of making their users more alert to the tests' inadequacies seemingly made them more obtuse to their shortcomings. No doubt the great difficulties which the standardization of a new adult scale presented, also had something to do with this feeling. But whatever the reasons, the continued use of children's scales for adult testing has no scientific justification. The scales now in use fail to meet some of the most elementary requirements which psychologists ordinarily set themselves when standardizing a test. The first deficiency is that they have not been standardized on a sufficient number of cases. Indeed most of them were never standardized on any adults at all. To see how serious this situation is, we list below the *individual* tests most commonly used in this country and the number of adults on whom the needed norms

---

[3] Terman and Merrill: *Measuring Intelligence.* Boston, 1937.

were ostensibly computed when the tests were first standardized. (See Table 1.)

It thus appears that with the possible exception of the Army Performance none of the currently used scales meets the very first prerequisite of a valid intelligence examination, namely the condition of having been standardized on a sufficiently large number of cases. The seriousness of this failing is shown by the fact that no published studies with these tests have confirmed the norms which the authors posited for them. Most of these studies, it is true, were again made with relatively small numbers of subjects, but in every one involving populations of any considerable size, as for example the population sample of the soldiers of the U. S. Army, used to obtain M.A. equivalents for the Alpha and Beta tests, the results showed that the original Stanford-Binet

TABLE 1

TEST	NUMBER OF ADULTS
Stanford-Revision of the Binet........................	62*
Kuhlmann-Binet.......................................	Not specified
Yerkes Point Scale.....................................	73
Pintner-Paterson Performance.........................	0
Army Performance Scale...............................	260
Terman-Merrill Revision of the Stanford-Binet...........	0

* Terman speaks of the tests having been given to 150 migratory workers but the scores obtained from these subjects do not seem to have been used in the final standardization. See Terman: *The Measurement of Intelligence.* Boston, 1916. Pp. 54–55.

norms needed immediate discarding. According to these norms no less than 34 per cent of the "flower" of American manhood would have had to be classified as mental defectives[4]. Such a number is palpably absurd, but perhaps no more astounding than some of the earlier estimates of the incidence of mental deficiency among delinquents, which ran as high as 90 per cent.[5]

A more obvious shortcoming of intelligence examinations now used for adults, and one that has often been noted, is the unsuitability of much of the material that forms part of the examinations. Many of the test items do not seem to be of the sort that would either interest or

[4] Using 16 years as an adult denominator and an I.Q. of below 75 as indicative of mental deficiency. The figure 34 per cent is derived from the data furnished in table 54, *Army Memoirs*, p. 391. This is for English-speaking Whites. For the colored population, Southern drafts, the per cent of defectives by the same criterion is almost doubled.

[5] Pintner, R.: *Intelligence Testing.* New York, 1931, 2nd ed., pp. 375–377.

appeal to an adult. The early lay critics of intelligence tests emphasized this fact particularly. Although their criticism was often exaggerated, it contained more than a grain of truth. To ask the average adult to say as many words as he can think of in three minutes, or to make a sentence of the words *to asked paper my teacher correct I my*, and assume that he will be either interested or impressed, is expecting too much. The average child generally responds to such questions as a matter of course. The average adult will, as often as not, start wondering as to what possible purpose or meaning the tests can have. Such remarks as, "That's baby stuff," "Why do I have to do this?" and "I never had that in school," are very common, particularly among the less alert subjects. Asking the ordinary housewife to furnish you with a rhyme to the words, "day", "cat", and "mill", or an ex-army sergeant to give you a sentence with the words, "boy", "river", "ball", is not particularly apt to evoke either interest or respect.

Apart from the matter of interest and appeal, there are other serious objections to the type of material generally employed in children's tests which make them unsuitable for adult use. One of them is the fact that credit for correctness of response so often depends upon the individual's capacity to manipulate words (or objects), rather than upon comprehension of their meaning. Thus, a subject asked to make a sentence of the words, *for the started an we country early at hour* might think that the main idea to be apprehended, and therefore expressed, is that somebody started somewhere at an early hour. Nevertheless, "We started early at an hour for the country", is marked as a failure.[6] The subject must say, (to be credited with a correct response), "We started for the country at an early hour", or at least, "At an early hour we started for the country". Unfortunately, many items on current scales call for an accuracy of precisely this sort.

Another limitation to the use of tests on adults, originally standardized on children, is that many of these tests lay altogether too much emphasis on speed as compared to accuracy.[7] This does not imply that speed of response is not important in measuring intelligence. Actually there is a high correlation between speed and accuracy. Indeed, in the case of children at least, it would seem that of the two, speed alone is often the better measure in the sense that it correlates higher with other global ratings of intelligence. In the case of adults, however,

[6] Cf. Terman, L.: *The Measurement of Intelligence*, p. 218.

[7] This emphasis, to be sure, varies widely in different scales. In the Binet, for example, speed of response is of secondary importance, but in most performance tests it is given considerable weight.

general experience would indicate that speed alone is not the better measure. This is particularly true for older subjects who do badly on nearly all "speed" tests. A number of explanations have been offered for this fact. The one which is of particular pertinence to our discussion is the possible influence of the different attitude which adults take toward set tasks or set situations.

When you tell a child, "Put these blocks together as fast as you can," the chances are he will accept the instructions at their face value. One cannot be so sure of a similar acceptance in the case of the adult. He might be a type of individual characterizing the attitude, "look before you leap", or "first try to figure the thing out". In that case his attitude might only serve to get him a lower intelligence rating. On many performance tests the difference of a few seconds in the time taken to complete a set task often reduces a subject's score considerably.[8] Facts like these do not, of course, imply that time scores cannot be used in testing adult intelligence, but they do show that their evaluation and interpretation may be considerably different from that which we place upon them in the case of children.

The foregoing considerations illustrate some of the more important reasons why tests standardized on children cannot be used on adults. We have yet to mention the most fundamental of all: the fact that adult intelligence cannot be evaluated in the same terms as those generally employed in defining juvenile intelligence. We refer to the definition of intelligence in terms of mental age (M.A.) levels and mental age scores. The concept of mental age, fundamental as it is to the definition of juvenile intelligence, may be grossly misleading when applied to the definition of adult mental capacity. A mental age score of 12 years, for example, in a child of twelve does not represent the same level of mental ability that it would in the case of a man of forty. Even more misleading is the use of the M.A. as a basis for calculating adults' indices of brightness (I.Q.'s) by methods identical to those employed in the case of children. The continued use of such methods by psychologists is due in part to the fact that children's tests have continued to be their main instruments for measuring adult intelligence, and in part to the fact that the significance and implications of the M.A. and I.Q. are still not fully understood by many. In view of the important rôles which the M.A. and I.Q. play in all contemporaneous attempts at evaluating and measuring intelligence, the criticisms we have just made are obviously very serious. It is important to discover whether they are justified and, if so, to see how they can be remedied.

[8] For example, completing the Seguin Form Board in 10 seconds earns the subject an M.A. score of 15 years; in 13 seconds, an M.A. score of only 13 years.

CHAPTER 3

THE CONCEPTS OF MENTAL AGE AND INTELLIGENCE QUOTIENT

The term mental age, as now used in psychology, was first coined by Binet, who offered it as a way of defining different degrees or levels of intelligence. The novel point was that he proposed to define these levels in terms of the measured abilities of children at different ages. This presupposed that intellectual ability could be measured and that it increased progressively with age. Both of these assumptions have proved correct. Binet's great contributions, however, were more specific. (1) He devised a series of graded intellectual tasks whereby intelligence could in fact be effectively measured; (2) he described a mode of evaluating the results in terms of age units such that the average child of 6 might be said to have a mental age of 6, the average child of 9 a mental age of 9 years, and so on. The technique of scoring tests in terms of age units has come to be known as the mental age method, and the scores obtained by this method as mental ages (M.A.'s).

The method by which an age-intelligence-scale is devised is briefly as follows: A series of intellectual tasks of varying difficulty is assembled and administered to subjects of different age groups. The responses are scored and collated, and, on the basis of the per cent of individuals passing and failing the various tasks at different ages, certain of them are selected as suitable tests. The tests selected are then ordered according to difficulty and combined into groups usually of six or eight to form various *year levels*. The number of tests per year level determines how many credits are assigned to each test. For example, if there are six tests per year, each test passed counts two months. The final score or M.A. which an individual gets on the tests is the sum of the partial credits he obtained for the tests passed at different year levels, expressed in months and years, plus a certain bonus for tests which it is assumed he could have passed if the tests had been given him.[1] The sum of both, expressed in months and years, is the individual's men-

---

[1] The bonus consists of the M.A. score automatically credited for items below the year level on which the subject has passed all tests. For example, if a child passes all tests at year IX (known as the basal year) he is given full credit (96 months) for all tests through year VIII, even though he has not actually taken the tests of the lower year levels.

tal age score. Thus if a child passes 6 tests at year IX, 4 tests at year X and 3 tests at year XII, his M.A. score is 12 + 8 + 6 + 96 (bonus) or 122 months. All this is, of course, quite familiar; but we have thought it worth while to summarize the actual procedure for obtaining a mental age in order to throw into focus a number of fundamental facts of which even psychologists sometimes lose sight.

 The first of these facts is that a *mental age*, however obtained, *is just a score*. Basically it differs in no way from any other type of score given in terms of the number of items passed out of a possible total. Thus when a child gets a mental age score of 122 months on the Binet Scale, the important fact is that he is credited with having passed 61 test items.[2] The fact that we multiply each item by 2 so as to be able to express the score in terms of months and years is primarily a matter of convenience. An intelligence rating expressed as a score of 61 points is as real and can be made as understandable as a mental age score of 122 months. It has the same arithmetical properties and the same possibilities of evaluation, including that of calculating intelligence quotients. Of course, it also has the same limitations.

 The second point of importance about the M.A. method of evaluating intelligence is that it inevitably limits the range of possible scores. Beyond certain points M.A. equivalents are impossible. These limits are reached, for any given test, whenever the mean scores made on the test cease to increase with advancing chronological age. The limiting mental age varies from test to test. Thus on the Manikin Test the mean scores cease to increase above age 8; on the Ship Test, above 12; in the case of Memory Span for Digits, they stop increasing at 14 and in the case of the Vocabulary Test, at about age 22.

 The point at which mean scores cease to increase with advancing age is in part dependent upon the difficulty of the test used and in part a function of the general maturation process. Thus in the case of the Manikin and Ship Tests the mean scores fail to increase with advancing age because the tests are too easy. In the case of the Memory Span for Digits and the Vocabulary Test the differences between the mean scores at higher ages disappear because the abilities measured by these tests no longer increase with age. Thus the ability to repeat digits stops improving at age 14, not because it is impossible to attain a higher score than those generally attained by the average 14 year old, but

  [2] Actually he will have been tested with considerably fewer items. This number 61 includes both the items actually passed as well as those for which he received automatic credit. See previous note.

because the mean scores for the average 16, 18, and 20 year old are no higher.

What is true of the various abilities considered individually is equally true of measures of these abilities when combined into "batteries" of tests to yield measures of general intelligence.   Beyond the age of 15, mean scores on practically all[3] intelligence scales cease to increase significantly with age.   Psychologists have generally interpreted this fact to mean that intellectual ability stops growing at about that age. With this general conclusion we are in agreement, but shall not pursue it any further at this time.[4]   Of more immediate concern to us here is is what bearing the fact that all intelligence scales eventually reach such a point may have on the concept of mental age.   The first implication is obvious: the mental age concept has a natural limit of applicability. When a test reaches a point beyond which mean scores on it cease to increase with age, then any higher scores for which the test allows can no longer be expressed in terms of mental age.

The fact that every intelligence scale attains a point beyond which mean scores for successive age groups no longer increase with age, does not mean, of course, that scores higher than those calculated at the limiting age levels, cannot be attained.   On the contrary, the fact that the mental age scores are average scores, shows that there must be a large percentage of individuals who attain higher scores than the mean. The only question is how to interpret, or at least make use of these.   One way is to assign hypothetical values or M.A. equivalents to them, based on the relative frequency of their occurrence; another is to accept them at their face value and to assume that if there were higher mental age scores they would increase with chronological age precisely in the manner in which the scale provides for it.   In either case, we get what are obviously extrapolated values, that is, M.A.'s which are only hypothetically related to the actual data, and whose maximal values are limited only by the range of the test scores.   Thus, in the case of the Stanford Revision of the Binet it is possible to obtain an M.A. of 19 years and 6 months, on the Otis Tests of Mental Ability an M.A. of 18 years and 6 months, and on the Terman-Merrill Revision of the Binet an M.A. of 22 years and 10 months.   With these limits, we are not particularly concerned, nor with the doubtful statistical procedures by

---

[3] This is not true of intelligence scales like the Otis Self-Administering Tests of Mental Ability, which are markedly influenced by educational factors.

[4] See Wechsler, David: *The Range of Human Capacities*. Baltimore, 1935, Chapter 8.

which they have sometimes been obtained. But it is very important to appraise their possible psychological significance.

A mental age score above an age beyond which mean scores increase with age, e.g., an M.A. of 20 years, can have only one of two meanings. The first and most important one is that which it could have had, if it signified the same thing as that which is implied when we say that a child has a mental age of 7 or 8 or 10, namely, that it represents the average mentality of the average individual of that age, expressed in months and years. Such an interpretation for a mental age of 20 years is clearly incorrect. The average mental age of the average 20 year old is not 20 but 15 years. The second possible meaning of mental age of 20, is that it represents a measurable level of intelligence that is above the average, the precise amount of which for the sake of convenience, is expressed in the year-month notation. In that case, however, the above notation acquires an altered connotation and can only add confusion to the original concept. To speak of an individual having an M.A. of 20 years is both practically and scientifically meaningless.

What we have said thus far does not, of course, deny the value of the mental age concept altogether, but only points to its inevitable limitations. The most important of these limitations, as we have just seen, is that the M.A. method of defining intelligence cannot logically be used to define levels of intelligence higher than that obtained by that age group beyond which M.A. scores cease to increase with chronological age. The precise age at which this occurs is still in dispute. It cannot, in fact, be definitely fixed because the mental age limit attained is a function of the actual tests used, and there can be no possible agreement so long as different intelligence scales are composed of different batteries of tests. Present day evidence, however, is that the age beyond which M.A.'s generally cease to increase with chronological age is not far from 15 years. In the opinion of the writer, the mean for all tests pooled together would probably be a little higher.[5] But whether the mean *adult* M.A., as this limiting value is called, be 14 or 16, the fact is that the M.A. method of measuring intelligence breaks down even before either of these ages is attained. Actually, it begins to fail about age

---

[5] In all probability the age of maximal functioning mental ability falls between 22 and 25 years, but the psychometric differences between ages 15 and 25 are generally so small and influenced by so many factors that they may be disregarded for all practical purposes. According to the results on the Bellevue Adult Scale the age of maximal mental functioning ability falls at approximately age 22.

12, for though the means of the actual test scores continue to increase with age above that age, they do so with progressively diminishing and ultimately negligible amounts. That they do fail is of particular moment in calculating indices of brightness or intelligence quotients. Before considering this problem any further, therefore, we shall find it necessary to consider the meaning of these indices.

The most universally used of all indices of intelligence is the *intelligence quotient* (I.Q.). It is generally calculated by dividing a subject's mental age (M.A.) by his chronological age (C.A.). Thus if a child of 10 attains an M.A. of 12, his I.Q. is 1.20 or, omitting the decimal point, 120. As thus defined, the intention of the I.Q. is straightforward and easy enough to comprehend. But its full meaning really depends upon what we understand by the terms M.A. and C.A. The meaning of an M.A. we have already discussed at length. It is a test score, for convenience expressed in a month-year notation. But what is a C.A.? We do not, of course, refer to its literal definition, namely the life or chronological age of an individual at the time he is examined, but its meaning as a part of the I.Q. formula. Let the reader pause and try to answer the question for himself. If he has not given it much thought before, it is probable he will find the task far from easy. Nor is he likely to find the answer by consulting the average text-book. Most of them will define an I.Q.; some an M.A.; none, so far as we know, a C.A. This omission is unfortunate, because much of the nonsense which has been written about the intelligence quotient may be attributed to the failure of its critics to understand what a C.A. really is. Nevertheless, the definition of the C.A. in the I.Q. formula is almost glaringly obvious.

Like the M.A., *a C.A. is just a score.* It is a score which the examiner assumes would be the score of an individual of a given age if his ability corresponded exactly to that of the average individual of his own (the subject's) life age. Thus, if a given individual's age is 8 years, his C.A. score, if he were an average 8 year old, would also be 8 years. If his life age were 12 years and 9 months, his C.A. score, assuming him to be a normal individual, ought likewise to be 12 years and 9 months, and so on. A well standardized scale is one where the tests are so arranged as to make this assumption warrantable and at least approximately correct.[6] But in any case the important fact is that the C.A.

---

[6] Actually this has been shown to be the case for the midyear points only; for example, that the average 9½ year old child attains a mental age of 9½ and hence an I.Q. of 100. But it has not been shown for the average child of 9 years and 2 months, the average child of 9 years and 9 months, etc. It is probable, however,

is merely a converted score just like the M.A.   The thing that makes
them alike, however, is not the fact that they have the word *age* in
common, but the fact that they are both test *scores* measured in identical
units.

Bearing these facts in mind we may now define an intelligence quotient
in terms of what it actually represents: An intelligence quotient is the
ratio between a particular score which an individual gets (on a given
intelligence test) and the score which an average individual of his life
age may be assumed to attain on the same test, when both scores are
expressed in the same notation (e.g., in terms of months and years).
The usual formula

$$I.Q. = \frac{M.A.}{C.A.}$$

should really be stated as follows:

$$I.Q. = \frac{\text{attained or actual score}}{\text{expected mean score for age}}$$

The great value of the I.Q. is that it furnishes us with a method of
defining *relative* intelligence.   It tells us in the first instance how bright
an individual is compared with one of his own age.   But it tells us, or
at least is intended to tell us, even more than that.   The I.Q. is offered
as an index which is independent not only of the particular score which
an individual makes on a particular scale, but also of the particular age
at which he happens to make it.   It is thus a measure which presum-
ably defines the relative brightness or intellectual possibilities of an
individual more or less permanently.   Under ordinary conditions an
individual's I.Q. is supposed to remain the same throughout life, or at
least throughout the age limits covered by the scale.   Psychologists
refer to this property as the constancy of the I.Q.

The constancy of the I.Q. is the basic assumption of all scales where
relative degrees of intelligence are defined in terms of it.   It is not only
basic, but absolutely necessary that I.Q.'s be independent of the age at
which they are calculated, because unless the assumption holds, no
permanent scheme of intelligence classification is possible.   If an individual at one age attained a certain I.Q. and when examined a few

---

that within the limits of ages 5 to 12 years the deviations from the mean at any
given intermediate age would not be very great, and the correspondence of the
C.A. and M.A. values may for practical purposes be assumed to hold.

years later another I.Q., or if a particular I.Q. meant one thing at one age and quite a different thing at another, the I.Q. would obviously have no practical significance. It is, therefore, highly important to ascertain whether I.Q.'s, as now calculated, do in fact remain constant.

The facts regarding the constancy of the I.Q. are essentially of two kinds. The first pertains to the mean values of the I.Q. at successive chronological ages. In the case of most of the better standardized tests, it can be readily shown that, at least for the standardizing samples of population, the mean I.Q.'s over the middle portions of the scale, are regularly found to be about 100. The fact that they generally do not deviate more than two or three points from this value is interpreted to show that the I.Q. remains constant from age to age. This interpretation, however, goes beyond the fact. The only legitimate conclusion that can be drawn from them is that the I.Q.'s not far from the average will remain constant. It does not necessarily imply that I.Q.'s at any considerable distance from the mean, let us say one or two standard deviations from it, (for example, I.Q.'s of 85 or 70) will also remain constant. That will depend not only upon the average values of the I.Q. at different ages, but also on their respective variabilities at these ages. Hitherto, it has been assumed that these variabilities were the same or differed by no greater amounts than might be expected from sampling errors. In point of fact, however, little evidence has been produced to test this assumption which remains distinctly controversial.

The early standardizations of the Binet Scale contained little data which would enable one to evaluate the variability of the I.Q. at different ages. It was not until Burt's[7] revision appeared that such data became available. Burt himself did not actually take up the problem of the variability of the I.Q. (or mental ratio, as he called it) but did furnish data from which this variability might be calculated. One is able to do this because he gives for each life age, not only the mean M.A. score for each age, but also its standard deviation (S.D.).[8] Using these figures one may calculate what I.Q. may be expected for an individual of any given age, whose position is any given S.D. distance from the mean. If all I.Q.'s were constant, not only at the mean, but any distance from it, all individuals deviating by the same fractional standard deviation from the mean would have the same I.Q.'s. Actual calculation, however, shows that this is generally not the case.

Analysis of Burt's figures reveals that except between ages 6 and 10

[7] Burt, Cyril: *Mental and Scholastic Tests.* London, 1933.
[8] Loc. cit., p. 145.

the difference in variability of the I.Q. is so great as to significantly alter its value. For example, at the distance of 2 standard deviations from the mean an individual at age 6 attaining that rank would get an I.Q. of 76; at age 10, he would get an I.Q. of 81; at age 14, an I.Q. of 84.

More direct evidence of variability of I.Q. with age is furnished by the statistics of Terman and Merrill in their new revision of the Stanford-Binet. Their tables[9] are worth examining in detail. They contain some very significant surprises. In the first place, even the mean I.Q.'s show great variability, differing by as much as 9 per cent at different ages; for example, from a mean I.Q. of 109.9 at age $2\frac{1}{2}$ to a mean I.Q. of 100.9 at age 14. But even more significant are the differences between the standard deviation of the means at different age levels. These differ by as much as 7.5 units, and in consequence give rise to significant deviations from the I.Q. expectancy. Thus, the standard deviation for the mean I.Q. at age 12 on the Revised Stanford-Binet (Form L), is 20.0, and at age 6, only 12.5. Accordingly, depending upon the age at which an individual is being tested, he may obtain different I.Q.'s even though his relative brightness remains unchanged. Thus, supposing him to be an individual whose position is 2 standard deviations from the mean, he would get at age 6 an I.Q. of 75 and at age 12 an I.Q. of 60. This would imply that an I.Q. of 60 at age 12 means the same as an I.Q. of 75 at year 6.[10]

We have just shown that I.Q.'s calculated by the M.A. over the C.A. method do not remain constant for individuals whose ratings are any considerable distance above or below the average of their age group. It also appears that the method does not furnish constant values even for mean I.Q.'s except at certain ages. This becomes apparent if instead of comparing the mean I.Q.'s at different ages, one compares the original test scores from which they were derived. The most effective way of doing this is by plotting original test scores directly against chronological age, without any further manipulation of the data than a prior transmutation of the scores into units of equal amount. We have done this with intelligence tests obtained with the Bellevue Intelligence Scale, and the resulting growth curve is shown in figure 1.

[9] Terman and Merrill: *Measuring Intelligence*, pp. 36–40.

[10] Terman and Merrill are inclined to account for the large fluctuations in variability at certain ages as being primarily due to sampling errors or to the influence of pubescent changes. But though it is true that such differences are not obtained at all ages, they are by no means exceptional.

The curve shown in figure 1 is a logistic curve typical of all growth phenomena. As such it shows at once that intellectual growth does not proceed by equal amounts throughout its development. Accordingly, any method of calculating I.Q.'s which assumes a linear relationship between chronological and mental age cannot possibly give constant values for any considerable portion of the growth period.

The assumption of the linear relationship between M.A. and C.A. made by current methods of calculating I.Q.'s leads to certain inevi-

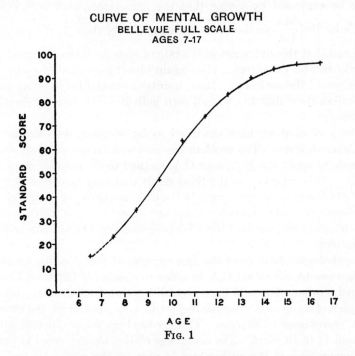

CURVE OF MENTAL GROWTH
BELLEVUE FULL SCALE
AGES 7-17

AGE

Fig. 1

table consequences. The first of these is that for the average individual, the mean value of the I.Q. will change from age to age. At early age levels or at other periods where the mental growth is rapid, the I.Q. will tend to be above the mean of the entire population; at the upper ages where mental growth is slower, it will be below the mean. Thus on the Stanford-Binet (original standardization), the mean I.Q. for ages 3 to 5 is approximately 102; for ages 14 and 15 it is more nearly 98. On the new or revised Stanford-Binet where the mean I.Q.'s are systematically above 100 for all ages, those between ages $2\frac{1}{2}$ to 5 average about 105; whereas those at ages 14 and 15 average about 101.5.[11]

A second result that might be expected from a study of the mental growth curve is that a child's I.Q. would tend to fall off as he grew older, and that this falling off would be more marked in the case of the mentally retarded than in the case of the normal or superior child. The explanation of these phenomena resides in the particular logarithmic relationship that connects mental with chronological age. In a gross way this may be expressed by saying that the numerators used in calculating I.Q.'s by the $\dfrac{MA}{CA}$ method increase more slowly than do the denominators and that this difference in the rate of increase is most marked in the case of mental defectives. Here again observation confirms what may be expected theoretically. Thus, results[12] obtained by retesting mental defectives show that I.Q.'s of all such individuals decline systematically with age.[13]

Much of what we have discussed so far concerns the calculation of I.Q.'s for children. The problem becomes more acute when an attempt is made to apply the M.A. over C.A. method to the calculation of adult I.Q.'s. This brings us to the third result that may be expected from a study of the growth curve, namely the ultimate arrest of mental growth. The successive increments by which test scores increase with advancing chronological age, not only diminish progressively, but ultimately vanish altogether.

Psychologists have from the first recognized that dividing an adult's M.A. score by his actual C.A. in order to obtain his I.Q. would lead to absurd results. To avoid these absurdities, they have generally adopted the plan of using as devisor the highest C.A. beyond which the observed M.A. scores cease to increase. This age has been set by different authors at from 14 to 18 years. The actual age chosen has depended in part on the experiences of the author and in part on the particular scale em-

[11] It should be added that the discrepancies would be much larger if the scaling methods employed did not compensate for them by using different criteria in selecting the tests at different age levels. At the lower ages, authors of tests usually require 60 to 70 per cent of "passes" for locating a test at a particular age level, whereas at the upper ages only from 50 to 60 per cent is required.

[12] See particularly, Kuhlmann, F.: Results of repeated mental re-examination of 639 feeble-minded over a period of ten years. *J. Appl. Psychol.*, 1921, V, 192–224.

[13] Incidentally, the fact that the I.Q.'s of individuals of low intelligence tend to decrease markedly with age entails some paradoxical consequences. One of them is that after being sent to a special school for several years, a mentally retarded child might well come out with a lower I.Q. than when he entered.

ployed. But apart from the fact that the assumed age has varied from test to test, the fixing of it at any particular point has introduced an assumption which has served to destroy the meaning of the I.Q. altogether. This assumption is that M.A. scores remain constant throughout adult life or, at least, up to the point where senility begins. If this were true, the curve of mental growth from age 16 onwards would be a straight line parallel to the C.A. axis. Actually, it is no such thing, but a curve which decreases more or less regularly with increasing age as shown in figure 2.

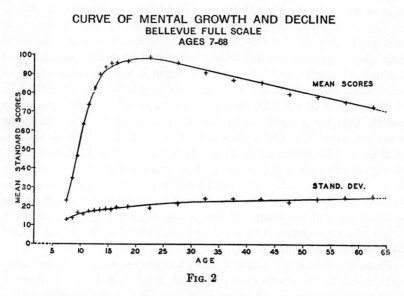

CURVE OF MENTAL GROWTH AND DECLINE
BELLEVUE FULL SCALE
AGES 7-68

Fig. 2

The curve shown in figure 2 is based upon the data obtained with the Bellevue Intelligence Examination for ages 7 to 65. We have already discussed the characteristics of it up to the age of puberty. The part which interests us now is that portion of it that describes the observed changes in mental ability from about 14 years onwards. We might add that the curve which we give here is very similar to the one that we derived[14] from the studies of Miles[15] and those of Conrad and Jones.[16]

[14] Wechsler, D.: *The Range of Human Capacities*, p. 85.

[15] Miles, W. R.: Measurement of certain abilities throughout life span. *Proceedings National Academy of Science*, 1931, XVII, 627–633.

Miles, W. R., and C. C.: Correlation of intelligence scores, age, etc. *Amer. J. Psychol.*, 1932, XLIV, 44–78.

[16] Jones, H. E., and Conrad, H. S.: The growth and decline of intelligence, etc. *Gen. Psychol. Monog.*, 1933, XIII, 223–298.

What they all show is, that beginning at an age varying from 15 to 22, all scores of mental ability, far from remaining constant, start to fall off. The point at which the falling off begins and the rate at which it progresses will vary from test to test and cannot be fixed. It is true that for most intelligence scales the difference between ages 15 and 25 are for most practical purposes negligible, but above that age the decline becomes appreciable and increasingly important. After 35, they begin to decrease so fast that the use of a single denominator for calculating I.Q.'s for adults will introduce serious errors. To calculate an I.Q. for a man of 60 by dividing his M.A. score by 15, is as incorrect as to obtain an I.Q. for a boy of 12 by dividing his M.A. score by 15. Nevertheless that is precisely what the general practice has hitherto been. All adult I.Q.'s have been almost universally calculated by using some assumed constant denominator. The effect of using a single denominator for calculating I.Q.'s of adults is to destroy the very basic concept of the I.Q.

The essence of the I.Q. concept is that part of its definition which asserts that for a valid evaluation of an individual's brightness, one must compare his mental ability to that of the average individual of his own age. The actual method by which this is done is of secondary, though not negligible importance. The essential thing is that the I.Q., however obtained, takes into consideration the age of the subject. As soon as the age factor is discarded, the I.Q. ceases to be an I.Q. in the original sense of the term. If this is correct, it follows that all adult I.Q.'s which are obtained by dividing an individual score (M.A.) by any fixed denominator, are not I.Q.'s at all.

From the theoretical point of view, the precise value of the denominator used, that is whether the adult M.A. is taken as 14, 15 or 16 years, is of no consequence. All are equally fallacious in the sense that they assume that mental ability (as measured by tests) remains constant after any one of these ages. That unfortunately is precisely what most psychologists have assumed ever since the I.Q. was introduced. The result has been that in-so-far as adult ratings are concerned, psychologists have been really not getting I.Q.'s at all; instead they have been calculating various indices of mental efficiency. They have been comparing adults not with individuals of their own age, but with those of some favored, usually optimally functioning, age group. In brief, by assuming a fixed adult mental age, psychologists have been calculating not intelligence quotients but efficiency quotients.

Our investigations into the nature and meaning of the I.Q. have led us to some very disturbing conclusions: First, we found that even if

I.Q.'s as now calculated could be said to be constant about the mean, this could in no way imply that they were also constant at all other points. Next, we found that the M.A. over the C.A. method could not possibly give constant I.Q.'s for all ages, because the assumed linear relation between C.A.'s and M.A.'s does not in fact obtain. Finally, we were forced to the uncomfortable conclusion that most adult I.Q.'s as hitherto obtained, were not I.Q.'s at all but some sort of efficiency quotients.

If these conclusions are correct, they suggest that the current method of calculating I.Q.'s is in urgent need of revision. To some this might further convey the belief that the entire method of evaluating I.Q.'s is invalid. The latter, however, would be an unwarranted conclusion. It is true that when M.A. scores are plotted against chronological age, the relationship observed is not a linear one, but if we examine the curve of mental growth we will find that this relationship does hold over certain portions of it. Thus although the curve shown on page 27 is far from a straight line, the section of it from approximately age 7 to 10 is pretty close to being one. This means that the I.Q.'s between these ages will remain approximately constant. With a little leniency we might say that the straight-line relationship is sufficiently good to give valid results from ages 4 to 12 or 13. But below,[17] and particularly above, these limits the linear relationship does not hold at all.

Again if we examine the latter portion of the curve of mental ability we note that although it does not remain parallel to the abscissa above age 15 as would be required by the assumption of a single adult M.A. denominator its decline up to about age 25 is relatively slight. Accordingly one might allow that I.Q.'s calculated by the M.A. over the C.A. method would remain fairly constant over this age span. Here too, with a little leniency, we might extend the age limits a few years, say up to 35. But above this age the decline of the curve becomes so marked that, as we have already noted, the fixed denominator assumption will give entirely invalid results.

We shall now proceed to describe a method of calculating I.Q.'s which will make allowance for the form of the curve for mental growth and also, as we now know, of mental decline. This method was arrived at only after a variety of statistical procedures had been tried out. All of them had this in common, that they made use of scores which had previously been transmuted into units of equal amount. This was achieved in the usual way by expressing our raw scores in terms of

[17] This portion is not shown in our curve.

standard deviation units.[18]   Before making use of these results, however, it was necessary to define zero intelligence. This problem, as might have been expected, presented the greatest difficulty.

The zero point in a scale of mental measurements, like that of any physical scale, may have one of two meanings. It may signify 'just not anything' of whatever it is we are seeking to measure, as in the case of the zero of the absolute temperature scale, or merely represent some defined point of reference from which we find it convenient to start our measurements, as the freezing point of water in the centigrade scale. In either case, its explicit definition is imperative to enable us to express scalar amounts as multiples or fractions. All I.Q.'s, of course, are precisely such multiples or fractions. Their magnitude obviously depends upon the points of reference from which they are being calculated. In the case of the M.A. over the C.A. method of calculating the I.Q.'s the zero point for both the numerator and denominator is the assumed age of the child at birth. In point of fact this assumption is incorrect. A child at birth does not have zero intelligence nor for that matter zero chronological age. When a child is born it is already nine months "old" and manifests a certain amount of intelligence. Whatever the situation, however, it could not be used as a point of reference for a scale like ours. Accordingly we are forced to look for another point of reference to define our zero, that would be related in some quantitative way to actual test scores.

A number of suggestions have been made by various writers as to how zero intelligence might be defined in terms of scores. The most cogent one is perhaps that of Professor Thurstone[19] who defines it "as the amount of test performance at which variability vanishes." Such an amount, it might appear, ought not to be difficult to determine for any given scale. All that is seemingly necessary is that we find a point below which no test score of any kind is possible. But the situation is not so simple. The reason is that what we are seeking is not a point on our scales beyond which there are no lower scores but really a point corresponding to a degree of intelligence below which intellectual ability may, to all intents and purposes, be said to be non-existent. That, of course, is quite a different matter. An individual failing to make any score on a given test might still make some sort of score on a much easier test. For example, a zero score on the Army Alpha is equal to a

---

[18] See appendix.
[19] Thurstone, L. L.: The absolute zero in the measurement of intelligence. *Psychol. Rev.*, XXXV, 1928.

score of about 12 on the Army Beta;[20] and there are other tests still easier than the Army Beta on which individuals can obtain some sort of score, even when unable to do anything on Beta. We therefore cannot take the lowest score attainable on any particular scale as the true zero point of intelligence. Some other method of arriving at it is necessary.

The usual way out of the difficulty has been to turn to the probability ✓ curve for an inspired guess. The technique consists of assuming a zero point so far from the mean of the group tested that the slight amount of ability this assumed point represented would make it highly improbable that any individual could be so ill endowed as ever to reach it. In terms of units of deviation, custom has tended to set this point at −5 S.D. from the mean, and our first I.Q. Tables were calculated on this basis.

I.Q. tables calculated by setting a zero point at −5 S.D. from the mean, gave us fairly satisfactory intelligent quotients. The method of obtaining them, however, seemed altogether arbitrary. We really had no rationale for the particular limits which we had chosen. It is true that when calculated with the zero limit set at −5 S.D. we obtained I.Q.'s that were not very much different from those we could obtain by the M.A. over C.A. method, after transmuting the sigma scores into the equivalent M.A.'s, nor indeed very much different from those we eventually obtained by the method we finally adopted. But we could offer no justification for our procedure, other than that of matter-of-fact empiricism. Moreover, when we set the point at −5 sigma, we discovered considerable irregularity in the I.Q. limits for our various age groups. In particular, we found that I.Q.'s below 100 tended to be lower, and I.Q.'s above 100 higher than seemed warranted. For all these reasons, we decided to abandon the idea of defining zero intelligence and to seek instead a defined base that was at once more rational and less difficult to manipulate.

The base which we finally chose to define, was that amount of intelligence which was represented by the individual who was one probable

[20] Conversely, a score of zero on the Army Beta would be equal to a score of about −71 on Army Alpha. The reader who is puzzled by these numbers, should recall that mathematically 0 is an indeterminate quantity. In psychology it means so small an amount of ability as to be just insufficient to enable its possessor to obtain the lowest possible score on a given test. Each test will therefore have a different zero point. Realization of this fact will show why scores on different tests forming a single battery, cannot be added together unless they have been previously equated against one another.

error away from the mean. We chose that distance because, through almost universal acceptance, the deviation −1 P.E. is used as the dividing line between individuals who are referred to as average (normal) and subaverage (below normal). According to this view, an average individual is a person who falls within the middle 50 per cent of the group, a range which on the normal probability curve is defined by the value +1 to −1 P.E. from the mean.

After setting −1 P.E. as the definable point from which our I.Q.'s were to be calculated, we next had to decide upon the value of the I.Q. which should be assigned to it. We say we had to decide because the absolute numerical value of the I.Q., as we trust the reader is now convinced, is altogether a matter of convenience. An individual's I.Q., as we have so often insisted, merely defines his relative position among the group with which he has been compared. The important fact about it is this relative standing and not the numerical rating which we may happen to assign to it.

The numerical value of an I.Q. has no more fixed meaning than a passing mark on a scholastic examination. We can, *ad lib.*, set the passing mark at 60, 70 or 90 without altering its implication, if by passing we mean the attainment of certain relative excellence or level of efficiency. In this sense, the meaning which any mark has is derived from its relative position among the set of marks that are being evaluated. For example, a mark of 90 may mean very superior or barely passing, depending upon the total range of the marking scale. It is the same with I.Q.'s. In the final analysis the level of intelligence which any I.Q. represents, will depend not upon its absolute, but its relative magnitude.

While the numerical rating that can be assigned to an individual attaining any distance from the mean (in our case −1 P.E.) is altogether a question of convenience, certain practical considerations limit the particular values which we may employ. The most important of these is the value of the mean I.Q. Here the historical definition has set it once and for all at 100. For all other I.Q.'s there is no such historical, nor statistical cogency. The only limitation imposed upon us is that I.Q.'s of individuals below the mean must be less than 100. But in choosing a base from which all I.Q.'s were to be calculated, it was obviously a matter of common sense to select such value for it as would be in line with the order of numerical values of I.Q.'s now in general use. In the case of most intelligence scales, an I.Q. of 90 has come to be interpreted as the lowest limit of what is generally called average intelligence. Since the distance −1 P.E. from the mean designated the lower limiting value of the category "average" in our own classification, we decided to use 90 as the I.Q. against which the distance of −1 P.E. might conveniently be equated.[21]

By equating the distance −1 P.E. against the I.Q. of 90 we at once defined, not only this particular I.Q. but all other I.Q.'s as well, because the equation by which this is done automatically defines the zero point.[22] This zero point is obviously that S.D. distance from the mean which gives us an I.Q. of 90 for any individual who attains the position of −1 P.E. from the mean. Having obtained this zero point, it is then a matter of simple arithmetic to draw up one's I.Q. tables. All that is necessary is to determine the mean and standard deviation of one's distribution, prepare a table of "z" scores, and by the formula $\dfrac{X - z}{X}$ obtain for each actual score the corresponding I.Q. This is the method we used for establishing our I.Q. tables.

Having described a new method of calculating I.Q.'s, we shall now briefly summarize its advantages over those currently in use: First, it dispenses with all assumptions as regards the precise relations between intellectual and chronological ratings of growth, and in particular, assumptions as regards the rectilinear relation between the M.A. and C.A. Secondly, in the calculation of adult I.Q.'s it relieves us of the need to commit ourselves to any fixed average adult mental age. Each age defines its own adult denominator. Thirdly, the method enables us to calculate I.Q's which maintain the same meaning throughout the life of the individual. Fourthly, it retains the original and only important meaning of the I.Q. namely, that of an index of relative brightness.

So much for the meaning, implication and method of calculating a true I.Q. All of this, however, is only a means to an end,—the classification of intelligence itself. The purpose of an I.Q. is to enable us to tell how bright or how stupid a person is, and how on the basis of test scores to classify him scientifically, with respect to what we are pleased to call his native intellectual endowment. This is a large order, and we shall need a full chapter to see how it may be done.

[21] From a statistical point of view, the use of the probable error has several advantages. First, the P.E. or any multiple of it is a very definite measure. Second, it is a measure that is influenced relatively little by extreme or accidental cases. Third, it possesses certain mathematical properties which are related to other fundamental measures of variability as well as to the normal probability curve as a whole. Lastly, it involves us in no assumption which experience cannot either verify or disprove.

[22] See Appendix 1.

CHAPTER 4

THE CLASSIFICATION OF INTELLIGENCE

When psychologists speak of classifying intelligence, they use the term in a somewhat specialized sense. The purpose of a mental classification is not, as in most other scientific classifications, "the detection of the laws of nature." It does not correspond, for example, to the chemist's arrangement of the elements into a periodic table or even the zoologist's subdivision of animals into vertebrates and non-vertebrates and then again into their various orders. The psychologist's effort at classifying intelligence is more like what the layman does when he tries to distinguish the colors of the rainbow. The analogy is more than a superficial one. General intelligence is a non-interrupted continuum like that of a rainbow spectrum. One level of intelligence merges into the next like colors seen through a refracting prism. Levels of behavior which present certain patterns (or hues, to return to the color analogy) are called defectives, others a little farther up the scale are called borderline, still others dull-normal and so on until we reach the other end of the scale where they are labeled very superior, precocious or genius. The borderline runs into the dull-normal and the high average into the superior just as the orange-yellow runs into the yellow, and the deep violet into the indigo. In both cases it is convention or custom which has assigned them their respective names.

The earliest classifications of intelligence were very rough ones. To a large extent they were practical attempts to define various patterns of behavior in medical-legal terms. These terms, like idiot, imbecile and moron, coined by the early writers on the subject, still form part of our present day terminology. The contribution of modern psychology has been not so much in the matter of defining new configurations of intelligent behavior as in giving precision to the already available concepts, through the introduction of quantitative methods. A mental defective is now defined not merely as a person who "through congenital arrest or imperfect mental development is incapable . . . of managing himself or his affairs with ordinary prudence," but as one who on standardized tests fails to attain an I.Q. or an M.A. of a particular level. In brief, psychologists have attempted to classify intelligence by means of quantitative measurements. This has been a great step forward. The progress to be realized is like that achieved by physicists in designating colors by their wave-lengths instead of their hues.

While the theoretical advantages of classifying intelligence quantitatively are obvious, the practical gain of such classifications is not always as apparent. The reason for this is that the merit of any quantitative classification necessarily depends on the validity of the data employed in arriving at it. These data, in the field of mental classification, usually consist of measures of brightness derived from one or another intelligence test. The measure of brightness most commonly used is the intelligence quotient. It is for this reason that we devoted such considerable space in our last chapter to the discussion of the I.Q. But the calculation of a correct and constant I.Q. is only the first prerequisite for its use as a basis of classification. We still have to decide as to the meanings we can attach to our indices, however obtained.

TABLE 2

Classification of intelligence according to Terman

I.Q. RANGE	CLASSIFICATION
Below 70	Definite feeble-mindedness
70–80	Borderline deficiency
80–90	Dullness
90–110	Normal or average intelligence
110–120	Superior intelligence
120–140	Very superior intelligence
140 and above	Genius or near genius

In practice the procedure has consisted of pairing certain familiar qualitative terms against I.Q. ratings falling within certain limits. Thus in Terman's classification, individuals attaining I.Q.'s below 70 are designated as mentally defective, those between 80 and 90 as dull-normal, those between 90 and 110 as average, and so on. According to Kuhlmann, the I.Q. limit for the corresponding categories are: mentally defective, below 75; borderline, 75–84; dull, 85–94; average, 95–104. And other writers have used still other delimitations.

When one examines the various I.Q. classifications that have been offered, a number of questions present themselves. The first is why the limiting I.Q. values are the ones given and not some others. As an example we may consider Professor Terman's original classification which is reproduced in table 2. The first thing that strikes us is that the limiting second cipher of each new class is a zero. Thus the category borderline begins at 70 I.Q., the category dull-normal at 80 I.Q., the category average at 90 I.Q., and so on. It is difficult to conceive of any statistical procedure which would give such neat correspondence. It is possible that the limiting numbers actually obtained were sufficiently near the even decades so that, allowance being made for the variability of the measuring instrument, it may have been permissible to round off the numbers. But the actual chance of each of them beginning with the zero is only 10^{-7}, that is, one in 10,000,000.

A more serious objection to Professor Terman's I.Q. classification than the improbability of all class intervals beginning and ending where they do, is that we are furnished no rationale for the choice of the indicated class intervals. We are not told why an I.Q. between 70 and 79 rather than between 72 and 84 was chosen to denote borderline intelligence, or an I.Q. between 110 and 119 rather than between 113 and 126 to signify superior intelligence. There is an implication that in some way the intervals used are based on the normal curve of distribution. But there is no explicit statement that such a scheme was intended. In any case, we have no way of determining from the class limits themselves what that scheme may have been.

Our comments on Professor Terman's I.Q. classification hold equally for all others published. We have chosen it to illustrate the shortcomings of current classificatory schemes not because it is the most vulnerable, but because it is the most familiar of any now in use. For all practical purposes it may be said to have become the standard scheme of mental classification in this country. The Terman classification is being used not only for I.Q. ratings obtained on the Stanford-Binet, but for I.Q.'s derived from a host of other tests for which they cannot possibly hold. For the latter misapplication Professor Terman is, of course, in no way responsible. Indeed he has on different occasions cautioned psychologists against this practice. Little attention, however, seems to have been paid to this admonition. We have seen equivalent Binet I.Q. ratings reported for nearly every intelligence test now in use.[1] In most cases the reporters proceeded to interpret the I.Q.'s obtained as if the tests measured the same thing as the Binet, and the indices calculated were equivalent to those obtained on the Stanford-Binet. Thus an I.Q. of 75 on an Army Alpha, a Pintner-Paterson or even a Porteus-Mazes Test might alike be interpreted as signifying borderline intelligence; an I.Q. of 85 on any of these, as dull-normal

[1] Including such as were derived from single test scores, like the Porteus Mazes, the Healy P.C II, and the Trabue Sentence-Completion Tests.

intelligence, and so on. The examiners were seemingly unaware of the fact that identical I.Q.'s on the different tests might well represent very different orders of intelligence.

But let us return to the question of what I.Q. limits ought to be assigned to the various qualitative categories of intelligence. Clearly the basis of any scheme will, in the last analysis, be largely a matter of convention. This follows from the fact that the absolute value of an I.Q. is a purely arbitrary number. Its magnitude, as we have seen in the last chapter, can be manipulated to suit the convenience of the investigator. Accordingly, every author of a test is in a position to devise his own I.Q. scale. A free exercise of this privilege would, however, lead to confusion, because one would not be in a position to interpret the I.Q.'s of any given scale without detailed knowledge of the author's standardizing technique. Some agreement, both as to system of notation and interpretation of results, is obviously necessary. Such agreement could best be achieved through conventions established by an international meeting of psychologists and psychiatrists. Unfortunately authors of tests are far from ready for such agreement. One is therefore left in a position of either having to adopt schemes of classification already in vogue, or risking further complication by the addition of others. We have tried to compromise with the situation by devising a scheme of I.Q. classification, which though new, does not differ[2] too much from those in current use. This scheme of classification is given in tables 3 and 4.

The basis for our classificatory scheme is the definition of intelligence levels in terms of statistical frequencies. Each intelligence level is defined as a class interval embracing a range of I.Q.'s falling at such and such distance from the mean, where these distances are expressed as multiples of the probable error. Thus a mental defective is a person who falls at a distance of 3 or more P.E. below the mean. In terms of percentile ranking he falls approximately among the lower 2.2 per cent of the total population. Similarly a person of borderline defective intelligence is an individual who attains an I.Q. that falls between a deviation of −3 P.E. and −2 P.E. from the mean or in terms of percentile rank a position anywhere from *circa* the lowest 3rd to *circa* the lowest 10th percentile. And so with the other categories. Our choice of the limiting points was only in part arbitrary. In the case of mental defectives we had available various estimates of the probable incidence

---

[2] When we say "does not differ too much" we refer only to the numerical magnitude of the I.Q.'s and not to the method by which the I.Q.'s were derived.

of mental deficiency in this country. These estimates, though varying greatly among themselves, gave a mean figure which was not far from about 3 per cent of the total population. It therefore seemed reasonable to us to define the mental defective group as those individuals who attain I.Q.'s falling at a distance of −3 or more P.E.'s from the mean. This distance is equivalent to about 2.2 per cent of the total area of the normal curve. For the intermediate categories such as borderline and dull-normal intelligence, as well as those of average, high-average,

TABLE 3

Statistical basis of intelligence classifications (theoretical)

CLASSIFICATION	LIMITS IN TERMS OF P. E.	PER CENT INCLUDED
Defective........................	−3 P.E. and below	2.15
Borderline........................	−2 P.E. to −3 P.E.	6.72
Dull Normal......................	−1 P.E. to −2 P.E.	16.13
Average..........................	−1 P.E. to +1 P.E.	50.00
Bright Normal....................	+1 P.E. to +2 P.E.	16.13
Superior.........................	+2 P.E. to +3 P.E.	6.72
Very Superior....................	+3 P.E. and over	2.15

TABLE 4

Intelligence classification according to I.Q.—ages 10–60 (actual)

CLASSIFICATION	I.Q. LIMITS	PER CENT INCLUDED
Defective........................	65 and below	2.2
Borderline........................	66–79	6.7
Dull Normal......................	80–90	16.1
Average..........................	91–110	50.0
Bright Normal....................	111–119	16.1
Superior.........................	120–127	6.7
Very Superior....................	128 and over	2.2

superior and very superior, we decided to use the intervening integral multiples of the probable error.

Our scheme of classification is symmetrical, comprising as many classes above the mean as there are below it. In the case of categories below the mean, it was easy to take over the terms now in general use. In the case of classes above the mean we lacked one verbal category to give us a symmetrical classification. We were confronted with the problem of deciding what to call the group plus 1 P.E. to plus 2 P.E.

above the mean. Since the individuals comprised in this category form a group of subjects who are as much above average as the dull-normal are below the average, a logical term that suggested itself was that of Bright Normal. The term is rather clumsy but better than most that come to mind. As a second choice there is the somewhat long but descriptive term High-Average-to-Superior, and we offer this as an alternative. It should be noted that the phrase High-Average-to-Superior does not have the same denotation it has in the Terman classification.

The final classification at which we have arrived, together with the percentage included in each category, is given in table 4. These percentages though justified by a rational statistic are, of course, in no wise definitive. If, for some reason, future experience would show that the present limits are not the best, they can be altered in the light of that experience. Indeed, if any one already disagrees with the limits as here given, he may substitute others of his own liking and use our own data with which to do it (table 5, p. 42). Our classificatory scheme, however, ought to serve as a model for others. More particularly we trust that the example set here, of presenting basic test score distributions with their appropriate constants, will be followed by other investigators. With such data available it would be a matter of simple arithmetic to equate any one scale against any other. This would render comparison of results obtained with different tests a matter of scientific evaluation instead of, as at present, a matter of arbitrary guessing.

The classification offered above, like all others making use of I.Q.'s, is based essentially on a statistical concept of intelligence. It differs from other classifications of this kind in that our statistics have been more rigorously developed, and above all by the fact that our assumptions have been more explicitly stated. But the important thing about all such classifications (whether one admits it or not) is that they abandon all attempts at an absolute definition of intelligence. An I.Q. merely tells you how much better or worse, or how much above or below the average any individual is, when compared with persons of his own age. What that average represents we really do not know. In a point scale it is some numerical score; in a mental age scale, an M.A. equivalent. Most people can readily see that a point score has no absolute significance, because among other things its numerical value is so obviously dependent upon the number of items that happen to comprise the scale. In the case of the mental age scores, even psychologists are often under the impression that we are dealing with some absolute quantity, and the impression is even more common among psychiatrists. There is a rather widespread view that in defining intelligence in terms of mental age, we are doing so in terms of some basic unit of amount. That, as we have seen, is a mistake. A mental

TABLE 5

Percentile ranks for I.Q.'s (Bellevue intelligence scales) ages 10–60

PERCENTILE RANK	I.Q.
1	59
3	68
5	73
7	77
10	81
15	85
20	89
25	91
30	94
35	96
40	98
45	99.7
50	101.4
55	103
60	105
65	106
70	108
75	110
80	112
85	115
90	118
95	123
97	125
99	130

age is just a test score and differs from other arithmetical summaries, only by the fact that it happens to be in a year-month notation. The mental age notation has a number of advantages, but among these is not the magical one of being able to transmute a relative into an absolute quantity. In brief, mental age is no more an absolute measure of intelligence than any other test score.

We have at this point returned again to the question as to what a mental age really is, because a number of authors, and no less an authority than Doll,[3] have suggested and indeed urged that intelligence be classified on the basis of mental age ratings rather than on I.Q.'s. Their arguments in favor of this change may be said to be of two kinds. The main argument against the use of the I.Q. for the classification of intelligence is the fact that the I.Q. does not remain constant. This criticism, as we have seen, is justified. But, as we have further shown, this is not the fault of the I.Q. but of the particular method by which it has been calculated.[4] The second important argument in favor of the M.A. over the I.Q. as a basis for classifying intelligence is that the M.A. does so in terms of fixed levels and hence definitely known amounts of intelligence. There is a further implication, though not stated in so many words, that an M.A. level can be looked upon as a sort of absolute measure. We have already shown that this cannot possibly be. But, in any case, it would be a mistake to set up the M.A. as a competitive base for the classification of intelligence. To do so would be tantamount to abandoning almost entirely the statistical concept of intelligence for which psychologists have so long worked.

One cannot emphasize too often the importance of the statistical concept of intelligence for the science of mental classification. It was first introduced in psychology by Galton when he defined genius. A genius, according to Galton, was a man "who [because of his eminent work] achieved the position of one in each million." Of course the genius' rarity or uniqueness is not the only characteristic which distinguishes him from the average man.[5] Genius is also determined by what a man does as well as the expertness with which he does it. The thing done must be in some way esteemed by those capable of judging its merits. From this point of view, men of genius, according to Galton, are those "whom the whole intelligent part of the nation mourn when they die, who deserve a public funeral, and whom future ages rank as historical characters." But with his own intuitive genius Galton realized that it is not possible to define various degrees of ability, however great and however measured, in terms other than those of relative position. A genius was one who with regard to any estimated ability attained a

[3] Doll, Edgar A.: Improper use of the I.Q. *Jour. of Delinquency*, 1920, V, pp. 67–70.

[4] This limitation is obviated by the method of calculating the I.Q. given in this book.

[5] For other concepts of genius see Wechsler, D.: *Range of Human Capacities*, Chapter VIII.

position of one in a million, just as "an eminent man was one who reached the position attained by one person in 4,000." Not being concerned in his studies of "Hereditary Genius" with the average type of individual, he did not have occasion to define the dull, average, or even superior. But if he had, it is clear that he would have defined them in a very similar way. We have, in a sense, continued Galton's task of defining these remaining groups as regards intelligence. Like geniuses, the average, dull and defective individuals are persons who, on a particular intelligence scale, reach a position attained by one person in such and such total number. Our statistical notation is somewhat different from Galton's but it can be readily translated into his. Thus our average individual is one who attains a position of plus 1 to minus 1 P.E. from the mean, which is the same thing as the position attained by one in every two persons. A superior person is one who attains a position of plus 2 to plus 3 P.E. above the mean, which is equivalent of saying that he is one person in 15, and so on with our other categories. Our scales do not pretend to measure genius. The highest rating we have is that of Very Superior Intelligence, that is, a person who attains a position of 3 or more P.E.'s from the mean. This is a position attained by one person in every 50. It is possible for individuals to obtain scores on our scales which would give them higher ranking, but we are rather hesitant about calling a person a genius on the basis of a single intelligence test score.

The statistical concept of intelligence and its logical implications are extremely difficult for some people to accept because at times it seemingly leads to impractical if not absurd consequences. Such conclusions do not devolve from the concept itself but may result from an incomplete understanding of it. This is perhaps best illustrated by the reactions of certain psychologists to the question of the need of special norms for special groups. Clearly the statistical definition of intelligence implies that norms obtained on any particular sample are valid only for such groups as the sampled population represents. It does not limit the *size* of the subsequent groups to which the norms be applied; these may be as large as the representativeness of the tested sample provides for; but it does put a restriction on the type of individual who may be included for classificatory purposes. Thus test norms obtained on Englishmen cannot be used for classifying Fiji Islanders.[6] This is

---

[6] It might be argued that this limitation holds only for Fiji Islanders in the Fijis and does not apply to a Fiji Islander in London. Here he has to match his wits with the average Englishman and could therefore be legitimately tested by

obvious to everybody. The principle involved, however, becomes less obvious when applied to less divergent groups; for example, the use of identical test norms for negroes with tests originally standardized on white populations; it becomes still less so when the differentiae which might distinguish the groups, such as "nationality", "economic condition" and "social status", are themselves hypothetical. Nevertheless, the limitations still hold. If, for example, social status *were* a factor that influenced these scores, norms obtained on any particular social group could not be used on any other which differed significantly from it with respect to this factor. If one did use them, the terms average, defective and superior would lose their statistical meaning.

Failure to understand this fundamental implication of the statistical concept of intelligence inevitably leads to confusion. You cannot on the one hand agree to define intelligence in terms of relative position and then disregard the rules by which such a classification is governed. When you do, incongruous and absurd consequences are inevitable. Thus L. S. Hollingworth rejecting the idea of separate norms for separate social classes writes: "If carried out to its logical conclusion this would mean that by measuring the inmates of schools for the feebleminded, we might obtain a norm which would be applicable to such inmates, on the basis of which they could be classified as 'normal.' "[7] This statement seems like a conclusive argument, but actually only shows how imperfectly its author has grasped the full statistical connotation of intelligence. She is quite correct in inferring that on the basis of norms obtained from a feebleminded institution, the average defective would rate as a normal intelligence. Indeed it is even conceivable that when classified on the basis of norms obtained on Fiji Islanders, many of the individuals of such an institution[8] might have to be classified as of superior intelligence. But what Dr. Hollingworth failed to see is that norms obtained on inmates of a feebleminded institution would be valid only for that institution, and that alone. The answer to

the same tests which we used on any other Londoner. The rejoinder is valid if by intelligence we mean intelligence as the Englishman conceives it. With this definition the Fiji Islander might well disagree. As scientists, we should at least allow him the opportunity of offering his own. It is possible that an Englishman tested with a Fiji Islander's test might not do very well either. The problem is obviously more complicated than this simplified statement of the case indicates. But we cannot dilate upon it without entering into a discussion which would carry us far beyond the scope of this book.

[7] Requoted from Wells, F. L.: *Mental Tests in Clinical Practice*, p. 60.

[8] Particularly if it were one "specializing" in high-grade defectives.

Dr. Hollingworth's quandary is that the subjects of her illustrative institution are not a separate but a selected population. They are merely the tail end of our larger population of which, for classificatory purposes, they form a part. They are not mental defectives because they happen to be in an institution for the feebleminded; they are in an institution for the feebleminded because they are mental defectives.

The great advantage of using the I.Q. as a basis for mental classification is that it does not permit us to lose sight of the fact that all measures of intelligence are necessarily relative. Nevertheless, for certain practical purposes, it is sometimes necessary to use test results *as if* they did represent absolute quantities. This is the situation when we use aptitude tests as measures of mental efficiency. In testing aptitudes, we may set up a minimal passing mark and then use this minimum as a standard for calculating indices of efficiency. The same sort of application may be made of intelligence tests. We may say, for example, that in order to be a good teacher or a good mechanic, a subject must have a minimal intelligence test score of such and such an amount. If now the I.Q. is used as a measure of the subject's intelligence, it is clear that the denominator used in calculating it assumes the rôle of the minimum score in the case of the aptitude test; and, if this denominator is constant, it will partake of all the properties of an absolute measure. Such application of the I.Q. is permissible, but when used in this way it is important to recognize that the I.Q. has been transformed into an E.Q. (Efficiency Quotient).

We have already referred to the difference between intelligence quotients and efficiency quotients. An intelligence quotient measures a person's ability relative to those of individuals of his own age group. For this comparison the entire group is assumed to be statistically homogeneous. In the case of an efficiency quotient we are not interested either in the person's age or any other factors which influence the I.Q. but only as to how his abilities compare with those of a fixed standard. Our point of view would be very much like that we would maintain in buying a machine. All that one is usually interested in when buying a machine is that it be capable of a certain amount of work in a given time and at a specified cost. The kind of material used or the time it took to manufacture it would, in most instances, be of little consequence provided the machine met our specifications. We can, if we wish, treat intelligence ratings in much the same fashion, but then it is only fair that we distinguish intellectual ability as a measure of intelligence from intellectual ability as a measure of mental efficiency.[9]

Although the I.Q. is the best single measure of intelligence, it is neither the only nor a complete measure of it. Intelligence, like personality, is too complicated an entity to be defined by a single number. It is a function of other factors beside sheer intellectual ability. We know that this must be so, because individuals having the same I.Q.'s may differ considerably as regards either their actual or potential capacity for intelligent behavior. These other factors,—drive, emotional balance, persistence,—are not always measurable or even easily discernible but have to be taken into account in concrete situations. In the practical classification of subjects, one often has to go beyond the point of merely obtaining an accurate I.Q. Sometimes it is necessary to take into account not only the subject's obvious and measurable responses during the examination, but also the record of his behavior prior to his coming for the examination.

Our last remarks suggest that in the definitive classification of a person's intelligence some regard must be paid to the subject's past history, that is, his social, emotional, and, in the case of adults, his vocational and economic adjustments.[10] The kind of life one lives is itself a pretty good test of a person's intelligence. When a life history (assuming it to be accurate) is in disagreement with the "psychometric", it is well to pause before attempting a classification on the basis of tests alone. Generally it will be found that the former is a more reliable criterion of the individual's intelligence. Inexperienced examiners are likely to over-look this fact, just as psychiatrists tend to over-emphasize it. Similar disregard of this fact is often met with in individuals who engage in what we may call *apersonal* psychometrics,—teachers who give group tests, school psychologists who are restricted to getting I.Q.'s, and college professors who merely write about them. Unfortunately, the medical profession, until recently, has been inclined to restrict the psychologist to just such apersonal psychometrics. Even more enlightened psychiatrists look upon an intelligence examination

[9] To meet the need of those who wish to use intelligence tests as measures of mental efficiency, we have calculated what we term Efficiency Quotients for the Full Bellevue Intelligence Scale. These are given and explained in appendix 2.

[10] Doll's Social Maturity Scale is an attempt to do this in a systematic way. See Doll, Edgar A.: A genetic scale of social maturity. *Amer. Jr. Orthopsychiatry*, 1935, V, 180–188.

as they do upon a Wassermann test; when an I.Q. does not come up to expectations, they feel privileged to disregard it. Apart from the fact that the analogy between a psychometric and a Wassermann test is at best a superficial one, our experience has shown that the average psychiatrist is no more expert in the field of intelligence diagnosis than the average teacher. Moreover, the rôle of a competent psychologist is not that of a laboratory technician. His techniques are not an end in themselves, but a means of diagnosis. More important than his ability to obtain an accurate I.Q. is his ability to interpret it correctly.[11]

Non-measurable factors enter into the classification of all levels of intelligence, but the evaluation of them is particularly important in defining the feebleminded group. To call a person a mental defective is a serious diagnosis. At its mildest, the result is to stigmatize the person so labeled; at its worst, it may determine whether he will be institutionalized for the greater part of his life instead of being permitted to work out his salvation in the community. In the case of the child, mental deficiency involves not only the general question of educability, but the specific problem of training and treatment. In the case of an adult it may also involve the question of legal responsibility. Mental deficiency is thus a medical and legal, as well as a psychological and social concept. This fact complicates the problem of classification. Each science necessarily has its own points of view, and this gives rise to the question whether any single system of classifying mental defectives can include them all. Our next chapter will take up this question.

[11] The interpretation of psychometric results, in our opinion, is or should be the job of the psychologist who administers them. Even the familiar I.Q., as we have seen, is a rather complicated quantity. It is not reasonable to throw the onus of interpretation upon the average doctor, teacher, judge and social worker to whom reports containing I.Q.'s eventually go. Unfortunately the common practice of sending numerical data to schools, social agencies and courts has in many instances served to deprive the psychologist of that function. The net result has been that the doctor, teacher, judge and social worker frequently take it upon themselves to do the interpretation. This is in part due to the fact that persons in administrative positions in time acquire a belief in their own expertness on a great many different subjects. In part, however, it is due to the fact that psychologists themselves have too often been remiss in the way that they present their results. A psychological report which contains two or three different I.Q.'s accompanied by a mass of technical analysis, is hardly what the lay person wants or can digest. In practical situations nobody is particularly interested in the particular score which a subject obtains on a particular test. What he wants to know is what that I.Q. means in terms of general or specific ability for adjustment.

CHAPTER 5

THE CONCEPT OF MENTAL DEFICIENCY

The concept of Mental Deficiency has, like many other concepts in psychology, undergone considerable modification since the turn of the century. This change has involved two separate, though not unrelated, alterations in point of view. The first pertains to the abstract definition of the term, the second to its practical application. Psychologists have not only sought to give a more definite answer to the question, "Who are the mental defectives?", but also sought to furnish quantitative methods for differentiating them. The shift in point of view has been from the older moral, medico-legal essays at abstract definition of mental deficiency to the current quantitative, statistical, practical methods of measuring it. Psychologists do not now speak of social defectives or moral imbeciles, but of mental ages and I.Q.'s. Accordingly a mental defective is no longer defined merely as one who because of arrested mental development, etc., is unable to handle himself or his affairs with ordinary prudence, but as an individual whose lack of intellectual endowment is such as to render him incapable of attaining a minimum score or rating on certain standardized tests, for example, an M.A. of 10 years, or an I.Q. of 70 on the Binet Intelligence Examination.

The definition of mental deficiency in terms of attained mental age or I.Q. levels on intelligence tests, represented a marked step forward but did not completely solve the problem of classification. The task still remained of arriving at (and, of course, justifying) the I.Q. or M. A. limits assigned to various degrees of mental deficiency as well as the category as a whole. And here we run into much the same difficulties that we met in the general problem of mental classification. The definition of mental deficiency is only a special or limiting case in the definition of levels of intelligence. Like the designations average, dull, superior, etc., it can only be delimited unambiguously in terms of statistical criteria. Accordingly, the most that we can say unequivocally, is that a mental defective is an individual who on a well standardized intelligence test attains a rating which places him among the lowest one, two, four or x-percent of the population. Of course this is not all that we can say about a mental defective. We can describe what he can or

49

cannot do, the chances of his reaching a certain grade in school, his likelihood of learning a given trade, and so on. All these are significant and useful facts to know, but in themselves cannot be used for psychometric classification.

The usual method of defining mental deficiency psychometrically is in terms of I.Q. or M.A. We have already discussed what these signify. It is important to reemphasize that their value as a basis of mental classification lies wholly on their statistical correlates. We may say that individuals who attain I.Q.'s below 70 are mental defectives so long as we intend, and the limit actually cuts off the lowest 2 or 3 or any other agreed upon percent of the general population. But we cannot use this criterion if in point of fact it does not agree either as to intent or fact. For example, the New York State mental hygiene law provides that individuals attaining I.Q.'s below 75 on the 1916 Revision of the Stanford-Binet can be classified as mental defectives. As it also states that I.Q.'s of adults are to be calculated on a 16 year basis, actual application of the criterion would automatically classify some 20 per cent of the white and a considerably larger per cent of the adult colored population of the United States as mental defectives. It is extremely doubtful if those who formulated the provision knew, much less intended, the provision to be as drastic as it would turn out to be if actually applied.

The statistical definition of mental deficiency for which we have argued differs from most current psychometric definitions in several respects. The most important of these differences is that it designates no precise mental age or I.Q. which specifically classifies an individual as a mental defective. It argues for the use of standardized tests, but at the same time implies that an identical M.A. or I.Q. may in the case of one individual denote deficiency and in the case of another fail to indicate it. There are three reasons for this. The first derives from our biological definition of intelligence which insists that intelligence involves other items than purely intellective factors; the second follows from our purely statistical definition of degrees of relative ability; and the third from our refusal to accept the current notion that mental deficiency is a unitary entity. The first two points have already been elaborated in previous chapters and we shall now only enlarge upon the last contention.

Mental deficiency, unlike typhoid fever or general paresis, is not a circumscribed entity.[1] A mental defective is not a person who suffers

[1] The remarks that follow are in part a reproduction of the author's paper on "The Concept of Mental Deficiency in Theory and Practice", *Psychiatric Bulletin* 1935, IX, pp. 232–236.

from a specific disease, but one whose general intellectual inadequacy allocates him to a social group whose level of functioning is such as to make it impossible for him to cope with his environment. Mental defectives are primarily individuals who because of lack of mental ability need special care, education and institutionalization. They are individuals who for reasons other than special physical or mental disabilities (neuroses, psychoses, etc.) are unable to care for themselves.

A mental defective is characterized not only by a lack of ability to care for himself but also by an incapacity to use effectively whatever abilities he does have. His actions are often not only senseless and inadequate but perverse and anti-social as well. He may be not only stupid but vicious, and the question arises why he is sometimes one and not the other? Is it due merely to the fact that he is unable to comprehend the significance of his acts or is his perverse behavior due to other deficiencies? What we are, of course, asking by these questions is whether mental deficiency, is, as is commonly held, exclusively a matter of lack of intellectual ability or whether it also includes inadequacies in other aspects of the individual's endowment.

The answer is that except in the case of individuals of very low intelligence (imbeciles and idiots) it is generally necessary to take into account factors other than sheer lack of intellectual ability in making a diagnosis of mental deficiency. This is particularly true of individuals who fall psychometrically into the moron, highgrade moron and borderline defective groups. Here an I Q. alone, however accurately determined, is often insufficient for a definitive classification. This is shown by the fact that there are many individuals with I.Q.'s above 70 whose behaviour is definitely defective. On the other hand there are individuals with I.Q.'s below 60 whose entire life history is that of a non-defective.

The following case illustrates that of an individual with a relatively high I.Q. who must nevertheless be considered a mental defective:

J. M., 26 years old, native white, was arrested on a charge of impairing the morals of a minor (a girl of 10 years). He is reported to have made similar attempts on several previous occasions and had, for some years, been a persistent problem on this account. The family states: "We have always kept an eye on him because we felt he would get into trouble."

Physical examination: Unattractive-looking youth who appears to be younger than he is. General physical and neurological examination as well as blood Wassermann is negative.

Psychiatric examination: Appears dull and indifferent and childish. General reactions, immature. Is careless about person, but able to take care of himself. Diagnosis: mental defective-moron.

Psychological examination: Stanford-Binet, 13 years 8 months, I.Q. (15 years) 91. Scatter IX–XVI, inclusive. Except for designs (patient had bad vision), no failures below XII year level.

Work history: Patient was never able to find work for himself but a number of jobs were procured for him by his father. These he was unable to hold for any length of time.

The case just cited is typical of many that come to the attention of any large clinic. Frequently the subjects are sex delinquents and, more often than not, individuals who have gotten into trouble with the law or otherwise proved themselves incapable of meeting the ordinary exigencies of social adjustment. On psychometric examinations they may rate dull-normal, or even average. Judged by social criteria they are mentally defective.

That such a group exists has been long recognized by those dealing first hand with delinquent and socially inadequate individuals. They are patients whom Tredgold[2] has called "individuals lacking both in prudence and moral sense" though yet suffering from no scholastic or educational disability. As Tredgold well points out, an individual falling into this group "far from being illiterate, may have quite a good range of educational requirements. He may be nimble-witted, a good conversationalist, plausible in argument and be able to give a good account of himself." In spite of this he is anti-social and requires supervision for his own welfare as well as for the protection of others. What he lacks essentially is an ordinary adaptiveness or "wisdom in the moral sense", and it is important to realize, as Tredgold insists, that such a person "is mentally defective in the usual and necessary sense of the term."

In contrast to the above, there is another group of individuals who systematically rate as mental defectives on mental tests, but, who can in no way be classified in this group when diagnosed on the basis of concrete social standards, i.e., in terms of capacity to adjust to the normal demands of their social and economic environment. They are frequently illiterate and, commonly, individuals coming from definite social strata where opportunity for education is small, and stultifying labor the general rule; many belong to what might be termed the "peasant type", as indeed they frequently are by origin. However, the first case of this type that came to our attention was a native, white Oklahoman of 28, who had come up for individual psychological exam-

[2] Tredgold, A. F.: *Mental Deficiency*. 5th Ed., Baltimore, 1929.

inations because he had failed to pass the Army Alpha and Army Beta intelligence tests. On both Stanford-Binet and the Yerkes Point Scale he obtained a mental age of less than 8 years. Nevertheless, before entering the Army he had gotten along very well, was supporting a family, had been working as a skilled oil-driller for several years and, at the time of draft, was earning from $60 to $75 per week. Incidentally, he was making the grade as a soldier, and would not have come to the attention of the authorities had he not failed on the psychological tests.

It would be possible to cite many cases,[3] particularly from among adults of foreign birth, who rate systematically defective even on non-verbal tests, but whose social life history of at least an adequate adjustment contradicts this classification. Nor can we disregard at this point the question of negro intelligence tests results, which if taken at face value, would necessitate our classifying over 40 per cent of that group as mental defectives. No one, we believe, at all in contact with reality, would venture such a conclusion, however much suggested by test results. In any case, actual clinical experience shows that there are certain individuals who regularly test as very inferior and frequently as mental defectives on standard psychometric tests but who, nevertheless, are able to adapt and adjust—make good housewives, adequate breadwinners, useful citizens and can and do get along not only in rural but urban environments. It is clear that these people are not mentally defective as defined by law or common sense. Nevertheless, by the tests available at present for measuring intellectual ability they are systematically selected as inferior individuals on a par with those who are recognized as needing institutional care as mental defectives.

From facts such as these it seems evident that there is not one, but several kinds of mental deficiency—that the concept of mental deficiency is far from a simple entity. There are at least two and probably three types of mental deficiency. The first is the intellectual defective, diagnosable as such by the usual psychometric tests; the second, the social defective for whom the life history of the individual is the most satisfactory criterion; and, third—the emotional or "moral" defective whose precise definition is extremely difficult to give, but whose existence, to any one who has had any first hand experience at a large clinic, is an observable reality. Between all three there is usually a certain degree of correlation, but this correlation is not sufficiently high to make any one an unfailing diagnostic indicator of the other.

[3] Two such cases are cited in Ch. 9, p. 130 (Case D. W.) and p. 132 (Case M. B.).

CHAPTER 6

THE PROBLEM OF MENTAL DETERIORATION

In speaking of mental deterioration much depends on what one means by "mental" and how one proceeds to define deterioration. By mental we shall mean primarily intellectual abilities,[1] and by deterioration any conspicuous falling off or loss in these abilities. Concretely, a person will be considered as giving evidence of mental deterioration when he is no longer able to carry on his intellectual tasks with the speed, accuracy or efficiency previously characteristic of his functioning level. The only condition to be added is that the loss must not be one which is due merely to lack of practice.

The definition of mental deterioration which we have just given is much broader than what is generally understood by it. Most psychiatrists and neurologists would not consider a mere falling off or loss in general capacity as an indication of mental deterioration. This is because they are primarily acquainted with mental impairment when associated with some organic or brain injury. But mental decline may and does occur independently of any specific mental disease. It is characteristic not only of such conditions as general paresis, cerebral arteriosclerosis, or chronic alcoholism but of all senescent decline. Nevertheless, for diagnostic convenience, mental deterioration may be said to be of two sorts—that which occurs after maturity with the natural increase of age, and that which is consequent to some brain lesion or prolonged mental disease occurring at any age. Psychiatrists and neurologists have been primarily concerned with the latter and have almost entirely disregarded what for want of a better term, we shall refer to as "normal mental deterioration". Psychologically, however, there is little difference between the two, except as regards the rate at which deterioration occurs and, in the case of traumatic injury, as regards the number of mental functions involved. The deterioration met with in normal old people is similar to that met with

[1] This is an arbitrary delimitation of the term. Emotion is no less mental than intellect, but the delimitation of the term when used in connection with deterioration corresponds to what is generally implied by it in clinical practice. Thus psychiatrists distinguish "emotional" from "mental," that is to say, "intellectual" deterioration.

in most organic brain diseases. Senility,[2] or extreme mental deterioration, is merely a terminal state of certain processes which begin relatively early in life and continue progressively with age. The net result of the accompanying changes is to impair all original endowment. Whether we wish to reserve the term mental deterioration to cover only the extreme losses of ability or prefer to apply it equally to the entire senescent decline is a matter of convenience. For an understanding of the impairment as a whole, however, it is essential that we have as full knowledge as possible of all changes which occur in human ability with age. It is these changes which we propose to discuss in this chapter.

The changes in human capacities which occur with age fall into two self-limiting epochs: (1) The period during which they increase and (2) the period during which they fall off with age. The first of these is the well known period of growth which need not detain us here. The second period is that of gradual decline, regarding which there is still much difference of opinion but whose main trends have been sufficiently established to warrant a general description. We have elsewhere summed up the main facts regarding the decline of capacities with age[3] but for the sake of completeness will briefly summarize them again.

Every human capacity after attaining a maximum begins an immediate decline. This decline is at first very slow but after a while increases perceptibly. The age at which the maximum is attained varies from ability to ability but seldom occurs beyond 30 and in most cases somewhere in the early 20's. Once the decline begins it progresses continually. Between the ages of 30 and 60 it is more or less linear. In the case of most abilities the decline between these ages may be described with good approximation by an equation of the first degree. These facts are graphically summarized in figure 3. The bold-faced curve is the smoothed line of means of Bellevue intelligence test scores for subjects from age 15 to 65; the light curve, that for Vital Capacity measures for the same age period. Both have been reduced to comparable scale units.[4] As will be seen the maximum of both curves

[2] Senility, unlike "senile psychosis," is not a clinical entity. Even the latter is seldom used alone. Usually there is some qualifying condition added; thus: senile psychosis with arteriosclerosis, senile psychosis with Alzheimer's disease, and so on.

[3] Wechsler, D.: *The Range of Human Capacities*. Chapter VII.

[4] The test-score means were derived from an abbreviated 8-test scale; the actual means for the Full Bellevue Scale are given on page 118. Those for Vital Capacity will be found in an article by Ruger and Stoessiger, *Annals of Eugenics* 1926, vol. II., pp. 85 and 104.

occurs in the age period 20 to 25, with that of Intelligence somewhat earlier than that for Vital (Lung) Capacity. Another point of interest is that the Intelligence Test curve declines at a faster rate than the curve of Vital Capacity. This may seem strange but is not an artifact. Contrary to common belief many of our intellectual abilities show greater impairment with age than do our physical ones.[5] The actual decline in any given case, however, varies with the ability in question.

The curve of mental decline shown in figure 3* is a composite curve. It is composite, first, in the sense that the points used in plotting it have been derived from measurements obtained on large groups and

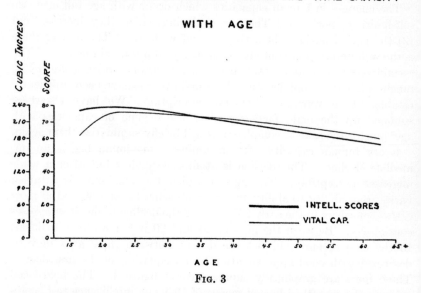

FIG. 3

not on single individuals. But it is also composite in the sense that the decline described represents the age changes in mental capacity, not with respect to any specific ability, but with respect to the average of a large number of abilities. The groups of abilities here considered are those represented by the tests which happen to constitute our

[5] The most conspicuous decline of all is shown in the sensory field. Vision and hearing fall off rapidly after 30. Their curves of decline, however, are far from straight lines. See on this point Ruger and Stoessiger, *op. cit.*

* See also figure 2, p. 29. The curve of mental decline shown by the heavy line in figure 3 has been "reduced" to make it comparable to the Vital Capacity curve given along side of it. It has also been "smoothed".

scale. A scale made up of a different set of tests might furnish an age curve which differed significantly from the one we obtained. To determine whether such were the case one would have to examine the same group of individuals with a large variety of scales, each as different from the other as possible. We were unable to do this. But, as a possible alternative approach, we compared the age curve obtained with the Full Scale with age curves obtained from combinations of only certain of the tests[6] and also with age curves obtained from the individual tests, taken separately. Individual age curves for six of our ten tests are given in figures 4 and 4A.

As will be seen from their examination, the form of all these curves is the same as that of the generalized curve given in figure 3. The decline of any given ability, like that of any combination of them, is essentially linear. The main difference between them pertains to the age at which the initial decline begins and more particularly to the rate at which the decline proceeds. Different mental abilities decline at different rates. That they do is psychometrically fortunate, because these differences can be made use of in determining mental deterioration.

The decline of mental ability with age is part of the general senescent process of the organism as a whole. Hitherto the common view has been that our mental abilities, unlike our physical abilities, remain relatively unimpaired until rather late in life (senility), except as an occasional consequence of disease or traumatic injury. This was an unsubstantiated hypothesis tenable only so long as no facts were at hand to oppose it. But the view still persists even though such facts are now available. Most people, including scientists, hate to believe that they are not as mentally alert at 50 as they were at 20. Part of this is due to a confounding of mental with practical ability, that is, a failure to differentiate between intellectual endowment and the success had in applying it. The latter is naturally dependent in no small measure upon experience. What one has lost through a falling off of native ability one may often replace by acquired knowledge. An old clinician may be a better doctor than a younger one, even though he possess less actual understanding of disease processes.

Another item which contributes to the biased attitude towards the facts of mental decline is the historical distinction between physical and mental. According to this distinction the latter is conceived of being higher, better or more important. Accordingly few people are

---

[6] For example, curves obtained from verbal tests alone, or performance tests alone.

concerned when told that at 40 they cannot hear or fight as well as when they were 20, but are quite "het up" when informed that they probably also cannot calculate or reason as well. There also exists a kind of hierarchy of relative values as regards the various mental

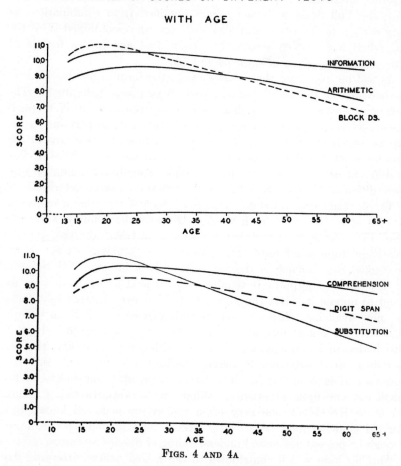

VARIATION OF SCORES ON DIFFERENT TESTS

WITH AGE

Figs. 4 and 4a

abilities themselves. Professor Cattell long ago called attention to the fact that people are ever ready to complain about their bad memory, but seldom of their poor judgment or common sense. But it is certain that memory is not the only mental capacity which declines with age, nor the one which is always most impaired by it. Conrad a.,.., Jones,[7] for example, found that older people (individuals over 50) did much better on the Army Alpha Test calling for general information, than on the one calling for abstract reasoning (the Analogies Test), and we ourselves have found that they do better on repeating digits forwards than in detecting similarities.

We have put forward the hypothesis that the decline of mental ability with age is part of the general organic process which constitutes the universal phenomenon of senescence, and have insisted upon the fact that the phenomenon begins relatively early in life. The evidence we have adduced for this hypothesis is the observed parallelism we have found in the rate of decline of various physical and mental abilities. Another line of evidence is furnished by neurological studies of the brains of senile individuals. These are not always clear-cut cases because they may be associated with special trauma or organic disease. If our hypothesis is correct, however, the same changes, though of course to a lesser degree, ought to be expected much earlier in life, say from 20 years onward. Up to the present, experimental data supporting this view have been lacking. This may be due to the fact that neuropathology has not been particularly alive to the problem, or, as is more probable, to the fact that neurological techniques are not sufficiently advanced to detect very small and gradual alterations[8] which may, and undoubtedly do, occur in brain tissue. There is, however, some indirect evidence that alteration of the brain begins at an early age, which may be considered as supporting our view. We refer to the progressive change in brain weight with age.

It has been known for some time[9] that the mean weight of the adult brain declines with age. The skull thickens and the brain shrinks. It we accept the brain as the organ of the mind, it is only reasonable to assume that even gross changes such as alterations of weight may also affect its function. Assuming that to be the case, we should expect that the changes in brain weight show some concomitance with alterations in general intellectual ability,—a fact which we thought might be demonstrated by an analysis of both in relation to the age factor. The graphs in figure 5 represent the result of such a study. They

[7] Genet. Psychol. Monog. 1933, pp. 260–261.
[8] Probably because most of these are atomic or molecular and therefore not discernible under the microscope.
[9] Pearl, R.: Variations and correlation in brain weight. Biomet., 1905, vol. IV, pp. 13–104.

are the age curves for intellectual ability and brain weight for ages 15 to 65. Necessarily they were not obtained from the same subjects. The age curve for intellectual ability is that obtained for subjects given the tests which were used in standardizing our Bellevue Scale; the brain weight curve is that computed from figures for brain weights of autopsied subjects of comparable ages, collected by Rössle and Routlet.[10] For purposes of comparison, the curves have been reduced to approximately the same scale. Inspection of these curves reveals a close parallelism between loss in brain weight and decline in mental

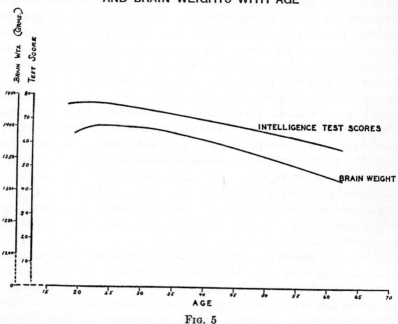

**VARIATION OF INTELLIGENCE TEST SCORES
AND BRAIN WEIGHTS WITH AGE**

Fig. 5

ability with age. It is probable that, with a different series of brain weights and a different series of tests, the similarity between the two curves would not be so marked. But the general parallelism cannot be ascribed either to chance or artifact. It is much better than that found between most physical and mental traits and as good as that found between curves for many mental abilities taken separately.

[10] Data given in Wertham's, F.: *The Brain as an Organ.* New York, 1934. The brain weights are those of males 16 years and over, averaged for five year periods.

The decline in the weight of brain, like that in intellectual ability, is essentially linear.[11] After reaching a maximum, at about age 20, the brain begins to decline in weight, somewhat irregularly at first, but after 25 or 30 at a fairly constant rate.

If our generalizations regarding the influence of age on mental deterioration are correct, it follows that mental deterioration in human beings begins at a relatively early age. However, to speak of a person in his early 30's as showing signs of deterioration because he already manifests some measurable decline of ability, would be stretching the term beyond its usual connotation. Clearly that is not what is implied by deterioration in the ordinary sense. It would seem desirable to restrict the term to only such impairment or losses in ability as are significantly greater than those due to the age factor alone. To do this we must necessarily know what the normal loss of ability is for the average individual and the mean limits of variability at all ages for the normal population. But even with these facts at hand we are only at the beginning of our task. To evaluate deterioration we must be able to measure it quantitatively.

The measurement of mental deterioration involves three separate problems: (1) The reliable measurement of the individual's actual or present functioning ability; (2) the evaluation of his previous functioning level; (3) the expression of the difference between the two in meaningful, quantitative terms. Up to the present, none of the three problems has had complete solution. We say none, although as regards the measurement of present functioning ability this statement is not altogether correct. We do have considerable means of measuring an individual's functioning ability, but these means, in general, are unsuitable for precisely those groups on whom they are most needed in studying mental deterioration, namely, the older adults. What we have said regarding the inadequacy of available general intelligence scales for the measurement of adult intelligence, holds equally for individual tests of mental ability. They have seldom been standardized for adults. The Bellevue Scales presented in this book are an attempt to furnish the necessary adult norms for such tests. By means of the tests which compose them we are now able to measure a fairly large number of intellectual abilities throughout the greater part of adult life, that is, up to the age of 60, and in some instances up to the age of 70.

The second step in the measurement of deterioration, namely, the evaluation of an individual's previous functioning level, presents a

[11] For further evidence on this point see Pearl, R.: *Studies in Human Biology.* Baltimore, 1924, pp. 58–65.

much more difficult problem. The reason is that in most cases we have no psychometric data by which such evaluation can be made. Few persons examined for mental deterioration have ever had a previous psychological examination. Yet, in order to make an accurate estimate of a person's normal functioning ability, we should have not only one but a series of psychometric examinations on him, done at various intervals and so far as possible with the same or comparable tests. That, however, is an ideal situation which cannot be realized at present.

In practice, it is necessary to turn to other sources of data that will enable us to appraise the subject's previous functioning ability. The data usually consist of facts gleaned from the subject's educational, vocational and social history. Thus, if from a subject's history we learn that he is a high school graduate, that he has held responsible positions for a number of years and that he attained some social recognition in his community, we can safely assume that he must have been a person of at least average endowment and that he should be able to perform certain mental operations which may be expected of individuals of comparable endowment. But information of this sort is of value only where the discrepancy between an individual's actual and expected functioning is considerable. Thus, if a formerly successful business man at age 45 attains an I.Q. of only 70, is unable to do simple calculations and can no longer repeat 5 digits, we should know at once that he has deteriorated. Degrees of deterioration of this sort, however, can ordinarily be detected without standardized psychometric examination.

We do not need tests to discover deterioration in an old paretic. The merit of psychometric tests is that they can show us small differences of ability, and their usefulness in the clinical field depends upon how well they can do this. Their value in determining mental deterioration must reside in their ability to detect changes in mental functioning long before they have so disorganized the behavior of the individual as to make them patent to all. For such purposes a general social and psychiatric history is insufficient as a base for comparison. We must either have psychometric records of previous examinations with the same or similar tests, or be able to use the results of the mental tests given at any specific examination as a means of inferring the probable previous ability of the individual. However, as already mentioned, few adults who come up for psychometric examination have had previous mental tests, and even fewer were done sufficiently long ago to enable us to make a comparison between their present and their former functioning. It is here that the age curves for separate abilities which we give in figures 4 and 4A are of value.

One of the interesting facts revealed by the age curves for different abilities obtained on the same groups of individuals, is that certain abilities decline more slowly with age than others. Thus, the abilities called for by the General Information and General Comprehension Tests hold up much better than do the abilities called for by the Substitution and the Memory Span for Digits Tests. This difference in rate of decline of various abilities suggests a possibility of estimating previous functioning levels. Thus, if the abilities which do not decline significantly with age were precisely those which were least affected by the deteriorative process, one could assume that scores which individuals attain on tests measuring these abilities represented their original or permanent endowment. If now we combined a number of these tests into a rounded scale, such a scale would furnish us a means of measuring mental deterioration as well as past functioning levels in terms of present functioning abilities. All that would be necessary would be to compare the mean score which a subject attained on the tests which remain relatively unimpaired with age, with the rating which he obtains on a group of tests which are relatively much impaired with age. The ratio or difference between their rates of decline would give us the required measure.

The method outlined above for comparing previous and present functioning ability in terms of test scores obtained in a single examination of a subject may be termed the *differential-test-score method* of measuring mental deterioration.[12] As we have just seen, it makes use of the fact that some abilities decline relatively little during adult life and others to a considerable degree, and assumes that the difference between their rates of decline in any given individual expresses his relative degree of deterioration. The usefulness of the differential-test-score method for evaluating deterioration necessarily depends upon the availability of tests with full age norms. Ideally, we should have to have available age curves for many different abilities, each measured in as many ways as possible with tests whose validity and effectiveness had been previously established. At present such tests are all too few, but the eleven subtests made available by the standardization of the Wechsler-Bellevue offers the possibility of trying out the method just discussed.

---

[12] Some attempt to use methods like the one just outlined has already been made by a number of psychologists. (Babcock, H., *Arch. of Psychol.*, 1930, no. 117; Gilbert, J. D., *Arch. of Psychol.*, 1935, no. 188; Shipley, W. C., *J. Psychol.*, 1940, 9, 371–377; Hunt. H., *J. Appl. Psychol.*, 1943, 5, 375–387.)

The first step in the application of the differential test score method is the optimal allocation of tests to the "Hold" vs. "Don't Hold" groups. In general, the tests which drop most markedly with age belong, as might be expected, with the "Don't Hold" and those which drop least, with the "Hold" tests. But another factor must also be considered, namely, the type of ability measured by the tests. There must be some functional similarity between the opposed or contrasted tests. If this is not the case, we risk making test combinations which, though showing significant differences, are likely to give spurious discriminants. For example, most abilities tapped by performance tests decline much more rapidly with age than those involved in verbal tests. At first thought it might appear that this situation could be capitalized by using verbal tests against performance tests as a ready means of obtaining measures of "Hold" vs. "Don't Hold" abilities. This, however, would be a mistake because, if we accepted differences between the scores on verbal and performance tests as a criterion of deterioration, all individuals who have relatively good verbal capacity would inevitably show greater mental deterioration as they grew older. This would follow from the fact that the differences between verbal and performance abilities automatically increase with age. On the other hand, people who are relatively good in performance tests would show lesser deterioration or indeed none at all, because the discrepancy between their verbal and performance scores would become smaller and smaller as they grew older. Accordingly, in assembling our "Hold" vs. "Don t Hold" batteries we have brought together approximately the same number of verbal as performance tests. The tests combined in each of the proposed categories are as follows:

Tests which hold up with age
   Information
   Comprehension
   Object Assembly
   Picture Completion
   Vocabulary

Tests which do not hold up with age
   Digit Span
   Arithmetic
   Digit Symbol
   Block Design
   Similarities
   (Picture Arrangement)

To obtain a measure of deterioration, one compares the sum weighted scores of the "Hold" tests with that of the "Don't Hold" tests, allowing for the difference in number of tests in each group, or for a more strict comparison the sum of the first four tests of the "Hold" with the first four tests of the "Don't Hold" group. The resulting comparison may be expressed either as a ratio or difference between the two sums. Naturally, if the result is given as a difference it must be expressed as a percent difference in order to take into account the absolute magnitude of the sums compared. Thus, if the sum of a subject's "Hold" subtest scores is 50 and the sum of his "Don't Hold" subtest scores 40, he shows a deterioration loss of 20% and efficiency quotient of .80. Deterioration is indicated if the percent loss is considerable or the efficiency quotient low, that is considerably below 100.

The problem, of course, is to define what is meant by considerable or significant loss. In the long run such a definition would have to be statistical in character and be based on a distribution of individual percents of loss or calculated deterioration quotients of a sufficiently large number of cases both normal and pathological. These data are not yet available, but it is possible to arrive at effective approximations by the use of tables 39 and 40 given in appendix 2. This table contains the mean scores of all the subtests at successive age periods. Summing the subtest scores of the tests composing each of the batteries compared, we can obtain the total weighted score that may be expected for the "Hold" and "Don't Hold" batteries at different ages. Next, it only remains to treat the resulting sums in the manner described above, and obtain what may be termed "normal" or average deterioration expectancies. These are given in tables 6 and 6A.

Table 6 was obtained as follows: at each age level sums were obtained of the mean test scores of the Information, Comprehension (or Vocabulary[13]), Picture Completion and Object Assembly tests, (Hold tests), and of the Digit Span, Arithmetic, Block design and Digit Symbol tests, respectively. The sum of the "Don't Hold" tests at each level was then subtracted from the sum of the "Hold" tests and the difference divided by the minuend. The result is expected normal percent deterioration loss. If instead of expressing deterioration in terms of a difference one wishes to express it as a ratio, the sum of the "Don't Hold" tests is

[13] In practice it will be found safer to use the Vocabulary than the Comprehension test.

divided directly by the sum of the "Hold," and the results so obtained constitute deterioration quotients. These are given in table 6A.

We may now define deterioration in the pathological sense: An individual may be said to show signs of possible deterioration if he shows a greater than a 10 percent loss, and of definite deterioration if a loss greater than 20 percent[14] than that allowed for by the normal decline with age. Obviously the larger the loss the greater the probability that we are dealing with true deterioration.

TABLE 6

Average (Normal) Deterioration Loss at Different Ages
(In percent)

HOLD − DON'T HOLD ÷ HOLD	AGES							
	20-24	25-29	30-34	35-39	40-44	45-49	50-54	55-59
Calculated Values.........	0.5	0	4	4	9	11	14	16
Smoothed Values..........	0	1	3	5	8	11	14	16

TABLE 6A

Average (Normal) Deterioration Quotients at Different Ages

DON'T HOLD ÷ HOLD × 100	AGES							
	20-24	25-29	30-34	35-39	40-44	45-49	50-54	55-59
Calculated Values.........	99.5	100	96	96	91	89	86	84
Smoothed Values..........	100	99	97	95	92	89	86	84

We shall now present a few applications of the procedure described above, restricting ourselves to the percent of loss technique as the preferred method.

On page 161 is cited a case of a man age 54 with symptoms of headache, dizziness and history of an old skull fracture. The case was used to illustrate the organic brain impairment pattern. But the psychometric also serves to illustrate what is not so obvious, a test score distribution indicating marked mental deterioration. This is not suggested by the subject's test performance as a whole, since his I.Q. is

[14] Losses of 10 and 20 percent correspond roughly to deviations of −1 P.E. and −2 P.E. from the mean at age 20–25. The mean loss at this age is, of course, 0. The equivalents at other ages may be assumed to be roughly of the same order, but the percent of loss must of course be calculated from the altered means at these ages (see table 6).

103 and shows no discrepancy between his total Verbal and total Performance ratings. If, however, we compare his scores on the "Hold" and "Don't Hold" tests we find the following: Information—11, Comprehension—11, Object Assembly–11, Picture Completion–10, Arithmetic–6, Digit Span–9, Block Design–7, Digit Symbol–4. The sum of the "Hold" tests is 43, that of the "Don't Hold" 26; from which by applying the method outlined above, the deterioration loss $\left(\dfrac{43 - 26}{43}\right)$, is found to be 40 percent or, allowance being made for his normal decline with age (see table 6), a net loss of 26 percent. This is obviously considerable; actually, the subject was unable to continue at his job. The method just described will be most useful in determining mental deterioration in organic brain cases, but it may also be applied in cases of Schizophrenia. Here special considerations arising from the peculiarities in test patterning of this group must be borne in mind. Thus, the not uncommon low score of the Schizophrenic on the Comprehension and still lower ones on the Picture Completion test (see Case S-2); or, again, the fact that schizophrenic patients do systematically worse on the Object Assembly than on the Block Design, and so on.

Another possible application of the method is in the appraisal of the reported effects of shock treatment, negative as well as positive. Here in addition to some of the considerations already mentioned, there is also the problem of practice effect inherent in all retest procedures, and in particular its differential effect on the various tests used. But perhaps the most serious limitation to the method as a whole is the assumed very high reliability of the tests themselves. Such high order of reliability does not in fact exist. For some of the tests, such as the Vocabulary, it is reassuringly high and perhaps sufficient, but for most of the others no such claim can be made. Nevertheless the method does prove effective in practice, and if the limitations discussed are borne in mind, may be applied with reasonable confidence.

A particular point worth calling attention to is the frequency with which certain functions are involved in the deterioration of mentally ill patients irrespective of the disease entity. Thus alcoholics (Korsakoff type), paretics, seniles and schizophrenics all do badly on Digits Backwards, Hard Associations, Reproducing Designs and the Digit Symbol Test. They do not, however, do so for the same reason. The paretic and alcoholic fail on repetition of Digits Backwards and on the Digit Symbol Test because of definite retention and learning disabilities, the dementia praecox patient because of poor attention, self-preoccupation and general inability to concentrate.[15] Nevertheless, from certain practical points of view, the disabilities may amount to the same thing. Both types of patients cannot be trusted to execute simple tasks or to follow complicated directions.

This brings up again the interesting question of the nature of the deteriorative processes. There is no doubt that, as a result of certain traumatic injuries, individuals show special disabilities. But the recurrence of like disabilities in different traumatic injuries strongly suggest the generalized nature of the deteriorative process. The brain acts as a whole and its impairment in one place affects its functioning as a whole. The fact that its disorganization is greater along one rather than another line is of secondary importance. For this reason it is perhaps not particularly important what tests are used in detecting it, providing they are such tests as are especially sensitive to the patient's intellectual functioning.

In general, mental deterioration is best revealed by measuring speed of response, learning and the ability to perceive new configurations, particularly spatial ones. Ordinarily, it is not the form of the test but the function it calls forth that determines its diagnostic value. One can measure speed of response almost equally well by counting the number of words the subject gives in three minutes, or by the number of A's he can cancel on a printed page in a like period. But it makes considerable difference when we study learning ability, whether we use "old" or "new" paired associates. Chronic alcoholics, for example, tested with a list of paired associates such as *come—go* and *Boston— Massachusetts* show little impairment, but when tested with a list of hard paired associates like *crush—dark* and *Appleby—Texas* will show considerable impairment. The reason is that while the test is of the same form, the functions involved are quite different. One requires the formation of new, the other merely the recall of old associations.

We have defined deterioration primarily as an impairment or loss of function. Sometimes this impairment manifests itself as a disorganization, sometimes as a mere regression to primitive types of response. Both occur in various types of organic brain disease. The disturbances met with in the visual motor field are particularly striking and have been extensively studied by Lauretta Bender by use of the Wertheimer

[15] This is the usual psychiatric interpretation. For a very different explanation, see Babcock, H.: *Dementia Praecox*. N. Y., 1935.

figures which she has standardized into a visual-motor Gestalt test.[16] We have applied her test to patients variously diagnosed as seniles, and found that the figures are reproduced by these patients as primitive loops or segments of large arcs, perseverated in a wavelike manner.[17] This is precisely the kind of thing that Bender found to be characteristic of children's efforts prior to the maturation of the psychomotor function, (at M.A. level of approximately 2 years) and in particular of mentally defective children of about this M.A. level. Veritably we must add another stage of Shakespeare's Seven Ages, the age of just plain *sans* everything.

[16] Bender, L.: The Visual-motor Gestalt Test and Its Clinical Use. *Research Monographs*, Amer. Ortho. Psych. Assoc., New York, 1938, particularly Chapter VIII.

[17] It is interesting to note that these changes are precisely those observed in patients with severe sensory aphasia. Seniles are, of course, frequently aphasic. Cf. Bender, L.: *Arch. of Neur. & Psych.*, 1933, XXX, 514–537.

PART II

THE BELLEVUE INTELLIGENCE SCALES

TEST MATERIALS described in the pages that follow may be obtained from the Test Division, The Psychological Corporation, 522 Fifth Ave., New York 18, N. Y.

CHAPTER 7

SELECTION AND DESCRIPTION OF TESTS

The first problem that confronts any one attempting to devise an intelligence scale is that of deciding upon the tests that should be included in the battery. This task is not a simple one, for, in addition to the necessity for fulfilling certain statistical criteria, there are a number of general considerations, which, independent of all other factors, restrict one's choice to a greater or lesser degree. One of these is the author's defined or implied view as to the nature of intelligence. Thus, if he believes that intelligence involves primarily the ability to perceive logical relations and to use symbols, he is very likely to favor tests calling for verbal, arithmetical and, in general, abstract reasoning abilities. If he believes intelligence also involves abilities to handle "practical situations", he is very likely to include at least some tests calling for performance and manipulative abilities.

The choice of tests is further restricted by the special requirements of the various types of scales themselves. Certain tests, for example, which are suitable for age scales cannot be used satisfactorily for point scales and vice versa. Thus items involving psychomotor ability, such as tying a bowknot and copying a diamond, are found excellent for age scales, but are almost useless for continuous point scales not only because of their limited range but by virtue of the fact that by increasing their complexity one alters the type of ability measured by the tests. For example, at age seven, ability to copy a diamond is a very good indication of the child's intelligence, but if we increase the complexity of this task, say by demanding the reproduction of a bisected rhomboid, we succeed in making the test more difficult but add little to its discriminative value, as a test of intelligence. And if we proceed to make the task still more difficult, we are likely to wind up with a test that measures primarily some specialized or even "new" ability. In this connection, it may be noted that the same difficulty inheres in all tests to a greater or lesser degree. Beyond certain points every test ceases to be an effective measure of the capacity which it was originally designed to measure either because superadded factors begin to enter into the relationship or because the curve of its measured function tends to reach an asymptotic level. Thus memory span for digits correlates with general intelligence up to a certain point, but beyond the ability to repeat 6 or 7 digits forward, its correlation becomes practically negligible. On the other hand, many performance tests (for example, the Ship Test) cease to be a measure of intelligence at about the 12 year level, because above this age, maximum scores are obtained by most subjects.

What is true for tests taken individually is true of them when combined into scales. Every mental scale eventually reaches a point or level beyond which increasing scores on it show relatively little correlation with intelligence as originally conceived. That is inevitable. But, of course, different scales may, and do, differ considerably as regards the location of the point where they cease to be effective measures of intelligence. Naturally, every author of a scale seeks to extend this limit as far as possible, but if the range of the scale is at all wide this desire to extend its limits entails serious restrictions in the choice of material. For it is unfortunately true that those tests which discriminate well at lower levels of intelligence generally do not do so at upper levels, and vice versa. It is for this reason, among others, that our scale does not go below the seventh year. We were unable to find any battery of tests which would discriminate below that year and still be valid for use with adults.

Yet another factor limiting the choice of possible test material is the degree to which one is ready to bow to the dicta of experience. It may seem like insisting on the obvious to assert that the worthwhileness of a test can be determined only by the way it shows up when actually tried out. It is surprising, however, how many tests that form part and parcel of most scales turn out to be poor indicators of intelligence when checked against clinical experience. A long list of such tests could readily be made. The thing that first calls one's attention to the possible inadequacy of these tests is that one often finds stupid people doing well and superior people not infrequently failing on them. These include such tasks as giving rhymes, checking letters, making designs, defining unusual words, repeating long series of numbers, putting together formboards, to mention only a few of the types of tasks frequently offered as tests of intelligence. It is the inclusion of items like these in our scales that often arouses the scepticism of the laity towards intelligence tests as a whole. This general scepticism is unwarranted, but it is unquestionably true that the purely statistical criterion of passing or failing an item at a given age level, is far from sufficient ground for accepting it as a valid measure of intelligence. Thus the fact that approximately as large a percentage of adults succeed in repeating 8 digits forward as in solving the ingenuity problem of year XVIII of the Stanford-Binet in no way proves that they are equally good tests of intelligence. In 15 years of continuous testing, we have not found a single person of inferior intelligence who has succeeded on the latter, though we have seen scores of mental defectives passing the former; and most clinicians, we believe, can testify to the truth of this observation.

The point we have been making is that all tests, in the long run, must be subjected to some effective experimental check-up, or practical criterion of validation. This pragmatic criterion of practical validity seems to have been insufficiently emphasized by the makers of test scales. Altogether too many items used in most intelligence scales have been included on the basis of purely statistical and a priori grounds. Unfortunately, this method of choosing test items is far from infallible. The only way one can know whether a test item is a really "good" measure of intelligence is by actually trying it out.

A priori prognostication is a very risky business, particularly with individual test items, as the following, from our own experience, shows. In collecting the items to be used for our Information Test, we included the questions, "How many pints make a quart?" and "How many feet make a yard?" as possible items for the lower end of the series. Both are questions commonly met with in various information tests, especially in the unstandardized ones of psychiatrists. Seemingly a knowledge of the correct reply is regarded as having some value by those who use these questions. The reader may agree or disagree as to their value, but it is unlikely that if he were asked to pass judgment on their respective merit, that he would rate either question very much better or very much worse than the other. In this, however, he would be mistaken. We submitted these two questions to several groups of known intelligence level and calculated the frequency at which each was passed by the several groups. Our data then showed that while the question, "How many pints make a quart?" was fairly good in the sense that it gave significant, discriminating differences between mental defectiveness, borderline and dull-normal individuals, the question, "How many feet make a yard?" was practically worthless, because the differences were small and negligible. Certainly no one would have predicted this result in advance. Now that we have discovered it, we must frankly admit we can offer no good reason for the fact.

The point of our illustration is that validation of any intelligence scale should be pragmatic. The scale must be not only statistically reliable, but discriminative with respect to the very thing we propose to measure (in our case, an intelligence level); and its validity can be determined only through actual experience. Ideally, the pragmatic test should be made, not only for the scale as a whole, but for every item that enters into it. In reality no intelligence scale (including our own) fully measures up to this requirement. We think, however, that the tests that constitute our scales conform more nearly to this ideal than do those of any adult scale now available. One reason we have been able to do this is that we have drawn so heavily on the experience of others. Our aim was not to produce a set of brand new tests but to select, from whatever source available, such a combination of them as would best meet the requirements of an effective adult scale.

In arriving at our final choice of tests we pursued the following procedure: (1) A careful analysis was made of the various standardized tests of intelligence now in use. These were studied with special attention to authors' comments with reference to the type of functions measured, the character of the population on which the scales were originally standardized, and the evidence of the test's reliability. (2) An attempt was made to evaluate each test's claim to validity as evidenced by its degree of correlation (a) with other recognized tests and, (b) more important still, with subjective ratings of intelligence. The last named included teachers' estimates, ratings by army officers (as in the case of the Army Alpha and Beta), and estimates of business executives (in the case of various tests which had been tried out in industry). (3) An attempt was made to rate the tests on the basis both of our own clinical experience and of that of others. (4) Some two years were devoted to the preliminary experimental work of trying out various likely tests on several groups of known intelligence level.[1]

On the basis of the data obtained from the above procedure, we selected 12 tests, the 11 presently to be described and the Cube Analysis.[2] These were given to the various populations to be described in the next chapter, and they form the basis of our several scales. The Cube Analysis test was discarded after being given to over 1,000 subjects because it showed large sex differences, proved difficult to get across to subjects of inferior intelligence, and because it tapered off abruptly at the upper levels. On the other hand, the Vocabulary Test was not added until a major portion of our subjects had already been

---

[1] Groups of 25 to 50 on whom we had intelligence ratings.
[2] Test 3 of the Army Beta.

examined, and for this reason was used for some time only as an alternate test.

The tests finally chosen were:

1. An Information Test
2. A General Comprehension Test
3. A Combined Memory Span Test for Digits Forwards and Backwards
4. A Similarities Test
5. An Arithmetical Reasoning Test
6. A Picture Arrangement Test
7. A Picture Completion Test
8. A Block Design Test
9. An Object Assembly Test
10. A Digit Symbol Test
Alternate—A Vocabulary Test

These tests have been combined to form four separate but interrelated Intelligence Scales, as follows:

I. The main *Individual Adult Examination* for ages 16 to 60, consisting of the first ten tests listed, but permitting a reduction of the number to as few as seven, depending upon their suitability to the subject.
II. *An Adolescent Scale* for ages 10 to 16, consisting of the same tests but separately standardized.
III. *A Performance Scale* consisting of five tests (tests 6 to 10 inclusive).
IV. *A Verbal Scale* consisting of five or six tests (test 1 to 5 and the Vocabulary as alternate).

By the *"Full Scale"* is meant either Scale I or Scale II, each of which consists of ten tests, plus the Vocabulary as an alternate. We shall now proceed to describe the individual tests which enter into any and all of the scales listed.

INFORMATION TEST

Questions formulated to tap the subject's range of information have, for a long time, been the stock in trade of psychiatric examinations, and prior to the introduction of standardized intelligence tests they were widely used by psychiatrists in estimating the intellectual level of patients. Psychologists, however, have generally been inclined to exclude rather than to make use of information items when devising intelligence scales. It was not until the development of the group test that such items found their way into the standardized intelligence examinations. It is probable, too, that their use here was largely inspired by practical considerations, such as the relative ease with which they lend themselves to scoring, rather than to any strong faith which psychologists may have had in the information tests as a good measure of intelligence. One had always to meet the obvious objection that the amount of knowledge which a person possesses depends in no small degree upon his education and cultural opportunities. The objection is a valid one, but our experience with the test has shown that it need not necessarily be a fatal or even a serious one. Much depends upon the kind of knowledge demanded of the subject and the type of question used in eliciting it.

The first strong support for range-of-information as a good measure of intelligence was furnished by the data obtained from the Army Alpha Examination. When the individual tests of the Army Alpha battery were analyzed with regard to their correlation with various estimates of intelligence, the information test, to the great surprise of many, turned out to be one of the best of the entire series. It correlated, for example, much better with the total score than did the Arithmetical Reasoning, the test of Disarranged Sentences, and even the Analogies Test, all of which had generally been considered much better tests of intelligence. Compared with the other tests on Alpha, the Information Test gave a much better distribution curve, showed a relatively small percentage of zero scores, and showed little tendency towards piling up maximal scores at the upper end. All this could not have been an accident, particularly in view of the fact that the individual items on the Alpha Information Test left much to be desired. The fact is, all objections allowed for, the range of a man's knowledge is generally a very good indication of his intellectual capacity.

In practice, the value of an information test will depend in a large measure on the actual items which are included in it. There are no universal principles which can serve as unfailing guides to "good" questions. In general, the items should call for the sort of knowledge that an average individual with average opportunity may be able to acquire for himself. Thus, "What is the height of the average American woman?" is a much better question than, "What state produces the most gold?" "How far is it from New York to Paris?" much better than "What is the distance from the earth to the sun?", etc. In general too specialized and academic knowledge is best avoided. "What does *ensilage* mean?" and "What is a *tetrahedron*?" are poor questions even for upper levels of intelligence. So are historical dates, names of famous people, whether of statesmen or movie actresses. But there are many exceptions to the rule, and in the long run each item must be tried out separately.

The twenty-five questions on our list are the final selection from some 75 which we tried out originally. The method employed in choosing the items was to present the questions, generally in sets of 25 to 30, to groups of individuals of known intelligence level.[3] Selection of the items was then made on the basis of the incidence of successes and failures among the various groups. A question was held to be a "good" one if it showed increasing frequency of success with higher intellectual level. Of course, not all questions were equally discriminative at all levels. Thus the question, "Where is London?" discriminates well between mental defectives and the borderline group and not at all between the average and superior. On the other hand, "What is the Koran?" does not discriminate at all at the lower levels (since practically every individual there failed it), but showed quite significant differences between the respective per cent of average and superior individuals who passed it.

The order in which the questions are listed roughly approximates their order of difficulty for our sample of the population. No doubt, in different localities, the order will be somewhat different; it will also be affected to some extent by differences of national origin. "Where is Rome?" will be passed almost universally by persons of Italian origin irrespective of their intellectual ability. More interesting than these expected variations are some very surprising results with respect to the difficulty of certain of the items. The question, "What is the population of the United States?" turns out to be inexplicably hard. It is surprising how many native Americans do not know even the approximate number of inhabitants of their own country. We have had estimates by college graduates from 10 to 300 million. On the other hand, more people can tell what a thermometer is than how many weeks there are in a year, and more can give the name of the inventor of the aeroplane than can give the author of *Hamlet*.

We shall now quote some comments about the test made by our examiners in the field, which will indicate some of the test's advantages and some of its limitations. "The test is of value because it gives the subject's general range of information"; "It often indicates the alertness of the person towards the world about him"; "It may reflect the social circle a person comes from; children from educated and intellectual

---

[3] Individuals for whom we had I.Q.'s or other intelligence ratings.

families more often give the correct answer to the question, 'Who wrote *Hamlet?'* "; "It presupposes a normal or average opportunity to receive verbal information. It is a poor test for those deprived of such opportunity as well as for those who have a foreign language handicap."

Altogether, the Information Test has proved one of the most satisfactory of our battery. It declines least with age and correlates second best with total score, ("r" = .67 ±.020).[4] Interestingly enough, it does not correlate as highly with rote memory (Digit Span) as it does with some of the purely performance tests, for example, the Block Design.

COMPREHENSION TEST

Tests of general comprehension have long been favorites with authors of scales, and our own results more than justify this popularity. General comprehension questions are to be found in the original Binet as well as in all of its revisions. They occur also in many group examinations, such as the Army Alpha and the National Intelligence Tests. The test as it appears on the individual and group examinations, however, cannot be said to be equivalent. One important difference is that on the group test the subject is asked merely to select one of a number of possible answers furnished him by the examiner. On the test given individually, the subject must furnish his own answer to the questions. The latter way of giving the test not only reduces the probability of the subject hitting upon a correct answer through sheer chance, but also enables the examiner to evaluate the subject's response even when it is incorrect. Indeed, one of the most gratifying things about the general comprehension test, when given orally, is the rich clinical data which it furnishes us about the subject. It is frequently of value in diagnosing psychopathic personalities, sometimes suggests the presence of schizophrenic trends (as revealed by perverse and bizarre responses) and almost always tells us something about the subject's social and cultural background. The variety of replies one gets to such a question as "What would you do if you found a letter that was already sealed, stamped and addressed?", or "Why does the state require people to get a marriage license?" is far greater than one would suspect, certainly far greater than an examiner could include in a multiple choice questionnaire. The following are sample replies to the former: "Bring it to the man's house". "Leave it there". "Open it and see if there is any money in it".[5] And here are some answers to the marriage ques-

---

[4] Inter-test correlations for all tests are given in Appendix 3.

[5] The first of these answers was given by a simple defective; the second, by a delinquent; the third, by a psychopath.

tion: "To prevent bigamy"; "For census purposes"; "To protect the morals of the community"; "To protect the honor of womanhood"; "So people will know they are married".

The twelve questions which form our test list were selected from some thirty in a manner similar to that employed for reducing the number of items on our information test. A few of the questions will be recognized as coming either directly from the Army Alpha or, in modified form, from those scattered among various tests discussed in the Army Memoirs. One or two turn out to be identical with some now appearing in the Terman and Merrill Revision of the Stanford—probably because borrowed from the same source. This duplication, however, will not seriously affect the usability of the items. Our experience has shown that the Comprehension questions are among those which suffer least from practice effect. It is curious how frequently subjects persist in their original responses, even after other replies are suggested to them.

Precisely what functions the Comprehension Test involves is difficult to say. Off hand it might be termed a test of common sense, and it is so called on the Army Alpha. Success on the test seemingly depends on the possession of a certain amount of practical information and a general ability to evaluate past experience. The questions included in our list are of a sort that the average adult may have had occasion to answer for himself at some time, or, in one form or another, have heard discussed by friends. Some of them, like the "Land" and "Marriage" questions, may seem unfair to young persons, and in particular to children. Indeed, when given to children, the answers to these questions show a considerable correlation with age and social maturity. Although bright young children are prevented from making high scores on the test, it seems, however, to have no serious effect on their final rating. These questions, it will be noted, involve no unusual words, so that even individuals of foreign background and bi-lingual homes have no difficulty in understanding them. We have, nevertheless, found that poor verbalizers and those unaccustomed to setting forth their ideas in words often make low scores on the test.

The Comprehension Test holds up very well with age and, even when it begins to fall off, drops less than most of our other tests. It correlates best with Similarities, and General Information and least well with the Digit Span and the Object Assembly. The correlation (r) with total score is .66[6] for ages 20–34 and .68 for ages 35–49.

[6] For probable errors of these and other "r's" given in this chapter, see tables 40–44.

ARITHMETICAL REASONING TEST

The ability to solve arithmetical problems has long been recognized as a sign of mental alertness. Even before the introduction of psychometrics, it was used as a rough and ready measure of intelligence. Now most intelligence scales include items calling for arithmetical reasoning in some form. The inclusion of such items is fully justified: Arithmetical Reasoning tests correlate highly[7] with global measures of intelligence.

In addition to being a good measure of general intelligence the Arithmetical Reasoning Test enjoys the advantage of being easily devised and standardized. But its merits are lessened by the fact that it is influenced by education and occupational pursuit. Clerks, engineers and business men usually do well on arithmetic tests, while housewives, day laborers and illiterates are often penalized by them. Another shortcoming of the test is that individual scores may be affected by fluctuations of attention and transient emotional reactions.

The general appeal and interest which the Arithmetical Test has for most adults should be especially mentioned. Most adults look upon questions in arithmetic as a task worthy of a grown-up. They may be embarrassed by their inability to do certain problems, but they almost never look upon the questions as unfair or inconsequential. Perhaps our choice of problems has something to do with provoking this attitude. All the problems touch upon commonplace situations or involve practical calculations. Moreover, they have been so devised as to avoid verbalization or reading difficulties.[8] The knowledge required to solve most of our problems is not beyond that taught in the first seven grades of school or what the average adult could acquire for himself in the course of ordinary business transactions.

While the influence of education on the individual's ability to answer arithmetical problems lessens the value of the test as a measure of adult intelligence, the effect of the interrelation between the two factors is not entirely negative. It appears that children who do poorly in arithmetical reasoning often have difficulty with other subjects. A number of our examiners reported they were sometimes able to diagnose educational abilities on the basis of scores obtained on this test, especially when supplemented by scores obtained on the General Information

---

[7] They do so, however, to a lesser degree than certain other tests that enjoy less popularity, e.g., the General Comprehension and Similarities tests.

[8] All but the last two questions are given orally, and even these may be read to the subject.

Test. The combined scores of these two tests frequently furnished an accurate estimate of the subject's scholastic achievement.

The correlations between the Arithmetical Reasoning Test and total scale score are neither among the highest nor the lowest obtained. They vary with the age at which they are calculated, being generally higher at the upper than lower ages. For the age group 20 to 34, the correlation between Arithmetical Reasoning and total scale score is .63, for the age group 35 to 49, .67. Though the test *versus* total scale correlations rise with age, the absolute scores on the test decrease significantly with age. Here again, the Arithmetical Reasoning Test occupies an intermediate position. It does not fall off as rapidly as most of the performance tests or Memory Span for Digits, but neither does it hold up as well as the Vocabulary, General Information or General Comprehension Tests.

MEMORY SPAN FOR DIGITS

There is perhaps no test that has been so universally used in scales of intelligence as that of memory span for digits. It forms part of the original Binet scale and all the revisions of it. It has been used for a long time by psychiatrists as a test of retentiveness and by psychologists for all sorts of psychological studies. Its popularity is based primarily on the fact that it is easy to administer, easy to score, and specific as to the type of ability it measures. Nevertheless, as a test of general intelligence it is among the poorest. Memory span, whether for digits forwards or backwards, generally correlates very poorly with all other tests of intelligence. The ability involved contains little of "g", and as Spearman has shown is more or less independent of the general factor. Our own results confirm these observations. For a long time we considered the desirability of eliminating the test from our battery altogether, but finally decided to retain it for the following reasons: (1) While memory span for digits backwards and forwards is on the whole a poor measure of intelligence, it is nevertheless an extremely good one at the lower levels. Except in cases of special defects or organic disease, adults who cannot retain 5 digits forwards and 3 backwards will be found, in nine cases out of ten, to be feebleminded.[9] (2) Special

[9] Rote memory more than any other capacity seems to be one of those abilities of which a certain absolute minimum is required, but excesses of which seemingly contribute relatively little to the capacities of the individual as a whole. The Memory Span for Digits test has the great merit of quickly indicating whether an individual has that relative minimum.

difficulty with the repetition of digits forwards or backwards is often of diagnostic significance. Obvious examples are the memory defects which constitute clinical symptoms in certain organic and other types of cases. A marked falling off in memory span is often one of the earliest indications of them.[10]

Low scores on the Memory Span Test are frequently associated with attention defects. Individuals with these defects seem to have a special difficulty repeating digits backwards. This deficiency is often referred to by psychologists as *lack of mental control*. The term is rather unfortunate as it implies, and is often interpreted as meaning not only an inability to hold things before the mind, but also as a lack of self-control, in the broader sense. Both are spurious generalizations. Nevertheless, the failure to repeat digits backwards does often correlate with difficulties of attention and lack of ability in doing intellectual work which requires concentrated effort. Knowledge of this fact is frequently an aid to clinical diagnosis. The question, however, still remains whether the digit-span test might not better be used as a supplementary test rather than be included in the general intelligence scale.

It should be noted that as included in our battery, memory span for digits forward and memory span for digits backward have been combined into a single test. This was done for two reasons: first, because of the limited range of each of them when taken separately. On memory span for digits forward, a score range of only 4 points (repeating 5, 6, 7, or 8 digits) includes about 90 per cent of the adult population, and about the same percentage is included by the ability to repeat 4 to 6 digits backwards. Such a range is obviously too small for a point scale. By combining the scores obtainable on both into one test measure, we succeeded not only in extending the test's range, but also in closing up wide gaps that obtain between successive scores when the tests are used singly. Our second reason for combining digits forward and digits backward into a single test was for the purpose of reducing the amount which each contributed to the total score. Considering their limited correlation with general intelligence, it did not seem reasonable to give them as much weight as the other tests of the

[10] Wells has pointed out that the relation between the number of digits that an individual can repeat forward and those he repeats backward is often of diagnostic value in certain organic cases. Alcoholics with Korsakoff syndrome, for example, do much better on digits forwards than on digits backwards. Where the discrepancy is large, it often indicates mental deterioration. See this point: Wells, F. L.: *Mental Tests in Clinical Practice*. Ch. VIII.

scale. If we had used each of them as a separate test, they could have together contributed $\frac{9}{11}$ instead of $\frac{1}{10}$ of the total score which they now do.

Memory span for digits is too familiar a test to need further analysis. We include, however, some comments made by various of our examiners as regards their experience with it. "The effectiveness of this test depends upon calmness and strict attention to the material presented. Care must be taken not to give the test when the individual is fatigued." "The test is sometimes influenced by the auditory factor. People with defective hearing sometimes fail on it because they do not hear the numbers distinctly." "It is really best for picking out mental defectives." The last comment corroborates the point we have stressed in our Introduction, namely that many of our abilities are such that they enter into intellectual functioning only as necessary minimum. Ordinarily, a person who cannot repeat 4 digits forward is so handicapped as far as intake of the external world is concerned that he will inevitably be unable to function above the mental defective level. Above a span of 5 or 6 digits, the value of further improvement in the capacity diminishes very rapidly. A good rote memory is of practical value but correlates very little with higher levels of intelligence.

As might be expected, memory span declines rapidly with age. It holds up better, however, than certain other abilities, for example, those tapped by the Picture Arrangement. It would seem, therefore, that older people have other failings of which they might much more reasonably complain than their poor memory. The r for the Digit-Span Test with total score is .51. It correlates best with Digit-Symbol and worst with the Object Assembly Test.

SIMILARITIES TEST

This test turns out to be among the best of our entire battery. But we did not include it in our testing program until several hundred subjects had been examined without it. We omitted the Similarities Test from our original selection because of the mistaken belief that it would be unduly influenced by the language factor. This view was largely due to our previous experience with the more difficult similarities items on the Stanford-Binet. Because we had found so many adults failing on the difference between "idleness" and "laziness" owing to their unfamiliarity with the word "idleness" and so many more on the difference between "evolution" and "revolution" because they had never heard of "evolution", we were inclined to doubt the possibility of devising a similarities test that would be free of linguistic difficulties at the higher levels. A little research soon showed, however, that it was possible to increase the difficulty of the items without resorting to unusual or unfamiliar words. For example, with the words "fly" and "tree", one can formulate the question, "In what way are a fly and a tree alike?" and this question is answered correctly by less than 20 per cent of the adult population. When words like these are chosen, the Similarities Test can be freed almost entirely from the linguistic factor. This will be obvious to the reader from an inspection of the paired words which we finally used for our comparisons.

Our final list of 12 selected from almost double the number is as follows:

Orange................Banana
Coat..................Dress
Dog...................Lion
Wagon.................Bicycle
Daily Paper...........Radio
Air...................Water
Eye...................Ear
Egg...................Seed
Wood..................Alcohol
Poem..................Statue
Praise................Punishment
Fly...................Tree

The Similarities Test has several merits. It is easy to give and appears to have an interest appeal for the average adult. It is the kind of test which has been recognized by all investigators as containing a great amount of "g". Over and above this, the test has certain qualitative features, the most important of which is the light which the type of responses received throws upon the logical character of the subject's thinking processes. There is an obvious difference both as to maturity and as to level of thinking between the individual who says that a banana and an orange are alike because they both have a skin, and the individual who says that they are both fruit. As already noted by Terman and others, it is not until the individual approaches adult mentality that he is able to discriminate between essential and superficial likenesses. But it is remarkable how large a percentage of adults also never get beyond the superficial type of response. It is for this reason that, unlike previous methods of scoring, the one employed in our scale distinguishes between superior and inferior responses by allowing different credits for each.   Thus, when the subject says an orange and banana are alike because "you can eat them" and a bicycle and wagon, "because they have wheels", he receives a credit of 1, whereas the responses, "both are fruit", and "means of conveyance", are scored 2.   This qualitative difference in response is of value not only because it furnishes a more discriminating scoring method, but because it is often suggestive both of the evenness and level of the subject's intellectual functioning.   Some subjects' total scores, even when relatively good, are largely made up of 1 credits, whereas the scores of others are of a varied proportion of 0, 1 and 2 credits.   The former are likely to bespeak individuals of consistent intellectual ability, but belonging to a type from whom no high grade of intellectual work may be expected; the latter, while erratic, have many more possibilities.

Our correlations for the Similarities Test are not as complete as those of other tests, but they are uniformly among the highest obtained either with the individual tests or with total score.   The test's r with the rest of the scale is .73.

PICTURE ARRANGEMENT TEST

This test consists of a series of pictures which, when placed in the right sequence, tell a little story.   The picture series are not unlike the short comic strips to be found in the daily papers.   The pictures are presented to the subject in a disarranged order and he is asked to put them together in the right order so that they make a sensible story.   The correct order is the one originally given to the pictures by the artist.

A test of this sort was seemingly first used by DeCroly.[11]   In 1917 several Picture Arrangement series were tried out by the Army psychologists, as subtests on a group examination, and found wanting; but another set (the Foxy Grandpa series) ultimately found its way into the Army Performance Scale.[12]   It was, however, not used to any great extent.   Nor have other tests of this kind,—possibly because of the difficulties in scoring as well as in getting up good sequences,—had great vogue in this country.   But recently Cornell and Coxe[13] again experimented with some picture series and included them in their scale.

The picture series which we have chosen for our test consist of seven

---

[11] DeCroly, I.: Epreuve nouvelle pour l'examination mental.   *Ann. Psychol.*, 1914, XX, 140–159.

[12] *Army Memoirs*.   Nat. Academy of Sciences, vol. XV, pp. 189 and 404.

[13] Cornell, E. L. and Coxe, W. C.: *A Performance Ability Scale*.   New York. 1934.

sets, three adapted from the Army Group Examinations and four entirely new ones selected from Soglow's well known "King" series which appeared in the *New Yorker* magazine several years ago. Those adapted from the Army Group Tests were completely redrawn and in some instances slightly altered as to content.

The set of pictures included in our battery represent the final choice from among more than twice that number originally tried out. They were selected on the basis of interest of content, probable appeal to subjects, ease of scoring and discriminating value. Any attempt to satisfy all these conditions was bound to occasion difficulties, and in spite of the considerable labor spent before making definitive choices, the final selection leaves much to be desired. The fault, however, is not so much with our particular selection as with the limitations inherent to all picture arrangement tests, namely their dependency upon actual content. It is of some moment whether the story told by the pictures is that of a bird building a nest, or a policeman pursuing a thief in a radio car. The former is a situation a country boy may grasp at once, the latter may puzzle him a good deal; and what holds for such simple situations plays an even greater rôle when the story told by the pictures is more complicated. Our aim was naturally to choose situations from the American scene, but by so doing we also succeeded in making a number of our pictures very puzzling to subjects of foreign origin. In some other instances, we found that subjects of a particular cultural level were rather favored by one or another of the series. For example, some of the Soglow pictures, which are not only among the best, but also among the most difficult, were surprisingly easy for the sophisticated type of individual.

In spite of the above limitations, the Picture Arrangement test has some very worthwhile merits. In the first place, it is the type of test which effectively measures a subject's ability to comprehend and size up a total situation. The subject must understand the whole, must get the "idea" of the story before he is able to set himself effectively to the task. There is, of course, some trial and error experimentation, but the subject is also called upon to attempt appraisal of the total situation more than in most other tests. Secondly, the subject matter of the test nearly always involves some human or practical situation. The understanding of these situations more nearly corresponds to what other writers have referred to as "social intelligence".[14] We ourselves, as already indicated, do not believe in such an entity. Our point of view

[14] Alas, both delinquents and psychopaths often do very well on this test.

is that social intelligence is just general intelligence applied to social situations. Nevertheless, we have observed that individuals who do fairly well on the Picture Arrangement seldom turn out to be mental defectives even when they do badly on other tests.

A word as to the method of scoring. In a test of this kind the question always arises whether one should allow part credit for possible but incorrect combinations. The answer depends upon how much the test gains, that is, improves its correlations with total score when such allowance is made. For our short picture series the gain was practically nil and accordingly our first three picture series were given either full or no credit at all depending upon whether they were or were not arranged in the exact way called for. With the longer picture series,— those consisting of 5 or 6 pictures,—some gains were to be had by crediting certain combinations. On these, partial credit is allowed for various imperfect arrangements providing they make "sense". What makes sense was determined by a group of four judges after inspecting actual arrangements obtained from over 200 subjects. In general, the number of credits assigned to imperfect arrangements were roughly proportioned to the frequency with which the several arrangements occurred. Experimentation with different statistical procedures showed that little if any advantage was to be had from refined scaling and scoring. The arrangements given in our manual cover pretty well most of the rational arrangements of pictures which the individual series permit. Occasionally, however, a subject does produce a different one for which he is able to give a convincing explanation, but for which no credit is allowed in our tables. In such cases; it will be found that disallowing the subject's response does not materially influence his total score on the test, but provision is made for the examiner to credit the subject with a reasonable additional score. More interesting than the question of credits allowed, however, in such cases, is the explanation which the subject may give for his unusual arrangement. Consistently bizarre explanations are suggestive of some peculiar mental orientation or even psychotic trend.

The Picture Arrangement test holds up badly with age and correlates poorly with the other tests of our scales. It correlates best with Picture Completion and Similarities, and poorest with Digit Span and Object Assembly. Its r with total score is .51.

PICTURE COMPLETION TEST

The name "Picture Completion" is usually associated with a test like the Healy Picture Completion II, in which the subject is required to complete the sense of a picture by selecting a best fitting piece from among several possible choices. The test presented here under the same name is somewhat different. It merely requires the subject to discover and name the missing part of an incompletely drawn picture. He is shown a picture, like a steamship minus its funnel or a watch with its second hand missing, and asked to indicate the missing part. In its present form the test is very much like that of the "Mutilated Pictures" of the Binet Scale, of which it may be considered an extension.

A test of this sort forms part of many Group Examinations.[15] Its popularity is fully merited[16] even though the procedures used in adapting it for group testing generally limit its possibilities. One of these limitations is that the subject is required to draw in the missing part; another that the number of items used have generally been too few and often far from satisfactory. Preliminary experiments with pictures previously used on group examinations showed that, for the most part, they were haphazardly chosen. Many of the items were much too easy and some unusually difficult. On the whole, the individual pictures showed little discriminative value.

Suitable items for a Picture Completion Test are hard to find and present a number of difficulties. If one chooses familiar subjects, the test becomes much too easy; if one turns to unfamiliar ones, the test ceases to be a good test of intelligence because one unavoidably calls upon specialized knowledge. The 15 pictures included in our test are the final selection from some 30 to 35 tried out over a period of six months with various groups of subjects of known intelligence levels. Each picture was tried out separately and admitted or rejected on the basis of its discriminating[17] value. While there are a few with which we are still not satisfied, our final set of pictures seems to be a satisfactory series. Altogether they have furnished a test which, next to the Block Design, turns out to be the best of our Performance Scale. The test is particularly good in testing intelligence at the lower levels. Ostensibly it measures the individual's basic perceptual and conceptual abilities in so far as these are involved in the visual recognition and identification of familiar objects and forms. To be able to see what is missing from

[15] Among the more familiar are the Army Beta, the Pintner Non-Language, the Haggerty Delta, the Detroit Kindergarten and some of the early forms of the Thorndike College Entrance Tests.

[16] On the Army Beta the test correlates .74 with total score and .72 with the Stanford-Binet Mental Age.

[17] The method by which this was done was similar to that employed in selecting the General Information items. See text and note on p. 79.

any particular picture, the subject must first know what that picture represents. But, in addition, he must be able to appreciate that the missing part is in some way essential either to the form or function of the object or picture. In a broad way, the test measures the ability of the individual to differentiate essential from unessential details. But we must note again that the ability of an individual to do this depends in a large measure upon his relative familiarity with the object with which he is presented, that is to say, upon the actual content of the picture. A person who has never seen or read about a steamship cannot be expected to know that all such boats have funnels and that these are generally to be found at the center of the ship. Unfamiliar, specialized and esoteric subject matter must therefore be sedulously avoided when choosing pictures for this test. However, this cannot be done altogether. If nothing else, there is always the factor of sex differences to be considered. For example, in examining the incidence of correct responses to our own series, we found that more men than women failed to detect the missing eyebrow in the picture of a girl's profile (item no. 14) and more women the missing thread in the drawing of the electric bulb (item no. 13).

The Picture Completion as given on the Bellevue Scale is not a timed test. Each of the items is exposed for 15 seconds, and this is more than sufficient for most subjects. Most responses are made in less than 10 seconds. When a subject fails to detect the missing part within 15 seconds, experience has shown that he is unlikely to do so thereafter. Increasing the time limit up to 30 seconds per picture had little effect on total scores.

The Picture Completion holds up with age better than most other performance tests. Its main limitation is its "low ceiling", that is to say, its relative inadequacy in discriminating between higher levels of intelligence (high-average and superior). There is a tendency for scores to pile up at the upper end of the distribution table. On the other hand, its discriminating power at the intermediate levels more than makes up for this limitation. As already noted, it is particularly effective in picking out mental defectives. Correlation with total score (ages 20 to 24) is .61. As regards individual tests, it correlates highest with the Block Design and lowest with the Memory Span for Digits.

BLOCK DESIGN

The Block Design test was originated by Kohs who offered it as a comprehensive measure of non-verbal intelligence. While we do not believe that any single test can be so used, our own results indicate that its author's enthusiasm for it is fully justified. The test turns out to be our best single performance item. It conforms to all statistical criteria for a "good" test. It not only correlates well with total score and individual test items, but is one of the few performance tests that seemingly does measure very much the same sort of thing that verbal tests measure. In fact, it correlates better with Comprehension, Information and Vocabulary than some of the verbal tests themselves. It is hard to explain the basis for its merits other than that the reproduction of the type of design devised by Kohs in some way involves both synthetic and analytical ability. Curiously enough, individuals who do best on the test are not those who see, or at least follow, the pattern as a whole, but such as are able to break it up into small portions. In this connection, the recent study of Nadel[18] on intellectual disturbances following certain (frontal lobe) brain lesions is of interest. As between "following the figure" and breaking up the design into its component parts, the patients with frontal lobe lesions in contrast to the normal control group used almost exclusively the former method.

The Block Design as adapted for our scale is basically similar to that employed by Kohs in his original standardization, but its content has been modified to a considerable degree. The most important of the changes introduced pertain to the reduction in the number of test cards used and the alteration in the figure patterns which the subject is asked to reproduce. The reduced number of designs was for the obvious purpose of cutting down the time allowed for any one test on our scale. Our Block Design Test consists of 7 instead of 17 figures, with a consequent reduction in the time required for completing the test from some 35 to somewhat less than 10 minutes. The change in pattern was effected, both to avoid reproduction of items used on other scales[19] and to eliminate the possible factor of color confusion. The original Kohs included figures made up of red, yellow, blue and white; ours makes use only of red and white. Our mode of presentation also differs somewhat, as may be seen by consulting the instructions given in our manual.

The Block Design is not only an excellent test of general intelligence, but one that lends itself admirably to qualitative analysis. One can learn much about the subject by watching "how" he takes to the task set him. We have already mentioned the matter of the differences in method that may be employed in assembling the designs,—to wit, that of

[18] Nadel, A. B.: A Quantitative Analysis of Behavior Following Cerebral Lesions. Arch. of Psychol., no. 224, New York, 1938.

[19] The Kohs cards form part of the Grace Arthur Scale.

following the figure as against that of breaking it up into its component parts. There is also a difference of attitude and emotional reaction on the part of the subject which gives us valuable information about him. One can often distinguish the hasty and impulsive individual from the deliberate and careful type, a subject who gives up easily or gets disgusted, from the one who persists and keeps on working even after his time is up, and so on of a number of other temperamental traits which manifest themselves not infrequently in the course of a subject's performance.

The test's value for diagnostic purposes is particularly worth mentioning. Patients with mental deterioration and seniles have particular difficulty in managing the test and often cannot complete the simplest design, however much they try. So do most cases of brain disease. The difficulty here seems to be a certain lack of synthesizing ability, or loss of the "abstract approach", in K. Goldstein's sense of the term. Nadel points out that in many cases of frontal lobe lesions, the patient's inability to reproduce the design could be explained on the basis of a loss of ability to "shift". Some of the patients seemingly did not know when the designs were finished, others had particular difficulty in attending to the figure's color and pattern simultaneously, and still others, or the same patients, would get stuck at certain portions of the figures, apparently unable to synthesize the rest of the pattern with it. Whatever the mechanisms involved, the Block Design is one of the best tests we have for showing up early as well as late disturbances in the higher perceptual processes.

Among examiners' comments on the test we find the following: "The test involves the ability to perceive forms and to analyze these forms." "It involves the ability to perceive pattern." "In the Block Design, speed and success (of reproduction) is largely dependent upon the individual's ability to analyze the whole into its component parts." "Older adults do not do so well on it." "It is very good for picking out low grade people." "Artists and artisans do much better on the test than others." "The Object Assembly and Block Design Tests seem to get at some sort of creative ability." "Some subjects are penalized by the time score and by the fact that they 'haven't played with blocks for a long time.' " "This test and the Object Assembly are perceptibly influenced by a person's occupation".

With the possible exception of the Similarities and the Vocabulary, the Block Design correlates more highly with total score than any of our other tests including the verbal ones. Its "r" with total score (for ages 35–49) is .73. Its highest single correlations are .60 with Information (ages 35–49) and .57 with Picture Completion (ages 20–34). Its lowest correlations are with Object Assembly .32 (ages 20–34) and Picture Arrangement .37 (ages 35–49). These correlations are more like those obtained with the verbal than with the performance items of the scale. In spite of its high correlations, the test does not hold up well with age. Persons over 40 do progressively worse at it as they grow older. Considering the fact that the test correlates highly with all measures of general intelligence, we interpret this decline as one of the best proofs of the natural falling off of intellectual ability with age. For the same reason it may be regarded as an excellent measure of deterioration, a conclusion which is amply confirmed by the study of individual cases.

DIGIT SYMBOL TEST

The Digit Symbol or substitution test is one of the oldest and best established of all psychological tests. It is to be found in a large variety of intelligence scales, and its wide popularity is fully merited. The subject is required to associate certain symbols with certain other symbols, and the speed and accuracy with which he does it serve as a measure of his intellectual ability. In deciding upon its inclusion in our battery, the only question in our minds was the degree to which the purely motor aspect of it might penalize the performance of adults. This motor factor turned out to be less important than originally suspected from certain points of view, and rather more important as regards certain others. In the case of illiterates who have not had practice in the use of pencil and paper, it is particularly disturbing. One does not ordinarily realize what a difficult task the formation of numerals and letters may be for a person who has never learned how to write. Such individuals approach the task much like a schooled person might when attempting to write the letters of a foreign language for the first time. The letters are not written but copied. Obviously, then, the test cannot be used on illiterates, and in the examination of such individuals, it is omitted from our scale. In the case of literate older subjects, the problem is of a different order. Here the difficulty is not lack of familiarity with paper and pencil, but that of motor set and motor speed. To the extent to which these correlate with an actual loss in learning ability, the factors cannot, of course, be said to lessen the value of the test. But the question is whether motor speed does not have an independent and disturbing influence. The actual facts are these; the mean scores on the Digit Symbol Test begin to drop after 25, and after 35, and especially 40, they taper off very markedly with age. All this would be very discouraging except for the fact that the falling off of ability turns out to be more or less proportional to the original capacity of the individual as measured by the total score on the scale. This is because there is a high correlation between test scores on the Digit Symbol and total scores on the scale as a whole; and to the fact that in the calculation of our intelligence ratings (see page 219) allowance is made for the decline of general ability with age.

We should note in passing that neurotic and unstable individuals also tend to do rather badly on the Digit Symbol (as indeed on all other substitution tests). The inferiority of neurotic subjects on tests of this kind was noted as long ago as 1923 by Tendler.[20] Tendler suggests that this is due to some sort of associative inflexibility in the subject, and a tendency toward mental confusion. More obviously neurotic subjects do badly on this test because they have difficulty in concentrating and applying themselves for any length of time and because of their emotional reactivity to any task requiring persistent effort. The poor performance of the neurotic represents a lessened mental efficiency rather than an impairment of intellectual ability.

The Digit Symbol Test incorporated in our scale was taken from the Army Beta.[21] This particular form of Substitution Test (originally devised by Otis) has several advantages over many of the others commonly used. One is that it comprises a sample demonstration which permits the examiner to make sure that the subject understands the task. Another is that the subject is required to reproduce the unfamiliar symbols and not the associated numerals. The latter fact lessens the advantage which individuals having facility with numbers would otherwise have. The only change made from the way the test is administered is in the matter of time allowance. The two minutes allowed on the Army Beta was found to be too long. There was a tendency for scores to pile up at the upper end. Reducing the time not only eliminated this shortcoming, but also improved the distribution of test scores when these were converted into standard deviation equivalents. Several different time allowances were tried out, and a period of $1\frac{1}{2}$ minutes was found to give best results.

The Digit Symbol Test correlates best with the Memory Span for

---

[20] Tendler, A. D.: The Mental Status of Psychoneurotics. *Arch. Psychol.* no. 60, 1923.

[21] It likewise forms part of the original Army Performance Tests; the test has also been included in the Cornell-Coxe Performance Scale.

digits and poorest with Object Assembly. Its correlation ("r") with total score is .673 for ages 20–34 and .697 for ages 35–49. As already mentioned, Digit Symbol performance declines rapidly with age.

OBJECT ASSEMBLY

The test which is included under this title, consists of three separate figure formboards, a *Manikin, a Feature Profile,* and a *Hand.* The Manikin is essentially the same as that devised by Pintner and first used on the Pintner-Paterson scale,[22] except that the suggested features

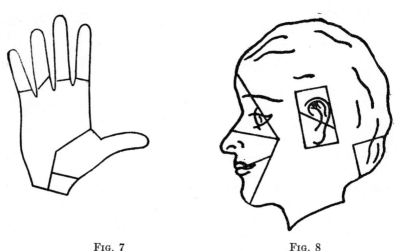

FIG. 7   FIG. 8

HAND AND FEATURE PROFILE

have been redrawn to make them more human in appearance. Our Profile resembles that used by Pintner-Paterson but differs from the original in several respects. It is a profile of a woman's head instead of a man's, the ear is divided into two instead of four parts, and a piece has been cut out at the base of the skull. The Hand is entirely new and was devised by the author. As presented to the subject, it consists of a mutilated hand from which the fingers and a large section of the palm have been cut away. The assembled Hand and our modified Profile are shown in figures 7 and 8. Details as to method of presentation and scoring will be found in the manual portion of the book.

[22] Pintner, R. and Paterson, R. G.: *Scale of Performance Tests.* N. Y. 1921.

The Object Assembly was included in our battery only after much hesitation. We wanted at least one test which required putting things together into a familiar configuration. Our experience over a long period with the commonly used formboards, had convinced us that whatever their merit when administered to children, they were generally ill-adapted for testing adults. Most of the standardized formboards are much too easy for the average adult, and at the high levels have very little discriminative value. The distribution tables[23] for these formboards moreover have unusually large scatter. Taken singly, the predictive value for most of them is nearly nil. The Manikin and Feature Profile seemed better in this respect than most of the formboards, but not much. Like all formboards, they also show great practice effects, and, therefore, are almost useless for retest purposes.

In spite of the foregoing limitations, the Object Assembly Test has a number of compensating features, and it is primarily because of these that we kept it in our battery. The first point to be noted is that while the test correlates poorly with almost every one of our subtests, it does contribute something to the total score. Secondly, examination of the Object Assembly scatter diagrams show that the low correlations it has with the other tests, are due primarily to the large deviations of a relatively small and seemingly special group of individuals. This means, perhaps, that the Object Assembly is a poor test only for certain types of individuals. If the test is appraised on the basis of criteria which are not influenced in a marked degree by the atypical individual, its rating is considerably enhanced. For example, if we consider mean scores alone, we find that the Object Assembly shows a rather good rise with age up to about 13 years, and a maintenance of the average adult norm considerably better than some of the other tests.[24]

The best features of the Object Assembly, however, are its qualitative merits. Various examiners have praised the test repeatedly, because "it tells you something about the thinking and working habits of the subjects." The subjects' approach to the task may in fact be one of several kinds. The first, is that of an immediate reaction to the whole, accompanied by a critical understanding of the relation of the individual parts. This is particularly true of responses to the Manikin test, where one can distinguish between the individual who recognizes from the

[23] For distribution tables, see Pintner-Paterson, op. cit., pp. 97–137.
[24] The test is weakest in the intermediate age range, i.e., from about age 15 to 30, where it is extremely erratic for individual cases. Part of this is due to its marked susceptibility to momentary changes of attention and interest.

start that he has a human figure to put together, from another, usually a mental defective, who has no idea what he is assembling but merely fits the pieces together by the trial and error method. A second type of response is that of rapid recognition of the whole but with imperfect understanding of the relations between the parts. This is best evidenced by the manner in which many subjects handle the Feature Profile. Still a third type of response is one which may start with complete failure to take in the total situation, but which after a certain amount of trial and error manifestation leads to a sudden though often belated appreciation of the figure. Such performances are most frequently met with in the case of the Hand. Altogether, then, we may say that the Object Assembly test has a particular clinical value because it tells us something about one's mode of perception, the degree to which one relies on trial and error methods, and the manner in which one reacts to mistakes.

Among the comments made on the test are the following: "The Object Assembly, like the Block Design Test, seems to get at some sort of creative ability, especially if the performance is done rapidly." "Successful reproduction of the Object Assembly items depends upon the subjects' familiarity with figures and their ability to deal with the part-whole relationship." "People with artistic and mechanical ability, seem to do very well on this test." "It sometimes reveals the ability to work for an unknown goal." "Some subjects continue working at putting together the Hand although they seem to have not the slightest notion as to what it is they are putting together." To this extent the tests are of value in revealing the capacity to persist at a task. Some subjects tend to give up very quickly and are discouraged by the slightest evidence of lack of success.

As already mentioned, the Object Assembly shows the smallest correlation with all other tests when taken individually or collectively. It correlates least well with the Memory Span for Digits and best with the Block Design. Interestingly enough, the correlation with total score in the case of adults, rises significantly with increasing age. Its "r" is .41 for ages 20–34 and .51 for ages 45–49. With respect to the particular abilities involved in this test, it would seem that older people react more nearly like children than do average adults.

VOCABULARY TEST

Contrary to lay opinion, the size of a man's vocabulary is not only an index of his schooling, but also an excellent measure of his general intelligence. Its excellence as a test of intelligence is seemingly derived from the fact that the number of words a man knows is at once a measure of his learning ability, his fund of verbal information and of the general range of his ideas. The one serious stricture that can be made against the Vocabulary Test as a measure of a man's intelligence is that the number of words a man acquires must necessarily be influenced by his educational and cultural opportunities. It is seemingly unfair to illiterates and persons with a foreign language handicap. Because of these possible limitations, the Vocabulary Test was included only as an alternate in the original battery. Our apprehension regarding the Vocabulary has proved unfounded, and it is now recommended as a "regular" test that should be included systematically when the Full Scale is administered.

The words included in our Vocabulary list were taken from one of the Funk and Wagnall's Standard (School) Dictionaries. The list was arrived at by choosing 100 words at random in the following manner: Beginning with an odd page, we selected every top word but one[25] in the left hand column of every fifth page and continued the process until we had listed 100 words. These 100 words were arranged in rough order of difficulty, divided into two lists of 50, each and given to experimental groups of known intelligence level. By this method the words which seemed to discriminate poorly between different intelligence levels, were quickly eliminated. After some further experimentation the two lists were consolidated into one of 60, then of 50 words, and finally cut down to the present list of 42. Their order of difficulty, at least for the individuals in the New York City area, is fairly consistent, except that there are always certain words which are especially easy[26] or hard for some individuals.

Apart from its value as a measure of intelligence, the Vocabulary is an especially desirable test to have on any scale, because of its qualitative possibilities. In defining a word, a subject gives us more than its mere meaning. In many instances he tells us a good deal about himself, or at least about the quality and character of his thought processes. These facts may not be immediately apparent but can be frequently brought to light by analyzing the formal and contextual aspects of the subject's response. There is an obvious difference in the reasoning ability[27] between two adults, one of whom defines a "donkey" as "an

[25] Omitting however, obsolete, technical or esoteric words.

[26] Since the war the words *nitroglycerine*, *espionage* and *hara-kari* have become much easier, and their altered difficulty must be allowed for.

[27] We entertained for a long time the possibility of using preciseness and accuracy of definition as a basis for scoring, but actual attempts to do so proved impractical.

animal" and the other who defines it in such terms as "it has four legs" or that "it looks like a jackass." Sometimes the quality of a subject's definition tells us something about his cultural milieu. The type of word on which a subject passes or fails is always of some significance. Dull subjects from educated homes often get uncommon words like "vesper" and "pewter" but fail on "gamble" and "brim"; the pedant will get "espionage" but fail on "spangle", etc. But perhaps more important than all these from a clinical point of view is the character of a definition as a whole in so far as it may give us some insight into an individual's thought processes. This is particularly true in the case of schizophrenics, the formal aspects of whose language disturbance is frequently diagnostic. We do not refer to such obvious aberrations as "neologisms", "word-salads", etc., but the more subtle ones pertaining to bizarreness of ideational content and peculiarites of expression.[28] Here are some examples of words defined by schizophrenics, which illustrate the kind of definition one meets with in such patients: *Plural*— "a way of thinking in grammar". *Bacon*—"part of pig associated with breakfast". *Armory*—"an institute of future training to no purpose, where guardsmen gather". *Guillotine*—"to disconnect a person's body by means of a knife". *Nail*—"a metal object used for putting things together". The last two though not strikingly aberrant, are of particular interest, because illustrative of the pedantism and rigidity so frequently met with in schizophrenia. Other vocabulary characteristics of schizophrenia are marked perseveration, redundancy of definition and incoherence of content.

In estimating the size of a person's vocabulary, items of the kind just discussed cannot enter into the evaluation   What counts is the number of words that he knows   Any recognized meaning is acceptable, and there is no penalty for inelegance of language. So long as the subject shows that he knows what a word means, he is credited with a passing definition. Most of the words on our list are easily scored either right or wrong, but to help beginners we have appended a list of criteria (in the manual part of the book) which will enable the examiner to score the doubtful responses more easily. The general rule when in doubt is to match the subject's responses against the acceptable definitions and to score accordingly. Wherever possible it is desirable to record the subjects' responses verbatim. This will not only provide for a subse-

[28] On this subject see for example, White, W. A.: "The Language of Schizoprenia," in vol. V. of the *Research Publications of the Association for Research in Nervous and Mental Disease*. Schizophrenia. New York, 1928.

quent re-checking, but also furnish the material for the qualitative analyses discussed above.

The Vocabulary Test correlates highly with our total scale (eta = .85). In the original standardization we did not have sufficient data to obtain its correlation with the separate tests of the scale, but subsequent studies by other investigators[29] show that they are of a high order. In conformance with the experience of other investigations our own results show that the Vocabulary Test holds up very well with age. Our results, however, do not confirm the view that it remains constant right up to senescence. Although the Vocabulary Test does not fall off with age nearly as much as most other measures of intelligence, it does fall off somewhat. This fact must be borne in mind when using the test for measuring mental deterioration.

[29] Goldfarb, W.: *Teacher's College Contributions to Education, No. 831, pp. 28–29.* (See reference 9.)

CHAPTER 8

POPULATION USED IN STANDARDIZING THE TESTS

In the present chapter we propose to describe briefly the chief characteristics of the population on which our scales have been standardized, and indicate the basis employed in arriving at our samples. It is clear, of course, that whatever the intrinsic merits of an intelligence scale, its diagnostic value must, to a large extent, depend upon the degree to which the characteristics of the originally tested groups will approximate those of the general population to whom the tests will be subsequently administered.

Statisticians are wont to sum up this condition by saying that the standardizing sample must be truly representative of the entire population. This is a very nice statement of the case, but in practice not a very helpful one. What we want to know precisely is what factors must be taken into consideration to assure us of such representative sampling. The formulae which statisticians generally furnish us merely afford us means of estimating the probability that a sample of such and such size will give us mean scores that will only deviate from that of the total population by such and such amounts. They tell us little about the qualitative differences which we are likely to find between our original sampling and the larger population to which the test may ultimately be given. For this we need to know a good deal about the qualitative characteristics of our group, and the variety of factors which inevitably act to differentiate various sub-groups in any large population. Unfortunately, this knowledge is not easily obtained, and even when at hand, extremely difficult to evaluate. Our own attempts to deal with the various problems presented leave much to be desired. We shall therefore limit ourselves to only a summary analysis of such of these influencing factors as we tried to deal with.

The first of these factors is that of age. In the case of children its bearing on test scores is so obvious that separate norms for different ages have been the rule almost from the first day that intelligence scales were adopted. But in the case of adults this has not generally been the case. The practice here (as for instance in the matter of calculating I.Q.'s) has been to treat all individuals from 15, 16 or 18, as an homogeneous group so far as the age factor is concerned.   This assumption is unwarranted, and, as we have seen, has led to serious difficulties. We cannot use the norms for a boy of 16 in evaluating the performance of a man of 60 any more than we can use the norms of a child of 6 in evaluating that of a boy of 16.   The age factor has to be taken into account, and we have done so by establishing different age norms for all ages up to 60.   The age distribution of subjects used in the standardizing sample is given in table 7.   It should be noted that the number

TABLE 7

Age distribution of subjects used in standardizing samples

CHILDREN		ADULTS	
Age group	Number of cases	Age group	Number of cases
7	50	17–19	100
8	50	20–24	160
9	50	25–29	195
10	60	30–34	140
11	60	35–39	135
12	60	40–44	91
13	70	45–49	70
14	70	50–54	55
15	100	55–59	50
16	100	60–70	85
Totals*..........	670		1,081

* These totals represent only the number of cases used to obtain the norms. The actual number of cases tested and from which they were "sampled" was much greater.   The actual totals (up to June 1938) were: ages 6–16, 1639 cases; ages 17–69, 1860 cases; total, 3499 cases.

of cases of each age level does not represent the total number of individuals tested, but only those we included in the standardizing sample.

The second important factor in the standardization of any intelligence test, especially one for adults, is that of education.   Practically all studies show that educational attainment (as measured by the number of years of school attendance) and intelligence ratings (as measured by test scores) correlate to a relatively high degree.   The correlation ranges in most cases from about .60 to .80.   For our own adult population we have found it to be .64 (and with mental defectives omitted, .53).   A correlation of this order might suggest that the ability to do well on intelligence tests is largely dependent upon formal education, and has so been interpreted by a number of authors.[1] The situation, however, is not so simple.

Although the correlation between educational attainment and intelligence level is high, it does not necessarily follow that the latter is dependent on the former. It might also mean that the education which an individual is capable of attaining, is dependent upon his intelligence. This is obviously the situation in the case of mental defectives. For example, a defective of 15 (Binet I.Q. of *circa* 65) is ordinarily not capable of going beyond the fifth grade in school. On the other hand, children of superior intellectual endowment are usually ahead of the age-grade placement, and, other things being equal, will by the time they are 15 attain greater scholastic achievement than the children of average intelligence. We do not cite these instances to prove that the amount of schooling an individual achieves depends primarily on his native endowment, but merely to show that the interpretation of the correlation between school achievement and intelligence scores is not so simple as some investigators have considered it. All intelligence tests are influenced by the amount of schooling that an individual has had, but this schooling must be understood in the larger sense. It includes not only education received in the class room, but also such as is self-acquired.

How to make allowance for the educational factor is not easy to say. Ideally it could perhaps be done by standardizing one's tests and obtaining one's norms on groups differentiated according to amount of schooling had. To do so, even for a limited number of categories, however, would require an enormous number of individuals. For example, if only five educational levels were taken into account we would have to increase our standardizing population fivefold, if eight categories, eightfold, and so on. That is hardly feasible at present. Some method of circumventing the problem is necessary. Such method would, of course, not take into account the individual case, but only the group as a whole. For example, it might be possible to select our standardizing group in such manner that the educational attainment of its average individual would be approximately equal to that of the average individual of the larger group for which the tests are destined. We have managed this for our age group 10 to 16, and the precise method by which it was accomplished will be presently described.

The task of compensating for educational difference in the case of

[1] Cf. Burt, C.: *Mental and Educational Tests.* London, 1924.

adults is a much more difficult problem. It is more difficult, not only because the actual educational distribution of the adult American population has not as yet been worked out, but also because the educational status must be set against other competing differentiae; for example, that of occupational status. The latter indeed offered a much more satisfactory basis of selection, and was the one ultimately chosen for our own adult sampling. Nevertheless, the question as to how our own sample compared as regards educational level with that of the population of the country as a whole, seemed one of considerable importance. We determined this by obtaining from the Educational Office of the Department of Interior[2] estimates as regards the percentage

TABLE 8

Percentages of U. S. population and Bellevue adult sampling in respective educational categories

EDUCATIONAL CATEGORY	ESTIMATED LEVEL OF EDUCATION OF U. S. ADULT POPULATION—AGES 21 YEARS AND OVER (1934)	ACTUAL EDUCATIONAL LEVEL OF BELLEVUE SAMPLING—AGES 20 YEARS AND OVER (1935-1938)
	per cent	*per cent*
College graduates..........................	2.93	5.10
Some college work........................	4.08	3.77
High school graduate (only)*............	6.85	10.81
Some high school work.	18.99	18.76
Elementary school graduate (only)*.....	18.68	28.85
Some elementary school..................	43.58	30.17
Illiterates.....	4.69	2.55
Total....	99.80	100.01

* The discrepancies in these categories are seemingly due to a difference in definition of what constitutes a public school and high school graduate (see text).

of individuals reaching various grades at school, and compared the distribution of this schooling with that of our own sample of population.

The estimated schooling of the American population as furnished by the Education Office, and the corresponding figures for the educational categories as found in our own sample, are given in table 8. The only major difficulty we had in making the comparison was in deciding whether 8th grade grammar school meant merely reaching the 8th grade

[2] We are indebted for this information to Dr. David Segal, Educational Consultant and Specialist in Tests and Measurements at that office.

or completing it, and similarly in the case of the 4th year high school. In our own sample, we set 8 years public school and 4 years high school as meaning either mere attainment or actual completion of these grades. There was also the question as to what the term illiteracy should embrace. According to our definition, it means no schooling whatsoever, whereas in the case of the Federal estimates it seemingly means not knowing how to read and write. These possible sources of error, notwithstanding, there is a rather remarkable correspondence between the educational level of the country as a whole and that of our sampling. It thus appears, that by following a sampling based primarily on the occupational distribution of our subjects, the factor of educational status took care of itself. The educational distribution of our sample is not very far from that of the entire United States. In fact, the median educational level of our subjects is practicaly identical with that estimated by the Education Office for the country as a whole.

A third factor which might be thought of as a possibly important item in the standardization of an intelligence test, is that of sex differences. With respect to this factor most of the available data relates to differences observed on test performances of boys and girls. Briefly summarized, the data show occasional significant, though generally small differences between the sexes as regards the efficiency on individual tests. For example, boys tend to do better on Arithmetical Reasoning, and girls better on Vocabulary tests.[3] But when the total score is taken into consideration, that is to say, when the individual tests are combined into batteries, these differences tend to cancel each other. It is not clear, however, whether this nullification of sex differences is due to a real averaging of these differences or to an artifact resulting from a special selection of tests. For example, in the New Stanford Revision, Terman and Merrill[4] eliminated such tests as they said were "unfair" to one sex or another. And we have done the same. Thus we dropped the Cube Analysis from our battery when we discovered that the mean scores for men and women showed systematically large differences in favor of the former. As our scales now stand, there are no statistically significant differences in total score between the sexes, although women tend to have higher mean total scores at almost every

[3] But that is not necessarily true at all ages. See on this point Terman, L. M.: *Intelligence of School Children*. Boston, 1919. For sex differences among adults see Jones, H. E.: of Conrad, H. S.: *Genet. Psychol. Monog.*, 1933, no. 6, pp. 260-261.

[4] *Measuring Intelligence*. Boston, 1937, p. 22.

year level. These small differences in themselves do not prove anything, but taken together with other evidence, have led this writer to the belief that it may be possible to demonstrate a measurable superiority of women over men so far as general intelligence is concerned. We do not have the necessary data as yet to back up this generalization, but we have more than a "sneaking suspicion" that the female of the species is not only more deadly, but also more intelligent than the male.

We now come to a group of factors which undoubtedly influences intelligence test results, but whose exact rôle is difficult to evaluate owing to our, as yet, limited knowledge of what the actual relationships between them may be. We refer to the factors of "race", social milieu and economic status. Here again, our view is that in an ideal standardization, there ought to be separate norms in each of these categories to make allowance for their respective influences. We do not think, however, that it is possible to do this at present, particularly when those to whom we might look for the facts are at so great odds among themselves as to what these facts are. In the case of our own standardization we have rather cut the Gordian knot than undone it. Thus, we have eliminated the "colored" vs. "white" factor by admitting at the outset that our norms cannot be used for the colored population of the United States. Though we have tested a large number of colored persons, our standardization is based upon white subjects only. We omitted the colored population from our first standardization because we did not feel that norms derived by mixing the populations could be interpreted without special provisos and reservations.

In eliminating the "colored" vs. "white" factor from our population problem, we do not, of course, avoid the question of race differences altogether. All that can be said about intelligence differences between the white and colored population of the United States, applies in a general way to differences in intelligence level between other "racial" groups. That such differences exist between various groups which constitute the white population of the United States there can be little doubt. To what extent, however, these differences need to be considered in an intelligence examination that could be used indiscriminately on all groups, cannot be easily answered. At all events, any attempt to make allowances for racial differences presents many practical difficulties, perhaps the greatest of which is the large number of individuals that one would have to examine in order to obtain any reliable norms. We do not say that this would not be a worthwhile endeavor, but it was a task which we were not equipped to carry out. We believe, however, that the differences that might be found between the English speaking white groups in the United States of different "racial" origin would not be very large. It seemed to us that if we omitted the non-English speaking population we could treat the remaining portion of the white population as a relatively homogeneous group,—at least in so far as their suitability as cases for our sampling was concerned. This is undoubtedly making a virtue out of necessity. The only justification we offer for this procedure is that we believe that, taken as a whole, our subjects represent a fair cross section of what may be called American intelligence.

Our subjects were chosen mostly from the City and State of New York, but these were matched against the total population of the United States in a manner presently to be described. Our total sampling is on the whole perhaps more representative of the State of New York than of the entire nation. But, according to results obtained with the Army Alpha Test, the mean intelligence level of the white population of the State of New York is not far from the average for the nation as a whole. For this reason we may assume that our mean scores will not differ much from those that may be obtained from the remaining population. Subsequent studies, however, will have to determine the legitimacy of this assumption.

We shall now describe the manner in which our actual sampling was achieved. For this it is necessary to distinguish between our adult and children's samplings. As regards our adult groups, the procedure was as follows: We tried to obtain individuals from all walks of life, and examined as many of these as were willing to take the tests, providing they were not mentally or physically ill and could understand and write English. In this way over 1800 adults, both male and female, ranging in age from 17 to 80 were examined. Transcripts of their examination were recorded on cards and put into a general file. This general file served as an "urn" from which cases could be picked at random to fill whatever criterion of selection might be decided upon.

After much consideration we felt that the most unbiased method of selection would be a sampling based upon the occupational distribution of the country's adult population. For the necessary data we turned to the United States Census for 1930 as the best source. The numerous occupational sub-divisions given in the census report were first combined into ten broad categories such as Agricultural, Manufacturing, Mechanical, Clerical, etc. From the figures given in the census tables, we calculated for each sex and for each age, the percentage of the total number of individuals engaged in the listed occupations.   This furnished us the figures given in table 9.

After this table had been devised, we merely went to our files and took from them such cases as would enable us to match the general occupational distributions of the census population.   The number of adults (ages 20–59) finally available amounted to approximately 1,000. The result of our own matching is shown in table 10.   As will be seen, our percentages for the various occupational categories, agree very closely, age for age and sex for sex (except for females above 50), with those determined for the country as a whole.

Owing to the predominately urban character of our own population, a certain amount of substitution was necessary.   For example, we did not have among our subjects any person employed in the extraction of minerals, and very few who might be classified as being engaged in agriculture.   It was therefore necessary to find cases, among our own occupational groups, which might be legitimately used in their place. A fair way to do this, it seemed to us, was to substitute individuals chosen from urban occupational groups which might have a mean intelligence rating of the same order.   To achieve this we turned to the tables furnished in the Memoirs of the National Academy of Sciences[5] wherein are listed the mean scores of the various occupational groups represented in the U. S. Army draft.   Checking on these mean scores, we looked for such urban occupations as showed intelligence ratings of about the same order as those of the agricultural and other groups which we were lacking.   Thus we found that barbers, bakers and teamsters could be substituted for farmers, and that other missing occupational representatives[6] could be similarly replaced.

A word as to the social status of subjects available for our testing program.   In general we can say that we included individuals from almost every social and economic class to be found in the City of New York.   Large numbers, however, were taken from special groups, such as persons attending Adult Education classes; workers, helpers and personnel of various hospitals of the city; members of several social organizations, like the "Y's"; political clubs and church auxiliaries, and, in the case of the older people, Homes for the Aged.   It should be noted,

---

[5] Tables 374–375 and 377, pp. 820–821 and p. 824.

[6] Where the numbers employed in any given occupational group were relatively very small in the U. S. Census, we did not bother with making the substitution. Our general rule was to disregard such occupational groups as showed an incidence of only 1 per cent of the total or less.

TABLE 9

Percentages of total white population in each occupational category—U. S. census, 1930

OCCUPATION	20-24		25-29		30-34		35-39		40-44		45-49		50-54		55-59	
	M	F	M	F	M	F	M	F	M	F	M	F	M	F	M	F
Total numbers per age in tens of thousands	466	480	424	432	405	405	417	401	373	346	329	302	281	259	222	206
	per cent	per cent	per cent	per cent	per cent	per cent	per cent	per cent	per cent	per cent	per cent	per cent	per cent	per cent	per cent	per cent
Agriculture	20	1	18	1	17	1	19	1	20	1	22	1	24	1	26	1
Forestry and fishing	1	0	1	0	1	0	1	0	1	0	1	0	1	0	1	0
Extraction of minerals	3	0	3	0	3	0	3	0	3	0	3	0	3	0	2	0
Manufacturing and mechanical	30	8	34	5	34	4	35	4	35	4	34	3	32	3	29	3
Transportation and communication	9	2	11	2	11	1	10	1	10	0	9	0	8	0	7	0
Trade	11	4	14	3	16	3	16	3	16	3	15	2	15	2	14	2
Public service	2	0	2	0	2	0	2	0	2	0	2	0	3	0	3	0
Professional service	4	8	6	6	5	4	5	4	5	3	5	3	5	3	5	2
Domestic and personal service	3	6	3	5	4	6	4	5	4	6	4	6	4	7	4	6
Clerical	9	14	8	9	6	5	5	4	4	3	4	2	4	1	3	1
Not gainfully employed	8	57	0	69	1	76	0	78	0	80	1	83	1	83	6	85
Total	100.0	100.0	100.0	100.0	100.0	100.0	100.0	100.0	100.0	100.0	100.0	100.0	100.0	100.0	100.0	100.0

TABLE 10

Percentage of Bellevue adult sampling in each occupational category—ages 20-59

OCCUPATION	20-24		25-29		30-34		35-39		40-44		45-49		50-54		55-59	
	M	F	M	F	M	F	M	F	M	F	M	F	M	F	M	F
Total number of cases	90	70	120	75	92	48	85	50	54	37	40	30	44	11	40	10
Agriculture equivalents*	22.2	0	19.2	0	17.4	0	20.0	0	18.5	0	22.5	0	25.0	0	25.0	0
Forestry and fishing	0	0	0	0	0	0	0	0	1.9	0	0	0	0	0	0	0
Extraction of minerals	4.4	0	2.5	0	3.3	0	2.4	0	1.9	0	2.5	0	2.3	0	2.5	0
Manufacturing and mechanical	30.0	7.1	34.2	9.3	25.9	4.2	36.5	4.0	35.2	2.7	35.0	3.3	36.4	0	32.5	0
Transportation and communication	8.9	2.9	11.7	2.7	12.0	2.1	10.6	2.0	13.0	0	10.0	0	4.5	0	7.5	0
Trade	11.1	2.9	13.3	5.3	15.2	4.2	15.3	2.0	14.8	2.7	15.0	0	13.6	0	12.5	0
Public service	1.1	0	1.7	0	1.1	0	2.4	0	1.9	0	0	0	4.5	0	2.5	0
Professional service	4.4	8.6	6.7	9.3	4.3	6.2	4.7	4.0	5.6	2.7	5.0	3.3	2.3	9.1	5.0	0
Domestic and personal service	3.3	7.1	3.3	8.0	4.3	6.2	3.5	6.0	3.7	8.1	5.0	3.3	4.5	9.1	2.5	10.0
Clerical	7.8	15.7	7.5	14.7	5.4	6.2	4.7	6.0	3.7	2.7	5.0	3.3	6.8	0	2.5	0
Not gainfully employed	6.7	55.7	0	50.7	1.1	70.8	0	76.0	0	81.1	0	86.7	0	81.8	7.5	90.0
Total	99.9	100.0	100.1	100.0	100.0	99.9	100.1	100.0	100.2	100.0	100.0	99.9	99.9	100.0	100.0	100.0

* Note: For occupations substituted for "Agriculture" category, see text.

however, that a substantial percentage of our subjects was obtained by visits to private homes. A certain number of the female subjects were parents of children brought to the Bellevue Mental Hygiene Clinic. A special source worth mentioning was the Coney Island beach, where one of our resourceful examiners went daily throughout a summer, and obtained volunteer subjects of both sexes. A detailed analysis of the sources is given in table 11.

Subjects chosen by the above procedure included very few individuals of mental defective level. It was necessary to supplement our general sampling by a certain number of low grade individuals, which would roughly correspond to the estimated incidence of defectives in the total

TABLE 11
Sources of adult sampling
Ages 16 to 69

SOURCE	NUMBER OF CASES
Homes of subjects (mostly housewives).......................	130
Political, social and fraternal organizations...................	126
Commercial establishments.................................	14
Federal project workers, hospital workers, including professional, clerical, skilled, unskilled and domestic workers.......	255
Hospital wards and clinics (non-mental cases)................	176
Transient Bureau (all types who happen to be passing through the city and are in need of temporary aid)..................	67
Summer resort (Coney Island Beach)........................	58
Adult vocational schools...................................	234
Day high schools..	48
Old age institutions.......................................	73
Total...	1,181

population. The percentage of mental defectives in the U. S. has been estimated very differently by different investigators,[7] but on the basis of our own experience, and of the consensus of previous investigators we fixed it at 3 per cent. To obtain a random sampling of the defectives themselves, we made use of patients coming to the Bellevue Psychiatric Hospital and of others already committed to various State Institutions. Over 200 such cases were available to us and from among these we were able to make a random selection at all ages and for both sexes. A special analysis of the entire group of mental defectives will

[7] See Pintner, R.: "*Intelligence Testing,*" pp. 336–340.

appear subsequently in a study devoted to the problem of the better classification of mental defectives.

The sampling of our children was a much simpler task, thanks in a good measure to the co-operation and assistance of the Bureau of Reference, Research and Statistics, of the Board of Education of the City of New York.[8] Our procedure was as follows: Consulting the Bureau of Reference, Research and Statistics, we obtained a list of available schools, which in their opinion might be called representative or aver-

TABLE 12

Age-grade distribution in public schools of New York City

Per cent of each age in each grade year, ages 7–16

GRADE-YEAR	AGE IN YEARS									
	7	8	9	10	11	12	13	14	15	16
Ungraded...............			1	1	1	2	2	2	1	
First...................	9	1								
Second.................	63	12	3	1						
Third..................	28	59	14	4	1					
Fourth.................		27	54	15	5	1				
Fifth...................		1	27	51	16	6	2	1		
Sixth..................			1	26	48	17	6	2	1	
Seventh................				2	24	42	17	7	3	1
Eighth.................					4	24	38	17	7	3
Ninth..................					1	7	27	38	20	8
Tenth..................						1	7	22	33	20
Eleventh...............							1	6	19	26
Twelfth................								1	6	17
Continuation Schools..								4	10	25
Total...............	100	100	100	100	100	100	100	100	100	100

This table was calculated from the 37th Annual Report of the Superintendent of Schools, City of New York, Statistical Section, tables 56, 108, 132, 179, pages 109, 177, 204, 259.

age. By representative schools is meant that the children attending them were not predominately of one racial or social group, and by

[8] We take this occasion to express our gratitude to the various Superintendents who gave us permission to test the children in the schools of the City, and for the kind co-operation of the Principals of these schools. We wish to mention in particular Miss Elizabeth A. Walsh, Director of the Bureau for Children with Retarded Mental Development, who assisted us in obtaining children of the ungraded classes.

average that they were schools, the pupils of which, as a group, were neither noticeably above nor significantly below the average in intelligence for the City of New York as a whole. At these schools we tested certain fractions of the population, depending upon the facilities and the age-grade range of the school. Usually not more than 100 to 150 children, chosen at random, were examined at any single school. At the end of a year we had some 1300 children from 6 to 17 years, tested at different times, at different schools[9] and by different examiners. These New York groups were supplemented by some 200 examined in Yonkers and

TABLE 13
Age-grade distribution of Bellevue samplings
Per cent of each age in each grade year, ages 7–16

GRADE-YEAR	AGE IN YEARS									
	7	8	9	10	11	12	13	14	15	16
Ungraded..............			2.0	3.3	1.7	1.7	1.4	1.4	2.0	
First...................	10.0	2.0								
Second.................	80.0	26.0	2.0							
Third..................	10.0	62.0	14.0	3.3	1.7					
Fourth.................		10.0	74.0	15.0	5.0	1.7				
Fifth..................		8.0	55.0	23.3	5.0	1.4	1.4			
Sixth..................				21.7	46.7	28.3	7.1	2.9		
Seventh................				1.7	18.3	31.7	15.7	2.9	2.0	1.0
Eighth.................					1.7	30.0	42.9	17.1	7.0	3.0
Ninth..................					1.7	1.7	28.6	48.6	21.0	8.0
Tenth..................							2.9	18.6	42.0	40.0
Eleventh...............								2.9	12.0	14.0
Twelfth................									4.0	9.0
Continuation Schools..								4.3	10.0	25.0
Total...............	100.0	100.0	100.0	100.0	100.1	100.1	100.0	100.1	100.0	100.0

New Jersey schools, making a total of approximately 1500. As in the case of our adult sampling procedure, we placed all these cases in a "statistical urn," and from this urn, made a random selection to conform to our sampling criterion. The basis of this final sample was a matching of our own population against the age-grade distribution of the City as a whole, as derived from the 1934 age-progress analysis of pupils in Elementary, Junior and Senior High Schools and various Continuation

[9] Of the Schools, 4 were in Manhattan, 3 in Brooklyn, 2 in Queens and 2 in the Bronx.

Schools of the City of New York.[10]   This general age-grade distribution for the City as a whole is given in table 12; the corresponding figures for our own matched sampling, in table 13.

The cases included in our standardizing children's sample do not represent all the children under 16 who were tested, but only those who were "matched" to fit our criterion, that is, the age-grade distribution of children in the New York Public Schools.   On the other hand, it includes a small percentage of individuals (*circa* 2 per cent) who were not in the public schools.   These are the lower-grade defectives who because of their limited endowment were not to be found in regular schools.   Our sources for these lower-grade defectives (also some of the higher types) were, again, patients up for commitment at the Bellevue Mental Hygiene Clinic, or cases already committed to some New York State Institutions for the feebleminded.[11]

[10] Superintendent's Report, 1934.
[11] Principally Letchworth Village.   We wish to thank Dr. Edward J. Humphreys, Director of Research, and Dr. Elaine F. Kinder, Research Psychologist, for the co-operation which made these cases available to us.

CHAPTER 9

STANDARDIZATION AND RESULTS

The intelligence examinations that are presented in this book are point scales. This means that an individual's intelligence rating is obtained, ultimately, from a summation of the credits (or points) which he is given for passing various test items. The first problem which confronts us in such a scale is to decide what portion of the total number of credits should be assigned to each of the tests. This is the statistical problem of "weighting". One way of meeting it is to let the test weights take care of themselves by simply allowing one point for each item correctly passed. Such, for example, is the procedure employed on the Army Alpha, where the number of items on the several tests determines the final amount that each test contributes to the scale. Another way is to use some predetermined scoring system that will fix in advance the proportion which each test contributes to this total score, irrespective of the number of items it may happen to contain. This, of course, requires an additional set of criteria, but has the advantage of compelling the author to evaluate his tests separately.

To determine the "value" of a test, however, is an extremely onerous procedure. From a statistical point of view the most valid method that can be employed seemingly is that of multiple correlations. But the results obtained thereby usually do not, in our experience, justify the amount of labor involved. In the end, the tests must be evaluated in the light of clinical experience. Whether a test is "good" or not must be determined eventually by the efficacy with which it measures the thing one wants it to measure.

Now that we have examined some 5000[1] subjects, we are in a better position to express a competent opinion regarding the merits of our individual tests. At the outset of standardization it seemed to us, in the absence of any definite knowledge, that the best assumption to make about the separate tests of the scale was that they were equally important.[2] Accordingly each test in our scale was made to contribute

[1] This number includes 2000 cases not used in the standardization.

[2] From a qualitative point of view, subsequent statistical analysis has not, as indeed was to be expected, fully confirmed this assumption. Some of our tests

the same possible maximal number of points as any other, irrespective of the number of items of which it happened to consist. There are a number of advantages in this procedure, the most important of which, perhaps, is that it allows for the addition or omission of tests from the scales without significantly altering the norms. When tests scores are expressed in terms of S.D. units and each test is equated to every other, any given test may be left out and any new test may be added and allowed for (up to a certain point) by simply prorating for it.

Weighting of the separate tests was performed in the following manner: Using the age group 20–34 as the standardizing group, we first distributed the raw scores of each test separately and calculated the usual statistical constants for them. From a comparison of these constants we then found that a scale of about 20 points would best fit our data. We accordingly converted the raw scores for each test into such a 20 point scale, setting a new mean at 10 and a new standard deviation at 3. This conversion was made by employing Hull's method.[3] The result of the conversion obviously was to equate all the tests against each other, so that all had identical means and approximately equal ranges of variability. Finally, we drew up a table of equivalents in which the original scores on each of the tests were expressed in terms of equal multiples or fractions of their new S.D.'s. It is these scores which were used in obtaining all our norms, and which must be employed to obtain a subject's final rating on any of the scales.

We shall now summarize the main results of our standardization. The first fact of interest is the rise and fall of total scores on the various tests with increasing age. These are given in tables 14–16. As will be noted, there is a progressive rise of mean score with age, which continues up to about age 18.[4] The curve plotted for the Full Scale means is given on page 29, and has already been discussed. As might be expected, the standard deviations for the lower ages are rather large for their mean scores. This indicates that the tests cannot be used below a certain age. The critical point seems to be about year 10, and accordingly our scales are to be used only from that age onward.

---

are better measures of intelligence than others. (See on this point comments on individual tests.) However, such attempts as we have made at more refined scoring do not seem to affect significantly our total score distributions. This experience agrees with that of the standardizers of the Army Alpha.

[3] The details of our statistical procedures are given in Appendix 1.

[4] Actually; age 22. The difference in mean score, however, between age 18 and 22 is negligible. The scores compared are the smoothed and not the calculated means.

The mean scores, even at an early age, however, furnish an opportunity for calculating equivalent mental ages, and although we have abandoned the M.A. as a base for calculating I.Q.'s, these equivalents are of some interest. They are accordingly given in table 17 for our three major scales. An important point to note is that there are no mental age equivalents for ages above 15½, and that beginning as early

TABLE 14

Summary of mean standard scores and sigmas

Ages 7 to 59

Full scale, 10 tests

AGE	CALCULATED MEAN	CALCULATED SIGMA	SMOOTHED MEAN	SMOOTHED SIGMA
7.5	27.2*	11.55	23.0	13.0
8.5	34.8	13.78	34.5	14.8
9.5	46.8	16.82	48.6	16.0
10.5	63.3	15.72	62.3	16.8
11.5	73.8	17.43	73.2	17.4
12.5	82.2	17.89	82.6	17.8
13.5	89.9	17.94	89.8	18.0
14.5	93.3	18.67	93.4	18.3
15.5	95.1	18.00	95.0	18.8
16.5	95.9	19.14	96.2	19.0
18.5	96.3	19.88	97.8	19.6
22.5	98.8	19.00	97.9	20.8
27.5	95.9	21.35	95.0	21.9
32.5	90.4	24.00	91.6	22.5
37.5	86.7	24.00	88.0	23.4
42.5	85.1	23.90	84.8	23.9
47.5	79.0	22.20	81.3	24.0
52.5	77.4	23.73	78.0	24.2
57.5	74.9	24.77	74.8	24.5

* The mean score for age 7 is obviously too high owing to the necessary omission of individuals in this age group of low defective intelligence. The Bellevue Scale does not extend sufficiently far down to permit their being tested with it.

as age 14, the differences between succeeding half year scores are so small as to make them unreliable. This would likewise be true of most other general intelligence examinations if the original raw scores were similarly transmuted into S.D. units.

A second point of interest is the change in test score variability with age. This change is best revealed by the ratio of the mean to the standard deviation, that is, the value of the coefficient of variation at

TABLE 15
Summary of mean standard scores and sigmas
Ages 7 to 59
Verbal scale, 5 tests

AGE	CALCULATED MEAN	CALCULATED SIGMA	SMOOTHED MEAN	SMOOTHED SIGMA
7.5	11.2	4.92	9.1	6.1
8.5	16.0	7.70	15.6	7.5
9.5	22.1	8.77	22.1	8.8
10.5	30.08	8.78	30.0	9.4
11.5	36.50	10.75	36.4	9.9
12.5	40.66	10.29	40.9	10.1
13.5	43.5	9.95	43.5	10.2
14.5	45.07	10.17	45.0	10.4
15.5	45.6	9.90	45.5	11.0
16.5	46.25	10.33	46.2	11.2
18.5	45.8	11.69	46.8	11.5
22.5	48.6	10.33	47.0	11.9
27.5	48.14	12.36	47.0	12.4
32.5	44.96	13.90	46.5	12.5
37.5	45.1	13.31	45.5	13.0
42.5	45.1	12.87	44.5	13.4
47.5	43.8	13.15	43.5	13.6
52.5	41.85	13.75	42.2	14.0
57.5	40.6	14.14	41.0	14.5

TABLE 16
Summary of mean standard scores and·sigmas
Ages 7 to 49
Performance scale, 5 tests

AGE	CALCULATED MEAN	CALCULATED SIGMA	SMOOTHED MEAN	SMOOTHED SIGMA
7.5	15.6	8.49	13.7	8.3
8.5	20.5	8.0	19.6	9.0
9.5	24.9	9.5	25.8	9.4
10.5	34.0	9.0	31.6	9.7
11.5	37.42	8.25	37.1	9.9
12.5	41.83	9.42	42.4	9.9
13.5	46.86	10.05	46.2	10.0
14.5	48.35	9.57	48.3	10.0
15.5	49.55	10.75	49.5	10.1
16.5	50.7	10.69	50.7	10.4
18.5	50.95	10.29	51.5	10.5
22.5	50.88	10.23	50.8	10.9
27.5	48.1	11.1	48.3	11.2
32.5	45.45	12.58	45.5	11.6
37.5	42.91	12.17	42.6	12.0
42.5	40.1	12.19	39.8	12.5
47.5	36.6	12.54	36.8	12.8

TABLE 17

Equivalent* mental ages for Bellevue Intelligence Scales

M.A.	FULL SCALE	PERFORMANCE SCALE	VERBAL SCALE	M.A.
7—0	22	15	10	7—0
7—3	24	16	11	7—3
7—6	26	17	12	7—6
7—9	29			7—9
8—0	31	18	14	8—0
8—3	34	19	15	8—3
8—6	37	20	16	8—6
8—9	40	22	17	8—9
9—0	43	23	19	9—0
9—3	46	24	21	9—3
9—6	49	26	22	9—6
9—9	52	27	24	9—9
10—0	56	28	26	10—0
10—3	59	30	28	10—3
10—6	62	31	30	10—6
10—9	65	33	32	10—9
11—0	68	34	33	11—0
11—3	71	36	35	11—3
11—6	73	37	36	11—6
11—9	76	39	38	11—9
12—0	78	40	39	12—0
12—3	80	41	40	12—3
12—6	82	42	41	12—6
12—9	85	44	42	12—9
13—0	86	45	43	13—0
13—3	88			13—3
13—6	90	46	44	13—6
13—9	91			13—9
14—0	92	47		14—0
14—6	93	48	45	14—6
15—0	94	49		15—0
15—6	95	50	46	15—6

* These M.A. equivalents may not be used to calculate I.Q.'s.

each age. These values (Pearson's C.'s of V.) are given in table 18. Our results show that in children there is a decline in variability and in adults an increase in variability with age. These results are in line with what has been found in other studies,[5] but interpretation of them is not easy. As regards the decrease of variability with age in the case of children, one possible explanation is that it is due to the leveling influence of education[6] and environment. Another possible cause is the factor of natural selection. If for no other reason than the effect of death in

TABLE 18

Coefficients of variation $\left(\dfrac{\sigma}{M} \times 100\right)$

Weighted scores (smoothed)

Ages 10–60

AGE	FULL SCALE	VERBAL SCALE	PERFORMANCE SCALE
10	26.97	31.33	30.70
11	23.77	27.20	26.68
12	21.55	24.69	23.35
13	20.04	23.45	21.64
14	19.59	23.11	20.70
15	19.79	24.18	20.40
16	19.75	24.22	20.51
17–19	20.04	24.57	20.39
20–24	21.25	25.32	21.46
25–29	23.05	26.38	23.19
30–34	24.56	26.88	25.49
35–39	26.59	28.57	28.17
40–44	28.18	30.11	31.41
45–49	29.52	31.26	34.78
50–54	31.03	33.18	
55–59	32.75	35.37	

cutting down extreme deviates, one ought to expect variability to decrease with age. But this factor should also operate in old age.

The fact that actual measures do not confirm this expectation, suggests other possible influencing factors. One is the lack of equivalence

[5] As for example those of Ruger, H. A. and Stoessiger, B.: On the Growth of Certain Characteristics in Man. *Annals of Eugenics*, 1926, parts I & II.

[6] See on this point Wechsler, D.: The Influence of Education on Intelligence. *Jr. Educ. Psychol.* 1926, XVII, pp. 248–257.

TABLE 19
Bellevue intelligence quotients
Means and standard deviations of Full-Scale intelligence quotients

AGE	NUMBER	MEAN I.Q.	S.D.
10	60	101.25	13.20
11	60	100.84	14.10
12	60	100.08	13.80
13	70	100.57	14.70
14	70	99.93	14.75
15	100	100.00	14.57
16	100	100.30	15.15
17–19	100	98.75	14.50
20–24	160	100.16	13.70
25–29	195	100.89	14.60
30–34	140	99.57	15.60
35–39	135	99.76	15.50
40–44	91	100.30	14.80
45–49	70	100.07	14.01
50–54	55	100.50	13.97
55–59	50	99.1	16.85
50–59	105	99.84	15.26

TABLE 20
Bellevue intelligence quotients
Means and standard deviations of Verbal I.Q.'s

AGE	NUMBER	MEAN I.Q.	S.D.
10	60	100.08	14.08
11	60	100.25	16.65
12	60	100.50	15.44
13	70	100.07	14.00
14	70	100.14	14.28
15	100	100.00	14.60
16	100	99.95	13.80
17–19	100	98.45	14.70
20–24	160	102.09	13.22
25–29	195	101.58	14.22
30–34	140	98.82	16.01
35–39	135	99.98	15.18
40–44	91	100.52	14.86
45–49	70	100.64	13.84
50–54	55	100.05	13.95
55–59	50	98.00	14.85
50–59	105	99.07	14.43

between physiological and chronological age. Some individuals grow "old" at a very much earlier age than others. Other factors are the mixed influences of education, vocational pursuit in a particular field over a prolonged time, and restricted environment. A fuller discussion of this question, however, would take us too far afield and we merely present it as a point for study and further investigation.

More important for our purpose than the variations of absolute scores with age is to discover the corresponding change in I.Q. when calculated in the manner described in chapter 4. In tables 19–21 we give the mean I.Q.'s and their S.D.'s for all ages—from 10 to 60—on our three

TABLE 21

Bellevue intelligence quotients

Means and standard deviation of Performance I.Q.'s

AGE	NUMBER	MEAN I.Q.	S.D.
10	60	102.50	13.57
11	60	101.50	12.60
12	60	100.17	13.42
13	70	101.07	14.62
14	70	100.50	14.19
15	100	100.05	15.70
16	100	99.75	15.15
17–19	100	99.10	14.30
20–24	160	99.00	14.37
25–29	195	100.22	14.31
30–34	140	100.00	15.78
35–39	135	99.13	16.21
40–44	91	100.47	15.04
45–49	70	100.64	13.10

major scales. The corresponding coefficients of variation for each scale are given in table 22. As will be noted, there is remarkable constancy of the I.Q. throughout. Not only the means, but also the S.D.'s remain approximately the same throughout the entire age range for which the scales are employed. It thus appears that our method of calculating I.Q.'s not only takes into account the change of test score with age, but that of the differences of variability of the tests scored at different ages. It should be noted that the mean I.Q. remains constant, not only in the Full Scale, but also in the case of the Verbal and Performance Scales. This may be interpreted as justification for our inclusion of both Verbal and Performance items in a single scale. More direct evidence on this question, however, may be had from a study of the mutual intercorrelations of the several parts when treated as separate scales. The correlations between them were as follows:

Verbal I.Q. $\times$ Full Scale I.Q., $r = .90 \pm .007$
Performance I.Q. $\times$ Full Scale I.Q., $r = .88 \pm .008$
Verbal I.Q. $\times$ Performance I.Q., $r = .71 \pm .018$

When test scores were used instead of I.Q.'s, the correlations were practically identical, thus:

TABLE 22

Coefficients of variation $\left(\dfrac{\sigma}{M} \times 100 \right)$

Intelligence quotients
Ages 10–60

AGE	FULL SCALE	VERBAL SCALE	PERFORMANCE SCALE
10	13.04	14.07	13.24
11	13.98	16.61	12.41
12	13.79	15.36	13.40
13	14.62	13.99	14.47
14	14.76	14.26	14.12
15	14.57	14.60	15.69
16	15.10	13.81	15.19
17–19	14.68	14.93	14.43
20–24	13.68	12.95	14.52
25–29	14.47	14.00	14.28
30–34	15.67	16.20	15.78
35–39	15.54	15.18	16.35
40–44	14.76	14.78	14.97
45–49	14.00	13.75	13.02
50–59	15.28	14.57	

Verbal Test Score $\times$ Full Scale Test Score, $r = .91 \pm .007$
Performance Test Score $\times$ Full Scale Test Score, $r = .90 \pm .007$
Verbal Test Score $\times$ Performance Test Score, $r = .67 \pm .020$

When corrected for attenuation the correlations between Performance and Verbal increase significantly, thus:

Verbal I.Q. $\times$ Performance I.Q., $r = .83$
Verbal Score $\times$ Performance Score, $r = .81$

Because of the high[7] correlation between our Performance and Verbal

[7] The high correlation obtained is due in part to the heterogeneity of our population as regards both age and I.Q. range. Other studies show considerably lower correlations between the Verbal and Performance I.Q.'s.

I.Q.'s it might be supposed that the two scales could be regarded as equivalent, but that is not necessarily the case. A high correlation between two tests signifies only that the tests measure the same trait or ability; it does not mean that they measure them to the same degree. It is possible for two tests to be perfectly correlated and still give far from equivalent ratings. This would happen if the individual measures entering into the correlation showed systematic constant differences. Thus, if I.Q.'s furnished by one scale were systematically 10 points lower than I.Q.'s obtained on a second scale, then the same individual tested with the two scales would obtain different I.Q.'s in spite of the fact that the two scales were perfectly correlated. If he obtained an I.Q. of 95 on scale A, his corresponding I.Q. on B would be only 85, or if 115 on B, an I.Q. of 125 on A, and so on.

In evaluating the equivalence of two scales where results are expressed in the same units, one must take into account not only the degree to which the scales correlate with one another, but the absolute amounts

TABLE 24

Analysis of differences between verbal and performance I.Q.'s
Median difference and interquartile (Q) ranges for undifferentiated groups

AGES	MEDIAN DIFFERENCE	Q	NUMBER
10–16	9.1	5.3	520
20–49	8.4	4.9	590

by which the individual measures differ. In practice it is best effected by averaging the observed differences without respect to sign. The median difference between Performance and Verbal I.Q.'s for our Scale is approximately 8.7 points. It varies with age and with the levels of I.Q. compared. The basic data from which these factors may be appraised are given in tables 23, 24 and 25. Discussion of them is left for our next chapter when we shall again have occasion to take up the problem of Verbal and Performance I.Q.

At this point we may just mention the fact that while the I.Q. differences between the Bellevue Verbal and Performance Scales are seemingly large, they are probably considerably smaller than would be obtained from a similar study between the Binet and any other Performance Scale now in use. We say probably, because we have been unable to find such studies in the literature covering any considerable number of cases. The best material available for such a study is that furnished by Grace Arthur in the standardization of the Scale bearing her name,[8] where correlation tables between Performance and Verbal (Binet) tests are given. From these tables we were able to deduce the approximate I.Q. differences between scores on Performance and Verbal for some 185 cases between ages 10–15 and found the median to be 11.0 points with an interquartile range of 5.84.

The usefulness of a scale depends not only upon the validity of its measures, but also upon the manner in which these measures distribute themselves within the limits of their range. In general it is desirable that the range be as wide as possible, that the measures be continuous,

TABLE 24
Median differences and interquartile ranges for different I.Q. categories

AGES 10-16				AGES 20-49			
I.Q. category	Median difference	Q	Number	I.Q. category	Median difference	Q	Number
79 and below	7.7	4.8	40	79 and below	12.6	5.5	74
90–110	8.2	4.6	287	91–110	7.3	4.6	405
120 and over	14.9	7.8	41	120 and over	11.1	4.7	62

TABLE 25
Per cent of cases with verbal higher and performance higher

AGES 10-16				AGES 20-49			
I.Q. category	Performance higher	Verbal higher	No difference	I.Q. category	Performance higher	Verbal higher	No difference
79 and below	67.5	25.0	7.5	75 and below	74.3	23.0	2.7
91–110	52.3	43.9	3.8	91–110	46.7	48.9	4.4
120 and over	12.2	82.9	4.9	120 and over	21.0	77.4	1.6

and that there be no piling up of scores at any point. Some authors also believe that the resulting frequency curve ought to be Gaussian or as nearly Gaussian as possible. The last requirement seems to be a result of the wide-spread but mistaken belief that mental measures distribute themselves according to the normal curve of error.

The distribution of our adult I.Q.'s given in figure 9 conforms to the first three criteria just mentioned: (1) The range of scores is approximately 8 S.D. (or in terms of I.Q., from I.Q. of *circa* 35 to an I.Q. of

[8] Arthur, Grace: *A Point Scale of Performance Tests.* N. Y., 1933, vol. II, pp. 58–61.

circa 155[9]).   (2) Our I.Q.'s are continuous within the defined limits.
All intervening I.Q.'s are not only possible, but actually occur.   (3)
There is no piling up of scores at any point of the scale, and particularly
not at the lower extremes (as in the case of the Army Alpha).   The
distribution of our measures, however, is not Gaussian.   As can be
seen from the figure 9, the histogram is considerably skewed in a negative direction.   A curve fitted to this data would be of the form of
Pearson's Type IV.   We have not gone to the trouble of actually fitting

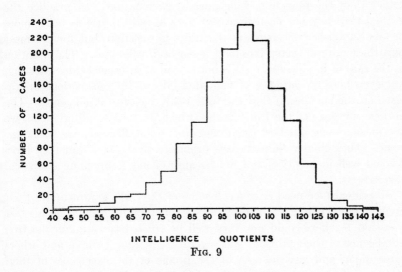

DISTRIBUTION OF FULL SCALE INTELLIGENCE QUOTIENTS
AGES 10 TO 60   1508 CASES

INTELLIGENCE   QUOTIENTS
FIG. 9

it but have calculated the necessary constants from which this may be
done.   These are given in the footnote below.[10]

We come at last to the most trying problem, that of validation.   How
do we know that our tests are "good" measures of intelligence?   The
only honest reply we can make is that our own experience has shown
them to be so.   If this seems to be a very tenuous answer we need only
remind the reader that it has been practical experience which has given

[9] The actual I.Q. range for any given age is a function of the age at which it is
calculated.   It varies from age to age.

[10] Mean = 100.11 β_1 = 0.2789 K_1 = 0.3973 $\sqrt{N\Sigma\beta_1}$ = 3.54
 S.D. = 14.69 β_2 = 3.6170 K_2 = 0.5668 $\sqrt{N\Sigma\beta_2}$ = 14.00
 N = 1508

(or denied) final validity to every other intelligence test. Regrettable as it may seem, empirical judgments, here as elsewhere, play the rôle of ultimate arbiter.[11] In any case, all evidence for the validity of a test, whether statistical or otherwise, is inevitably of an indirect sort and, in the end, cumulative rather than decisive.

The usual procedure for validating a new test has been to set as a criterion some well established test which has been accepted as a "good" measure of the trait in question and then appraise the validity of the new one on the basis of the degree to which it correlates with the already established test. The significance of this correlation will depend entirely upon the original criterion, and it is therefore the criterion itself, rather than the new test, which needs examination. In practice the general tendency has been to accept tests already in use as being more or less established measures of the traits in question, but for the most part these criteria themselves have never been validated. The situation in the case of intelligence tests is not so bad as in other fields of testing, but even here the absence of validated criteria imposes serious limitations on the conclusion that the tests really measure intelligence. The various revisions of the Binet Scales, which, in spite of all criticism, we accept as among our best single measures of intelligence, are no exceptions. Their final validation rests primarily on the fact that they have worked well in practice, and not because of any compelling statistical correlations.

As evidence we need only recall some of the early arguments in their favor. Thus, one of the reasons which Binet gave for devising his test was that teachers could not very well be trusted to estimate the true intelligence of their pupils. But several years later Terman and others came along and gave as one of the proofs of the excellence of their revisions of the scale the fact that I.Q. ratings correlated very highly with school progress. In other words, teachers' judgments which were first condemned were now used as supporting criteria for the validity of the tests. This obviously begs the question, but the dilemma involved is almost inevitable.

---

[11] The reader should not interpret this remark as an attempt on the part of the author to belittle either the importance or value of proper statistical methods. On the contrary, he is of the opinion that without intelligent and thorough statistical evaluation of one's data, little trust can be placed in one's results. The extensive statistical work done on the Bellevue Scales is perhaps the best evidence for that. But he is of the opinion that the task of validating a scale does not end but only begins with the statistical evaluation.

The trouble is not with the teachers' ratings. The same circularity is involved when ratings of any judges are set up as a criterion. In the case of the Alpha Tests, the estimates used at the beginning were those of Army officers; in the case of certain tests offered to industry, the estimates were of supervisors and executives. But these estimates were no more valid than those of the teachers. The tests were urged upon the Army and industry because it was pointed out that the estimates of officers and personnel managers could not always be relied on; then the tests were "sold" to them because they correlated well with practical judgments.

From what we have just said, it appears that every new intelligence test, unless it is merely intended as an alternate for an old one, must itself be validated anew. Such validation is especially necessary if, as in our case, we start with the view that the generally accepted criterion is not as valid as supposed. The Bellevue Scales were devised because of the belief that the Binet Scales were not sufficiently "good" measures of intelligence for adults. Otherwise, indeed, we should not have gone to the trouble of devising our tests. But we do not thereby deny the desirability of showing a correlation between them and other tests of intelligence.

No new test can be markedly out of line with established measures of intelligence and still claim to be "good" measures of it, because that would be tantamount to saying that all other tests were not reliable measures of intelligence. But the degree to which any new test correlates with established tests (e.g., the Binet) cannot in and of itself be accepted as a basic proof of the new test's validity. The test must be able to stand on its own feet. Its correlation with established measures of intelligence is only a minimum requirement. To meet this minimum requirement, a correlational study between Bellevue I.Q.'s and I.Q.'s obtained by the Stanford-Binet Test was made. The correlation for 75 cases (ages 14–16) was .82 ± .026. This is about as high as most other accepted tests of intelligence correlate with each other, and higher than a good many.[12] The results show that the Bellevue Scales measure about the same "thing" as the Binet, but of course leave unanswered the question as to which of them measures it better.

For other measures of validity, we made a number of separate correlation studies between test scores and judges' ratings. One of these

[12] For correlations between the Wechsler-Bellevue and other Scales see table 28, p. 134.

studies was between teachers' estimates and Bellevue Intelligence scores or I.Q.'s. The subjects for this study came primarily from our adolescent groups. One group consisted of students of a Trade School in the City of New York; another, of students from the General Commercial High School in Yonkers. An effort was made to have at least two ratings by different teachers for each subject. These ratings were averaged, distributed on a 6 point scale, and correlated against test scores by means of a four-fold contingency table. The correlation coefficients (Bellevue I.Q.'s against teachers' estimates) for the two groups were as follows:

> Teachers' Ratings (General H. S.) $\times$ Bellevue I.Q.'s, C = .43.
> Teachers' Ratings (Trade H. S.) $\times$ Bellevue I.Q.'s, C = .52.[13]

Our last method of validation was through comparisons of subjects' scores on the Bellevue Scales with estimates of their intelligence by psychiatrists, with records of their school history and with ratings obtained from other tests. These comparisons show that the Bellevue Scales not only provide reliable measures of intelligence when evaluated against clinical data, but do so more consistently than any other single scale. For example, in comparing the Stanford-Binet and the Bellevue Scales as regards degree of agreement with psychiatrist's diagnostic ratings, we found that the forecasting efficiency of the Bellevue Scale was more than five times that of the Stanford-Binet.[14] The psychiatrist's ratings consisted of the diagnoses 'recommended' or 'not-recommended' for commitment to a state institution for mental defectives; the test ratings were the I.Q.'s obtained by the diagnosed subjects on the two scales. The resulting correlations (bi-serial r's) were as follows:

> Binet I.Q.'s $\times$ Psychiatrist's recommendation, r = .33 $\pm$ .071
> Bellevue I.Q.'s $\times$ Psychiatrist's recommendation, r = .79 $\pm$ .048

But most of the "correlations" cannot easily be put into statistical form. They constitute a type of evidence which can best be put forward by citation of individual cases. We have many such cases at hand, but to cite any considerable number of them in full would require more space than we can give here. The following are only by way of illustration:

Case D. W. Male, age 39, born in Poland, has lived 22 years in this country.

---

[13] General H. S., N = 45; Trade H. S., N = 74.
[14] *The Relative Effectiveness of the Stanford-Binet and the Bellevue Scale, etc.,* by B. Balinsky, H. Israel and D. Wechsler. Amer. Jr. of Orthopsy., 1939, IX, 798–80:.

Occupation: window cleaner. Referred by Court on charge of disorderly conduct. Chronic alcoholic, also suffering from syphilis. Examined on 9/29/36 by a staff psychologist with the following results:

Stanford-Binet, 8 yrs. 4 mos. I.Q. (on 16) 52

Pintner-Paterson, M.A. 6-6

The examining psychologist's remarks are as follows: "One cannot rate the patient on the basis of test scores because the results of the psychometric test are at variance with clinical impressions. The patient is definitely inferior but in the examiner's opinion not of defective intelligence."

Re-examined on 10/1/36 with the Bellevue Intelligence Tests, the patient attained a score which gave him an I.Q. of 68 and a rating of borderline intelligence. This corresponded to both the psychologist's and the psychiatrist's estimate of the patient. It was clear also from the man's social history that he could not have been of so low an intelligence level as the Binet and Pintner-Paterson Scale made him out to be. In spite of his alcoholism and his syphilis he had managed, until recently, to get along tolerably well in the community and had worked fairly consistently until two years ago when, as the result of a fall, he had to be hospitalized. The subject obviously needed treatment both for his syphilis and alcoholism, but was not a suitable candidate for admission to an institution for the mentally defective.

Case S. A. Female, age 28, born in U. S. Occupation: nursemaid. Charged with prostitution and referred by Court for observation. Two years prior to present admission had been seen in Bellevue Mental Hygiene Clinic. At that time (1936) was examined with the Stanford-Binet and attained an I.Q. of 86. During present period of observation (October 1937) she was first retested with the Binet and then given the Bellevue Adult tests, with following results:

Stanford-Binet, I.Q. (on 15) 86

Bellevue Adult, I.Q. 68

Abstract of examiner's comments: Because of the apparent discrepancy between the clinical impression and the relative competence which the patient showed on the Binet tests, she was given a Bellevue Adult Examination which contains performance as well as verbal tests. Her scores on the separate parts of the Bellevue showed marked discrepancy, being relatively good on the verbal and markedly inferior on performance tests, but the final score which she attained on the Bellevue Full Scale gave a more appropriate index of her mentality than that obtained from either the Bellevue Verbal tests or the Stanford-Binet alone. The performance part of the Bellevue Test revealed the patient's vocational inaptitude, her defective motility and her marked inability to adjust to unfamiliar patterns. Altogether she functions as a borderline defective meriting commitment. No evidence of psychotic behavior was noted.

Case M. O. Male, age 15 years, 9 months, born in U. S.; school placement: ungraded class. He was brought to the hospital by the probation officer of the Children's Court because of persistent truancy. He was a neglected child without proper supervision. In 1927 the boy was in another city court and was remanded to the hospital as a possible mental defective. Returned to court with diagnosis, "not defective."

Bellevue Intelligence Examination (2/27/36): Score 96, I.Q.: 101, Rating: average intelligence.

Previous to this examination he attained I.Q.'s on the Binet ranging from 72 to 86. On recent Binet test (given 2/24/36) he made an M.A. of 13—7 and an I.Q. of 86. The psychologist's interpretation, notwithstanding the Stanford-Binet I.Q. of only 86, was: average intelligence. On the same day he was given a number of educational tests with the following results:

Woody McCall Arithmetic: 4th grade

Monroe Silent Reading: 8th grade

Monroe Written Spelling: 3rd grade

The child had been in the ungraded classes during the greater part of his school life. He resented being there and believed that he could do the work of the normal classes. In spite of his present school placement both the psychologist and the psychiatrist felt that this boy had good native endowment and did not belong in the ungraded class. The Bellevue tests showed that he was of average intelligence and that his educational disabilities could not be ascribed to mental retardation.

Case P. Q. Female, age 30, born in U. S. Occupation: registered nurse and social worker. Education: two years of college.

Revised Stanford-Binet (Form L), I.Q. 140

Bellevue Adult, I.Q. 117

Examiner's comments: This subject is employed in one of the mental hygiene clinics and known to both the examiner and psychiatrist who have had daily association with her. Our general clinical impression and that of the psychiatrist would be that the Bellevue Adult I.Q. of 117[15] is a more than generous estimate. The rating of high average is more in line with the general impression.

Case M. B. Female, age 40, born in Italy, lived in U. S. 25 years. Occupation: housewife. Education: 3rd grade.

Revised Stanford-Binet (Form L), I.Q. 58

Bellevue Adult, I.Q. 71

Diagnosis: borderline intelligence

Examiner's comments: Stanford-Binet I.Q. much too low. She worked from the time she was 12 until she was 30. The psychiatrist's impression is that the patient is of inferior intelligence but not as low as the Stanford-Binet would indicate.

---

[15] An I.Q. of 117 on the Bellevue rates Bright Normal.

RELIABILITY

The reliability of a scale is the consistency with which it measures the abilities it sets out to test.   It is concerned with two questions: (1) The limits between which any actual score may fall.   (2) The probability that an individual given the same tests on another occasion will make a like score.   As criteria of a scale's reliability, statisticians generally use one or several of the following measures: (1) the standard error of measurement, (2) the degree of correlation between the various portions of the scale, (3) the correlation between alternate forms of the same scale, (4) correlations between repeated administra-

TABLE 26

Correlation between various portions of the scale

	AGES	N	r^*	P.E.
4 tests × 4 tests†	20–34	355	.90	±.014
Verbal I.Q.'s × Performance I.Q.'s	20–34	355	.83	±.018

* Corrected for attenuation.

† The two groups consisted of Information, Digit Span, Picture Completion, and Block Design against Comprehension, Arithmetic, Picture Arrangement and Digit Symbol.

TABLE 27

Correlation between retests*

	AGES	N	RHO	P.E.
Children	10–13	32	.94	±.013
Adults	20–34	20	.94	±.018

* Given at intervals of one month to one year.

tions of the tests to the same individuals.   We have data regarding three of the above four.   The standard error of measurement ($\sigma_{1\infty}$) for the full Scale (I.Q.'s) whose mean and S.D. are respectively 100.11 and 14.69, is 5.674.   The correlation data are given in tables 26 and 27.

CORRELATIONS WITH OTHER SCALES

As a final set of data of general interest, we have brought together a series of reported correlations between the W.-B. and other scales.   These are given in table 28.   Examination of table 28 shows that the correlation of the Wechsler-Bellevue with other standard intelligence tests is generally high.   The correlations given in the table are all with the Full

TABLE 28

Correlations of the Wechsler-Bellevue Full Scale with other Intelligence Scales

TEST	SUBJECTS	"N"	"r"	SOURCE
Stanford-Binet 1916 Rev.	Adolescents, ages 12–16, male and female	75	.82 ± .03	Author (see p. 129)
Stanford-Binet 1916 Rev.	Male delinquent adolescents	61	.81 ± .03	Weider et al. (31)
Stanford-Binet 1937 Rev., L	M. H. Clinic clients, male and female, ages 15–24	55	.91 ± .02	Halpern (10)
Stanford-Binet 1937 Rev., L	College freshmen, female	112	.62 ± .04	Anderson et al. (1)
Stanford-Binet 1916 Rev.	College freshmen, male and female, ages 16–23	125	.57 ± .04	Fishbein (8)
Stanford-Binet 1937 Rev., L	Adult mental patients, ages 16–59	60	.93 ± .01	Benton et al. (2)
Stanford-Binet 1937 Rev., L	Mental hospital patients, male and female, ages 10–69	227	.89 ± .01	Mitchell (20)
Army Alpha	Adult female nurses	92	.74 ± .03	Rabin (21)
A.C.E. tests	College freshmen, females	112	.53 ± .05	Anderson et al. (1)
Morgan Mental Ability	College freshmen, male and female, ages 16–23	125	.62 ± .04	Fishbein (8)
Henmon-Nelson	Adolescents, male and female, ages 11–18	50	.81 ± .04	Wolfson (Unpub.)
C. A. V. D.	Male adults, ages 18–64	108	.69 ± .03	Goldfarb (9), Lorge*
C. A. V. D.	Female adults, ages 18–54	60	.39 ± .07	Ibid.
Otis S. A. (20 min.)	Male adults, ages 18–64	108	.73 ± .03	Ibid.
Otis S. A. (20 min.)	Female adults, ages 18–54	60	.53 ± .06	Ibid.

* The data are those of Goldfarb (9); the correlations were prepared for the author by Professor Lorge.

scale. Many of the cited studies also report separate correlations with the Verbal and Performance parts of the examination. Of these, the correlations reported for the Verbal part alone are usually almost as high and occasionally somewhat higher than those for the Full scale. Thus, Verbal × Stanford-Binet 1916, adolescents (2),* r = .87; × Stanford-Binet 1937 L, adult mental patients (10), r = .92; × Stanford-Binet 1916, college freshmen, r = .53; × Henmon-Nelson, adolescents, .80; × Morgan Mental Ability, college freshmen, r = .48; × C.A.V.D., adult males, r = .67. On the other hand, correlations of the Performance part of the W.-B. with other scales are systematically lower than that of the Full scale, and often markedly so. The corresponding Performance correlations for the groups just enumerated are .56, .73, .34; and .58, .34 and .44 respectively. In general, Performance correlations are better at lower than at higher intelligence levels, better for adolescents than adults, and poorest for college students

* The numbers in the parentheses are to the references cited in table 28.

CHAPTER 10

LIMITATIONS AND SPECIAL MERITS

In this chapter we propose to discuss the limitations and merits of the Wechsler-Bellevue Scale in the light of our experience with it as a clinical instrument. The scale has now been employed at the Bellevue Psychiatric Hospital, the Court of General Sessions of New York City and the Queen's General Hospital, for more than five years, during which time it may be said to have been under continued comparison with other standard scales. Since its publication, the scale has furthermore had wide trial in many sections of the country, recently among some of our armed forces; we have also had the benefits both of published reports and personal communications regarding its shortcomings and advantages. The following remarks are intended to summarize these findings and reactions as well as our own further experiences with the scale.

One of the first criticisms brought forward by examiners pertained to the differences in I.Q. between the Verbal and Performance parts of the Bellevue Scales when I.Q.'s were calculated separately on each part of the examination. Some of the examiners looked upon this fact as an advantage and others as a limitation. But from either point of view it again brought up the problem of the legitimacy of combining Performance and Verbal items into a single scale. The cases that came up for discussion were naturally those which showed large differences between Performance and Verbal I.Q.'s (10 to 15 points or more). Often they were subjects with special psychomotor or foreign language handicaps, but among them were many for whom no special defects could be posited. As these subjects were often hospital or clinic patients, the first question that suggested itself was how the matter stood when the scores of "normal" subjects were compared. Accordingly, we made a study of I.Q. differences obtained between the Verbal parts of our scale among various samples of our standardizing population. The results of this study have already been given (table 23, p. 125). The data comprises 590 cases between ages 20 to 49 and 520 cases between ages 10 to 16. The mean I.Q. differences between Verbal and Performance rating of the two groups were 8.4 and 9.1 I.Q. points, respectively. It should be noted that these differences could not have

136

been predicted from the degree of correlation between the two test batteries (.83), nor from their mean I.Q. values at any age. At no age were the mean Performance and Verbal I.Q.'s more than one or two points apart.[1]

The question arises what an examiner should do when he finds a large discrepancy between Verbal and Non-verbal I.Q.'s. Three solutions are possible. One is to give preference to one or the other of the test results; another, to use the higher of the ratings obtained; and the third, to resort to some method of averaging them. The first of these methods is seemingly the one most generally favored by psychologists when results are obtained with separate scales. Most psychologists when getting a large discrepancy between, say the Pintner-Paterson and the Binet, generally accept the latter. If a subject obtains an I.Q. of 85 on the Binet and 110 on the Pintner-Paterson Performance Tests, a very common rating given by psychologists is "Dull-Normal Intelligence with Special Manual Ability." ... This practice seems to us ill founded. We think it is incorrect because it not only assumes that there are different kinds of general intelligence, but because it further implies that the Performance tests are relatively unimportant as measures of general intelligence. Our Scale assumes the contrary. It was constructed on the hypothesis that an individual manifests intelligence by his ability to do things, as well as by the way he can talk about them.

The second method of treating discrepancies between Verbal and Performance I.Q.'s, namely, that of taking the higher of the two I.Q.'s as the true measure of an individual's intelligence, is likewise unsatisfactory. The main argument in its favor is, that by accepting the highest rating which a person makes, we are really getting what is most important, namely, a measure of his maximal functioning ability. Our own view that tests ought to be fitted to the subject would seem to favor this attitude. Also the fact that clinical experience often justifies the choice of the higher rather than the lower I.Q. Nevertheless, we are opposed to this selective procedure because we do not believe that any test which is either predominately Verbal or Non-verbal can alone completely measure an individual's general intelligence.

The third way of meeting the problem of discrepancies between Verbal and Performance I.Q.'s is to assume that neither is correct and that the true I.Q. of any individual with a discrepancy of this sort will

[1] The mean Performance and Verbal I.Q.'s for the entire population were 100.75 and 100.11, respectively.

generally lie at some intermediate point. The most probable value of this intermediate I.Q. will in most cases be obtained by averaging his different I.Q.'s. The Full-Scale Bellevue I.Q.'s are such averages. This results from the fact that they have been obtained from test scores to which both performance and verbal items have been permitted to contribute. As now constituted, the Full-Scale gives equal weight to performance and verbal abilities, since it is made up of five performance and five verbal tests. It is possible that some other combination, say one made up of six verbal and four performance tests would constitute a better scale, but whatever the final proportion between the two, the important consequence of our method of combining them is that the subject's I.Q. is always an average I.Q.

While insisting that intelligence ratings should be based on an averaged composite of Performance and Verbal test-scores, we should not go so far as to say that there may not be instances where such procedure would be unjustified. It would clearly be unfair to use a combined Verbal and Performance scale on subjects suffering from motor or visual defects or some special language handicap. One must also admit that from time to time one does encounter individuals, corresponding to what in the literature are referred to as persons "with special disabilities" who need special consideration. With such subjects it is often better to use one rather than another type of intelligence scale. But even in such instances, our own experience has shown that their "true" rating is never as high as that indicated by the results obtained with a type of test that favors them, just as it is never as low as that indicated by the tests which penalizes them.

In connection with the problem of discrepancies between I.Q.'s obtained from the Verbal and Performance part of the Bellevue, it should be noted that except for the I.Q.'s near 100, the I.Q. of a subject on the Full-Scale will seldom be equal to the exact average of his Verbal and Performance I.Q.'s, calculated separately. There will generally be a difference between them of one or two points, which will increase, as the I.Q.'s become smaller. Thus for mean I.Q.'s of about 60, the difference between the I.Q. of the Full-Scale and the I.Q. obtained averaging the Verbal and Performance parts may amount to as much as 4 or 5 points. Conversely, the Full-Scale I.Q. above 100 will tend to be a little higher than either Verbal or Performance I.Q. These discrepancies result from the fact that the I.Q. distribution curves for the Full, Performance, and Verbal scales differ somewhat in form. The discrepancies could be allowed for by establishing separate classifications for each of the scales, but the differences are generally so small that it did not seem worth while.

Another criticism of our Bellevue Scale made by some of the examiners was that the I.Q.'s obtained with it on older subjects were too high. By "too high" the examiners meant either that the Bellevue I.Q.'s were higher than those obtained with other scales, or that the individuals tested appeared to be of lower intelligence than the Bellevue I.Q.'s indicated. We have already pointed out why our adult I.Q.'s, particularly those for subjects 40 years and over, will be systematically higher than those obtained by present standard scales. Older subjects require a lesser absolute score to obtain the same I.Q. Thus, to obtain an I.Q. of 100 at age 25 a subject has to attain a test score of 95; at year 35, a score of 87; at year 45, a score of 81; and so on. But even when conceding the theoretical validity of the procedure, examiners found it hard to accept it in practice. Much as some of them tried, they could not convince themselves that a subject's age really influenced the I.Q. to the extent posited by the Bellevue Scale. This feeling continued primarily because they had been accustomed so long to obtaining I.Q. ratings with tests in which the age factor had been neglected. The Bellevue I.Q.'s seemed too high because in point of fact the Binet and other comparable I.Q.'s had always been too low. A similar explanation accounted for some of the impressions of examiners that the subject's intelligence was lower than the rating assigned to it by our scale. Here the difficulty was that most of the examiners attempted to interpret the test performance of the subject in terms of functioning levels primarily associated with children's M.A. scores. Using children's test scores, however, against which to match adult performance, is, as we know, quite invalid. A mental age of 12 years by a child of 12, may represent quite a different order of intelligence from what it does when attained by a man of 40. An examiner who has had little experience in testing adults really does not know what order of intelligence the scores made by them represent. In general he is more likely to be misled than helped by making use of criteria gained from the testing of children.

The problem of differences between I.Q.'s obtained on the Binet and other scales will necessarily prove an important consideration of those who contemplate using our tests. We have devoted considerable time to investigating the problem from various angles. Our results show that when such discrepancies occur, most of our clinical, social and vocational data confirms the Bellevue rather than the discrepant I.Q. This is particularly true of older individuals who have made low I.Q. ratings on the Stanford-Binet and considerably higher ones on the Bellevue Tests. Many of these are cases of subjects who if rated on their I.Q.'s attained on the Binet or similar tests would have to be classified as mentally defective, yet who could in no wise be so designated from a clinical point of view.[2] In such cases it was particularly gratifying to find that the Bellevue norms gave them I.Q.'s which were in accord with the general clinical impression (e.g., I.Q.'s more like 75 or 80 instead of 60 or 65). And the same might be said of many ratings which were above the defective level on the Binet but which again were increased by 10 or 15 points when the subject was tested with the Bellevue. The great advantage of the Bellevue Scale is that one is not nearly so often confronted with the problem one has when testing adults with other scales, of accounting for or explaining discrepancies between one's quantitative results and clinical impressions. The two generally agree.

We have thus far emphasized instances where the Bellevue I.Q. was higher than that of the I.Q. of the compared test. But we also had instances where the reverse was true, although these were generally rarer. Here again, however, clinical criteria, in the main, supported the Bellevue ratings. But we do not wish to convey the view that this was always the case. There were many instances where the Binet or the Army Alpha I.Q.'s did more nearly represent the subject's intelligence level as measured by clinical criteria. That, of course, was to be expected, and does not refute our main contention. No test can be so uniformly free from limitations but that another may not be a better measure for particular cases. Every experienced examiner will have found that for certain types of individuals[3] some tests are more suitable

[2] See for examples cases D. W. and M. B., p. 130 and p. 132.

[3] This is particularly true of mental patients where a difference of 20, or even 30 points in I.Q. between ratings obtained with different tests is not rare. Certain types of schizophrenic patients, for example, will do extremely well on tests like the Army Alpha and do very badly on either the Bellevue or the Binet Scales. This is seemingly due to the fact that the Army Alpha is made up of what we may call 'perseverative' tests. Many of the tests, e.g. the Opposites test, merely require the subject to repeat the same task over and over again. All he has to do to answer a question is either to cross out or underline words or numbers. That requires very much less adaptation or directed effort than responding verbally to unrelated questions following one upon another without any special continuity, as is required by most individual types of examinations. On the other hand, there are subjects who require continual stimulation and encouragement and who when left to themselves go altogether to pieces. With such subjects one gets far better results by using a personal type of examination like the Binet or Bellevue Scales. There are, however, many exceptions to the rule.

than others. In such instances it is up to the examiner to use what he thinks is the best instrument. The test must at all times be adapted to the subject.

Another point to which we have given much consideration is the desirability of using the term I.Q. to designate the indices which we have offered as measures of brightness. A number of psychologists with whom we discussed the problem thought that we ought not use the term, and curiously enough for two very different reasons. One group argued that the term I.Q. has been so long associated with the Binet Tests that to call our index by the same name would only lead to confusion, particularly in view of the fact that it is calculated in an altogether different manner. Another group argued that the I.Q., however calculated, had proved itself so inadequate and had so many drawbacks that it did not merit continuance. One psychologist went so far as to insist that the I.Q. had already "destroyed itself". We have not felt, however, that the arguments of either group are sufficiently cogent. In the first place, we may note that while the term I.Q. has been most frequently associated with the Binet type of test, neither the original definition nor present applications of it make it contingent upon the use of any particular kind of test. Actually the term I.Q. has been used to calculate indices of a large number of tests other than the Binet. The objections to this application derive not from the way the I.Q. is calculated, but from the altered meaning it acquires when applied to different kinds of tests. The essential meaning of the I.Q. is that it is an index of brightness obtained by comparing an intelligence test score of a subject with the average score of individuals of his own age. It is precisely to this essential meaning of the term that the Bellevue I.Q. conforms, only instead of stopping at year 15 or 16, to which the M.A. over the C.A. method of calculating restricts it, we have made possible its extension to ages above 16.

As regards the second argument that the I.Q. is such an unreliable measure that it is practically worthless, we must again take exception. It is true that the I.Q. as hitherto calculated neither remains constant nor equivalent throughout an individual's life span. In trying to make it so, Heinis and others have abandoned the term, and in recent years Kuhlmann has come out in favor of the *Per cent-of-Average* ratio. We think, however, that the term I.Q. is too happy a one to be abandoned. With a little effort it can be freed of most of the objections which have been raised against it. The method of calculating it offered in this book does precisely this. We think it is not too much to ask, that in view of the practical importance of the term, the old method of calculating it be so modified as to eliminate its shortcomings.[4]

A final word as to the numerical differences between I.Q.'s obtained by the method outlined in this book and those furnished by the M.A. over the C.A. method.   In particular we wish to indicate the order of I.Q. difference that may be expected between the Bellevue and Binet Scales with which they are likely to be compared.

In general *adult* I.Q.'s obtained on the Binet will differ from those obtained on the Bellevue Scale, in proportion to the degree to which the Binet fails to make allowance for the age factor.   Accordingly, I.Q.'s obtained on the Bellevue Scale[5] will show close agreement with those obtained on the various revisions of the Binet up to about age 15, because up to this age they both take into consideration the age factor. But from this age on the Bellevue I.Q. will begin to be systematically higher than the Binet I.Q.   Between ages 15 to 30 the differences will be small.   Beyond age 30 Bellevue I.Q.'s will grow larger and increase with the increasing age of the subject, so that when age 50 is reached they may be as much as 20 points higher than the Binet I.Q.

That the differences between adult I.Q.'s obtained with the Bellevue Scale and those obtained with other scales are not due to differences in the level of test performance, but rather to the methods by which these levels are interpreted, may be shown by recalculating I.Q.'s obtained in the latter scales, in a manner that will make allowance for the age factor.   When this is done, I.Q.'s calculated on a standard test like the Stanford-Binet or Amy Alpha will be found to approximate very closely the I.Q.'s obtained on the same subject with the Bellevue Scale. As many examiners using other scales might want to know what effect allowance for the age factor would have on their test results, we have prepared a table which will enable them to translate Binet into Bellevue I.Q.'s.   Table 45[6] shows what C.A. denominators have to be assumed when calculating I.Q.'s for adults at different ages by the $\frac{MA}{CA}$ method when the age factor is allowed for.   The table holds primarily for various revisions of the Binet Scale, but may be used on other tests which have been standardized against them.   Roughly summarized,

---

[4] Terman and Merrill have already begun to do this by using a sliding denominator when calculating I.Q.'s for ages 13 to 16.   All that would be necessary to make their method of calculating I.Q.'s applicable to adults would be to furnish proper denominators for ages above 16 in the same way.

[5] More specifically, the Verbal part of the Scale.

[6] See appendix 5.

our analysis showed that if 15 years is taken as the M.A. of the average adult, the mean I.Q. for persons between ages 15 and 30 will remain fairly constant. Continued beyond this age the use of a 15 year denominator results in a systematic drop in the I.Q. of about two-thirds of a point per year. This drop can best be compensated for by the use of an appropriate regression equation.[7] But sufficient accuracy is obtained by diminishing the assumed denominator by 6 months for every 5 years accretion in chronological age.

While the correction for age is probably the main cause for the differences in adult I.Q.'s obtained on the Bellevue and the Binet Scales, it is, of course, not the only factor. Other factors which contribute are: differences in the content of the respective scales; differences in the statistical procedure and, differences in the original populations used in the standardization. The Bellevue scale contains a considerably greater proportion of performance to verbal material than does the Stanford-Binet scale, so that the two scales do not quite measure the same thing or, if the same thing, not in the same way. We have already discussed the general argument for combining performance with verbal material, but regardless of the theoretic validity of this procedure the practical effect is to make for differences of achievement when individuals are tested with both scales. This is made manifest by differences in order of correlation between the Bellevue Verbal and Bellevue Performance with different forms of the Binet. Reported studies (see p. 134) show consistently high correlations (.60 to .85) between Binet and Bellevue Verbal I.Q.'s, but only low or moderate ones between Binet and Bellevue Performance I.Q.'s. In the latter respect, the results are no different from correlations obtained between Binet and other performance tests, but the fact that the Verbal and Performance tests correlate least at college level shows that the level as well as the range of intelligence of the groups compared must be taken into account in the interpretation of results.

The influence of the particular statistical procedures used in the standardization of the Bellevue scales is less patent, but one seeming effect has been a reduction in the range of I.Q.'s obtainable. The scale does not have either as high a "ceiling" or as low a "floor" as some other scales (e.g., the 1937 Stanford-Binet). This means that it is not possible to obtain as low or as high I.Q.'s on the Bellevue as on these other

---

[7] The regression of score on age for the Bellevue Scale is $y = .735\ x + 85.77$, where y = mean score at any age and x = the difference between 40 and the chronological age at which the score is desired. The equation holds only for ages 25 and over.

scales. The constriction of range may be considered a limitation or a merit of the Bellevue depending upon how one interprets extreme measures, but in any event, brings up the question of the diagnostic significance of the I.Q.'s. Obviously, when I.Q.'s of scales having different ranges are compared, the percent of population falling within certain I.Q. limits will not be identical. And, conversely, individuals obtaining identical I.Q.'s on the different scales may, in terms of percent of rating, represent different levels of intelligence.

Differences in the diagnostic significance of I.Q.'s obtained on different scales being primarily a function of their respective deviations, could theoretically be avoided if the test scores of the compared scales were given (as it has often been urged) in terms of standard deviation units. In the absence of this practice, valid comparison of I.Q.'s requires their equation to some common base, and, as a provisional attempt in this direction, we have drawn a table of equivalence between the full Bellevue, the "old" 1916 and the "new" 1937 revisions of the Stanford-Binet. The results are shown in table 46, appendix 6. Examination of the table shows that within the overlap of ages compared (ages 8–18) the I.Q. limits for the P.E. and percentile equivalents are approximately the same (i.e. within 5 I.Q. points) on all three scales, for I.Q.'s falling below the mean; that they are likewise very close between the 1916 Stanford for I.Q.'s above 100; but that the limiting I.Q.'s for both the Bellevue and the 1916 Stanford-Binet are significantly lower than those for the 1937 revision for I.Q.'s above 100. This last difference is particularly marked at the superior level of intelligence amounting to an average of 10 I.Q. points at deviations of 2 to 3 P.E. above the mean. It might be further noted here that comparative studies support these theoretical expectancies.

We have already noted the problem of the low ceiling imputed to the Wechsler-Bellevue Scale. Our own opinion is that this reduced ceiling as compared to other tests is not an accident of the construction of the scale, but represents a factual situation, namely that it is not possible to measure general intelligence beyond a certain level. I.Q.'s above 130, whether on the Bellevue or any other tests, do not represent superiority in intelligence level, but special aptitude in intellectual ability. A measure of such ability, of course, is desirable since it correlates well with academic educability and degree of scholastic success. To meet this need, we have extended the range of the Verbal part of the scale at the upper levels and by extending the maximum score possible on them from 17 to 18. These changes will not affect the scores of most of the weight has been given to the various factors which may have contributed to it. With these limitations in mind, the data given in table 30 may be accepted as clinically valid.

The second clinically useful feature of the Bellevue scale, is that the different mental abilities tested by it, may be compared at all levels of functioning. This is achieved through the fact that the same type of material is used throughout the scale, and because the individual sub-tests of the scale have been equated. This makes it possible to compare a subject's individual test scores and to look for significant test patterns. For any pattern analysis it is necessary to know the subtest score for any given total score, and the variations in these scores which occur with age. Since each of the subtests have been equated, the mean expected score on any given subtest for any given total score may be obtained with good approximation by dividing the total score by 10.

TABLE 29

Clinical Groups Generally Scoring Higher on Verbal Tests
    Organic brain disease
    Psychoses
    Psychoneuroses

Clinical Groups Generally Scoring Higher on Performance Tests
    Psychopaths (adolescent)
    Mental defectives

Thus, if a subject makes a total score of 95, the mean expectancy for any given subtest is 9.5; or, since the performance and verbal scores do not contribute identically equal amounts to the total score, a somewhat better approximation is obtained by dividing the sum of the verbal tests and the sum of the performance tests by 5 respectively. Thus, for a subject making a total score[2] of 95 with verbal and performance scores of 50 and 45 respectively, the mean expected scores for verbal tests would be 10 and for performance tests 9 points each. For the variations in subtest scores with age, separate data are, of course, necessary, and these data have been furnished in Tables 39 and 40, page 222.

The problem next arises as to what constitutes a significantly varying score. This necessarily has to be established both through clinical and statistical validation, and here again, not only for any given score but for all possible combinations of scores. While the data are available for such complex analysis, the multiple tables necessary for it have not

---

[2] These are, of course, the weighted scores.

crude way in psychiatry and neurology where specific disturbances or defects are considered pathognomic symptoms of various disease entities Familiar examples are the disturbances of association (flightiness of ideas) in manic depressive insanity and the memory defects in chronic alcoholism of the Korsakoff type. In so far as the diagnostic significance of large differences between verbal and performance ability as a whole is concerned, the general finding is that in most mental disorders impairment of functioning is greater in the performance than in the verbal sphere. This holds for psychoses of every type, organic brain disease, and to a lesser though still large degree, in most psychoneuroses. On the other side of the fence there are only two groups. One is the adolescent psychopath (without psychosis) and the other the high grade mental defective. Both of these do better on performance than on the verbal tests. It is interesting to note that both psychopaths and mental defectives differ from other psychopathic states in that they represent failure of functioning due to a 'lack of—' rather than a disturbance or disorganization of functioning ability.[1]

In appraising differences between verbal and performance test scores one must naturally allow for variability even among normal individuals. For subjects with I.Q.'s not far from the average, a variation of 8 to 10 points between verbal and performance in either direction is within the normal range. But the amount as well as the direction of the differences also varies with the age and intelligence level of the individual. Subjects of superior intelligence generally do better on the verbal, and subjects of inferior intelligence do better on the performance part of the examination. There are also racial (group) and cultural differences. We have made no systematic study of this aspect of the problem but experience shows that the psychometric patterns of colored subjects for example, need special interpretation. Our general observations also confirm the findings of older studies which show that Jewish children do better on verbal and Italian children on performance tests. Among adults, the nature of the subject's occupation is frequently an important factor, so that carpenters, as might be expected, will generally score higher on performance and lawyers, on verbal tests. All this means, of course, that a significant difference between a subject's verbal and performance score cannot be interpreted *carte blanche* but only after due

---

[1] Appreciation of this 'lack' helps us to understand why psychiatrists of the older generation used to refer to certain classes of psychopaths as "moral imbeciles". This appraisal of the psychopath agrees with Kahn's definition of psychopathic personalities as individuals characterized by quantitative divergencies in impulse, temperament . . . etc.

been made, but again may be had with sufficient approximations, by the following rule of thumb: For total scores on the full scale lying within the limits 80 to 110,[3] a difference of more than two points from the mean subtest score is significant. Thus, a subject making a total score of 95 with the following distribution of subtests:

Comprehension	11
Arithmetic	9
Information	10
Digit-span	7
Similarities	13
Picture Arrangement	9
Picture Completion	6
Blocks	11
Object Assembly	10
Digit Symbol	9

would manifest significant variations or differences in the Similarities, Picture Completion and Digit-span tests.

For subjects having total scores beyond the limits 80–110, the deviation of the individual's subtests from their mean, defining a significant difference may be roughly obtained by dividing the mean subtest score by 4. Example: Subject A makes a full score of 56. The mean subtest score is accordingly 5.6 points; one fourth of this is 1.4 points. Hence, any of his individual subtest scores which deviate by more than 1.5 points from this mean would be significant. Again, subject B obtains a full score of 132; mean subtest score is 13.2. Hence, for subject B any individual subscores would have to deviate by 3 points (actually 3.3 points) from the mean of the subtests in order to be significant.

The amount by which a given subtest must differ from the mean of the various subtests in order to be significant, is roughly proportional to the magnitude of his total score.[4] In certain instances where the discrepancy between performance and verbal is very large, it is desirable

[3] This represents a deviation of approximately ±1 S.D. from the mean of 95 at ages 20 to 35.

[4] This may be assumed if the correlation between variability and ability is small. Such seemingly is the case at least between the ages 20 and 40. Though the r's between them have not been calculated, a low correlation between ability (total score) and variability $\left(\frac{\sigma}{M}\right)$ would be in accord with the findings of most other investigators. Cf. *Bown, M.D.*, Variability as a Function of Ability, etc. Doctor's Thesis, Columbia Univ., 1941.

and often necessary to treat each part of the examination separately. This is particularly true in certain organic cases which show large discrepancies between verbal and performance as a whole but relatively little variation between the subtests constituting the two parts.   Case *O-1* given below is an example.

TABLE 30
Test characteristics of various clinical groups

A. Organic Brain Disease

Information	+	
Comprehension	+	except in paretics
Arithmetic	−	
Digit Span	− −	particularly digits backwards
Similarities	−	
Vocabulary	+ +	
Pict. Arrangement	0	
Pict. Completion	0	
Object Assembly	0 to − −	depending on type of impairment
Block Design	− − to 0	depending on type of impairment
Digit-Symbol	− −	

Verbal higher than Performance

Intertest Variability: Omitting the 2 or 3 tests on which subject is likely to do very badly, scatter of remainder generally small.

B. Schizophrenia

Information	+ to + +	
Comprehension	+ to −	depending on type of Schizophrenia
Arithmetic	0 to −	
Digit Span	0 to +	
Similarities	+ to − −	depending on type of Schizophrenia
Vocabulary	+ +	
Pict. Completion	0 to − −	depending on type of Schizophrenia
Pict. Arrangement	− to 0	
Object Assembly	−	
Block Design	0 to +	
Digit-Symbol	−	

Verbal generally higher than Performance

Sum of Pict. Arrangement plus Comprehension less than Information and Block Design.
Object Assembly much below Block Design.
Very low Similarities with high Vocab. and Inf., definitely pathognomic.

Intertest Variability marked; and in most cases greater between subtests of the Verbal than of the Performance part of the Scale.

TABLE 30—*Continued*

C. Neurotics

Information	+	
Comprehension	+	
Arithmetic	0 to −	
Digit Span	−	but unpredictable
Similarities	+	
Vocabulary	+	
Pict. Completion	0	
Pict. Arrangement	−	
Object Assemly	−	
Block Design	0	
Digit-Symbol	−	

Verbal generally higher than Performance.

Sum of Pict. Completion plus Block Design generally greater than Sum of Pict. Arrangement and Object Assembly.

Intertest Variability: moderate; less than in psychoses but greater than in normals or psychopaths.

D. Psychopaths (Adolescent)

Information	− to − −
Comprehension	0 to −
Arithmetic	−
Digit Span	0 to −
Similarities	− to 0
Vocabulary	0
Pict. Completion	+ to 0
Pict. Arrangement	+ + to +
Object Assembly	+ + to +
Block Design	+ to 0
Digit-Symbol	0 to −

Performance generally higher than Verbal.

Sum of Object Assembly plus Pict. Arrangement nearly always greater than the Sum of Block Design and Pict. Completion test scores.

Interest Variability: comparatively limited

E. Mental Defectives

Information	0 to −
Comprehension	+
Arithmetic	− −
Digit Span	− to 0
Similarities	0
Vocabulary	+ +
Pict. Completion	− to 0
Pict. Arrangement	0
Object Assembly	+

TABLE 30—*continued*

| Block Design | 0 to + |
| Digit-Symbol | − to + |

Performance generally higher than Verbal.

Intertest Variability: limited.

While Similarities and Block Design are generally at mean and occasionally above mean, high scores on either are counterindicative of Mental Deficiency.

Having determined how much of a test score difference constitutes a significant deviation, the general clinical problem of test patterning consists of establishing associations between particular test score divergencies, and specific clinical entities. This may be done in several ways, but the method which the author has found most adaptable for clinical use is that of "counting" or integrating signs. A "sign" or symptom is a low test score which has been found to be characteristic of, or associated with, a particular type of mental disorder or disfunction. Thus, if a low Performance and a particularly low Block Design test score has been found characteristic of organic brain disease cases, then a subject who does badly on both these items will be assumed to show two "signs" of possible organic involvement. This, of course, does not mean that it is necessarily an organic case, because there are other conditions which also show these "signs". But the first step always consists of noting the number of instances of relatively low or contrastingly high scores in the subject's test score distribution.

The above procedure, of course, implies a prior demonstration of the existence of established associations or correlations between particular test "signs" and disease entities. The extensive statistical work required for such correlations has only barely begun, but we have accumulated sufficient clinical experience with the Bellevue Scale to warrant a presentation of certain empirical findings which we believe will be of use to the clinician in his attempts at diagnosis. These have been put together in Table 30 which attempts to summarize the test patterning met with in various common mental disease entities. By test patterning here, is merely meant a summary of the various tests on which patients suffering from various mental disorders have been found to do particularly poorly or have shown significantly contrasting score differences.

The meaning of the symbols used in Table 30 are as follows: + and ++ signifies relatively good, high or considerably above the mean of the subject's remaining subtest scores; − and − −, relatively poor,

tortion in the patient's ideational processes. The schizophrenic misinterprets words just as he misinterprets reality, and his incongruent replies, like his bizarre ideas, are a product of this misinterpretation.

Another characteristic of the schizophrenic is his inability to deal with concrete and specific situations. He is oblivious to details and does not perceive ordinary likenesses and differences, difficulties which are often reflected by the poor scores he attains on either the Similarities or Picture Completion tests or both. Last but not least is the schizophrenic's unpredictability, so that now and again one finds patients who do well on one or several of the tests, failure on which we have listed as characteristic of schizophrenics. A thorough acquaintance with a particular case generally makes it possible to account for the contradictory findings, but the occurrence of such exceptions shows that the diagnosis of schizophrenic through psychometric "signs" or "patterns" is not a cut and dried affair. The cases we have used as illustrations are typical only in the sense that they are of individuals who manifest most or many of the signs characteristic of the schizophrenic group as a whole.

3. *Psychopaths.* The most outstanding single feature of the adolescent psychopath's test pattern is his systematic high performance score as compared with his verbal test score. Occasional exceptions occur but these generally reflect some special ability or disability. Also worthy of note is the good score frequently made by the psychopath on the Picture Arrangement test, a finding that is surprising because this test has been interpreted as measuring social intelligence. If this interpretation is correct, a distinction must be made between understanding and resultant behavior. Psychopaths generally have a grasp of social situations, but they are inclined to manipulate them to their own advantage in an anti-social way. The point cannot however be pushed too far because there are many exceptions to the rule, particularly in the case of extreme psychopaths who are not only perverse in their behavior, but distorted in their social comprehension. The psychopath's test performance as a whole is characterized by a breeziness and self-assurance which contrasts markedly to that of a neurotic. He is not bothered by contradictions and, when not ornery, takes everything in his stride. His abstract thinking is generally below average and this is frequently indicated by a low score on the Similarities test. He also tends to do poorly on Arithmetical reasoning; but in this connection it must be noted that the mean Arithmetic subtest score for the normal adolescent (ages 12 to 16) is systematically lower than his mean score on the remaining tests of the scale.

The test pattern just described is based primarily on the performance of male adolescent psychopaths. Further experience has shown that it is also applicable to the adult male psychopath; but a study now under way[5] indicates that it may not have the same diagnostic value in the case of the female psychopath. There is seemingly an important sex difference. One feature, however, common to both male and female adolescent psychopaths is a relatively low score on the Information test. This may be due in part to the educational retardation (truancy, etc.) often associated with adolescent delinquents, but the low Information nevertheless holds up as a consistently reliable sign.

4. *Neurotics.* The neurotic generally does poorly on tests which require immediate effort. He is inclined to look upon each task as a challenge and is apprehensive of the impression he may make on the examiner. The result is that he is often "blocked", overcritical and erratic. These characteristics may be evidenced on any test but are best revealed by the neurotic's performance on the Object Assembly and the Digit Span. Though the neurotic seldom puts the Object Assembly together in an absurd fashion his effort is characterized by a great deal of trial and error. The absence of absurd configurations is what often distinguishes neurotics from organic cases who also make low scores on this test. The neurotic's successes and failures on the Digit-Span test are unpredictable. He often fails on an easier digit series and passes on a harder one; frequently too, he repeats as many and sometimes more digits backwards than he does forwards.

Although the neurotic's performance is generally lower than his verbal score, exceptions are not uncommon, particularly in hysterics and obsessives. Many of the latter are preoccupied with numbers and often do surprisingly well on both the memory span and on the arithmetic tests. Neurotics engaged in clerical work may also get relatively high scores on the Digit Symbol. The low score of the neurotic on the Picture Arrangement test is frequently associated with lack of social alertness and reflects their common inability to deal with social situations.

Neurotic anxiety often manifests itself in the subject's hesitation, unexpected failures and balking at various test items. Patients with anxiety neuroses and neurotic depression require, as might be expected, continued reassurance. Neurotic patients generally overestimate their own intellectual ability. Test variability in neurotics is greater than that of normal subjects but less than that of psychotics.

[5] By F. Halpern at the Bellevue Psychiatric Hospital.

5. *Mental defectives.*   Mental defectives do not ordinarily present any special diagnostic problem except where the social rather than the intellectual prognosis is the paramount issue, and in a small number of cases which have to be differentiated from simple schizophrenics.   In differentiating between simple schizophrenia and mental deficiency, the most critical tests appear to be Arithmetic, Similarities and Block Designs.   Schizophrenics may on occasion get high scores on any or all of these tests, but the mental defective, almost never.   These three tests also differentiate between borderline and the definite mental deficiency.[6] In a recent study comparing these two groups we did not find a single mental defective who attained a score equal to the lower limits of normality.   This is in contrast with what happens in the case of the Digits-Span and the Object Assembly tests on which defectives will not infrequently obtain non-defective and even average scores.   Mental defectives, especially older subjects, tend to do particularly well on the Vocabulary test.   That is to say, the mean score of the group as a whole on this test is significantly higher than that of any other subtest, and this in spite of the fact that mental defectives generally score higher on the Performance than on the Verbal part of the scale.

6. *Intertest Variability.*   The notation 'large intertest variability', particularly as it applies to schizophrenics, requires some special comment.   In a recent study Magaret (18) has reported that the intertest variability of this group of patients on the Wechsler-Bellevue is not particularly large and, in any case, not significantly greater than that met with in mental defectives.   These findings are not only different from our own observations but also contrary to the clinical experience of other investigators, both with the Bellevue and other scales.   The discrepancy was hard to account for until further examination of Magaret's data showed that her findings were primarily due to the method used in calculating the intertest variability.   This method consisted of subtracting the mean variability of each subtest from the mean of all the tests, and then taking the average of these deviations as a measure of the variability of the group appraised.   Now the effect of getting a measure of variability from a mean of the means is simply to obliterate the variability arising from individual differences.   An illustration will make clear how this effect is achieved: Suppose two subjects each have a total

[6] A Study of the Sub-tests of the Bellevue Intelligence Scale in Borderline and Mental Defective Cases by D. Wechsler, H. Israel and B. Balinsky.   American Journal of Mental Deficiency, 1941, XLV, 555–558.

score of 70 on the Full Scale and an hypothetical subtest distribution as follows:

Subject A		*Subject B*	
Information..................	4	Information..................	10
Comprehension...............	5	Comprehension...............	9
Arithmetic...................	10	Arithmetic...................	4
Digits.......................	3	Digits.......................	11
Similarities..................	9	Similarities..................	5
Picture Arr..................	9	Picture Arr..................	10
Picture Comp................	4	Picture Comp................	10
Block Design................	4	Block Design................	10
Object Assembly.............	12	Object Assembly.............	2
Digit Symbol................	10	Digit Symbol................	4

The mean subtest score of each of the subjects is 7, and the mean deviation of the subtests from this mean 3.0, a deviation which of course is considerable. If the subtest scores of both are combined, the mean subtest score of the two subjects taken as a group is again 7, but the mean deviation from the mean becomes exactly 0. Thus the averaging of the individual subjects' scores has served to obliterate the variability of the group. In estimating the subtest variability of a group it is necessary to first treat each individual separately, that is, first obtain the subtest deviations from each subject's own mean and only afterwards average the deviations so obtained. When this is done, the variability of psychotics shows up considerably greater than that of either normal or defective subjects.

The data given in Table 30 will be valuable to its user in proportion to his familiarity with the Scale as a whole and his clinical acquaintance with the disease entities. They are not intended, nor can they be used as psychometric short cuts to psychiatric diagnosis. But they can be of considerable differential aid if the examiner is aware of the statistical and nosological problems which all such tables present. Thus, a careful examination of the table will show that the same tests are recurrently failed by different clinical groups. For example, all groups except the psychopaths and mental defectives do less well on performance than on verbal tests. Again, Digit Symbol as a "do-bad-on" test is common to the neuroses, organics and many psychoses; and nearly all subjects with mental disorders do relatively well on Vocabulary and Information. Accordingly, it is not merely the incidence of a given "sign" but the character of the other "signs" associated with it in combination, that determine its diagnostic significance. In general, the problem of diagnosis by test score differentiae resembles medical diagnosis through physical signs. A listing of mere symptoms met with in different diseases would show relatively little correlation between any one sign and any one specific disease entity, for the reason that the same symptoms are met with in many different diseases. An elevated temperature is characteristic of pneumonia, erysipelas, abscess of the arm, etc. None, therefore, would make a diagnosis of pneumonia on high temperature alone. However, if the high temperature were accompanied by consolidation of the lungs, it would quite obviously indicate an active pneumonia; if it were accompanied by a "butterfly" rash with raised edges, erysipelas, and so on.

In addition to assuming a correlation between "sign" and disease entity, the diagnostic technique just illustrated also assumes some differential or critical score method of evaluation.[7] But as the reader will have observed, no attempt has been made to furnish such critical scores for any of the disease entities listed. There are several reasons for this omission. In the first place, none has been statistically validated. But even if this had been done, the writer would have been extremely loathe to present such critical scores for fear of conveying the impression that all that is necessary to make a diagnosis is an ability to look up a table of interpreted scores. That such apprehension is not unwarranted, is attested by the wide incidence of such tables furnished by the authors of personality, neurotic inventory and delinquency scales. A more important reason for omitting critical scores which might be used directly for diagnosis is that our list of "signs" is concerned only with the presence or absence of significant test scores. Such simple dichotomy obviously does not take into consideration the factors of configuration and of degree of concomitance of "signs," which, as we have just noted, are at the very root of the problem of valid diagnosis. The appraisal of concomitance and interpretation of configurations cannot be made through simple statistical procecures, and at this stage

[7] The method of counting and subsequently interpreting "signs" suggested above is, of course, only one of several possible ways of evaluating the sort of data we have been dealing with. Instead of treating the individual test scores separately, an obvious next step would be to try combinations of certain selected tests, as for example, the sum of the Object Assembly and Picture Arrangement versus the sum of the Block Design and Picture Completion test, etc. Or, instead of dealing with sums, one might use ratios between the scores of certain tests or combination of tests, as I. Rabin has done (Test Score Patterns in Schizophrenia and

of our knowledge, is provisionally best replaced by clinical judgment and experience.

In general, the greater the number of "signs" associated with any given mental disorder manifested by a psychometric, the greater the probability of a correct diagnosis being made on the basis of the examination. However, the presence of only one or two "signs" when very marked, may be definitely pathognomic. For example, a very low Block Design score combined with a very low Object Assembly test score is definitely indicative of organic involvement, although some of the other signs may be absent. Sometimes, the "signs" are more numerous but not very decisive, and in these cases adjuvant aids must be taken into consideration. For example, mental defectives occasionally show test score distributions very much like that found in psychopaths. In such a case, the global intelligence rating of the individual may well be the most important differential determinant. For example, if along with the other "signs", the subject had an I.Q. of 65, the chances would be that we were having to do primarily with a mental defective, although presence of the added "signs" would indicate that we were dealing at the same time with an unstable and not easily adjustable defective.

On the other hand, it is sometimes extremely useful to distinguish between what might be termed "soft" and "hard signs". "Soft signs" are differences in test scores which deviate only slightly from the normal or expected mean, but which are nevertheless similar in direction to those met with in given disease entities. "Hard signs" are test score differences which show marked divergence from the normal or expected mean score. "Soft signs" are ordinarily passed over because they are within the normal range of variation. But their systematic presence is very important because they sometimes enable one to make a diagnosis before definite or full blown physical symptoms are in evidence. A striking case of this kind was that of a 19 year old boy who was admitted to the hospital after an attack of dizziness and transient loss of memory. He had experienced several similar attacks before, which the mother described as of short duration. She said, "He [the patient] did not seem

---

Non-Psychotic States, April 1941 meeting of Eastern section of A.P.A.), and as we have suggested in the discussion of indices of mental deterioration (p. 66). Finally, there is the technique of the multiple regression equation. This would be the most valid method of all, but its application to the problem of diagnosis would be beset with many difficulties, not the least of which would be the inability of most clinicians to apply it.

to remember and couldn't get himself together". The only event which the patient himself associated with his last attack was that on the night before he had "drunk two coca-colas". A neurological examination on admission was essentially negative. He improved very quickly and was discharged after a short period of observation with a tentative diagnosis, largely based on the patient's attitude toward his illness, of conversion hysteria. During this first stay, a psychometric examination (Wechsler-Bellevue) revealed a number of "soft signs" which led the psychologist to suggest the possibility of organic involvement. As there was no medical substantiation at the time of an organic brain disease, no special regard was paid the psychologist's observation. Three months later the patient was readmitted to hospital with a full blown brain tumor.

We shall now present a series of cases to illustrate the diagnostic possibilities of the method above described, making use, so far as possible, of the tabular data given on pages 150–151.

ILLUSTRATIVE CASES

Organic Brain Disease

Information............	14
Comprehension.........	12
Arithmetic.............	9
Digits..................	13
Similarities.............	11
Verbal................	59
Picture Arr.............	9
Picture Comp..........	8
Block Design..........	4
Object Ass.............	1
Digit Symbol..........	3
Performance..........	25
Verbal I.Q..............	115
Performance I.Q........	74
Digits forward........	8
Digits backward......	6

Case O-1. Male, age 34, showing definite neurological signs including marked hydrocephalus, facial weakness, slight tremor, absent abdominals. Also suggested Babinsky on left side with mild postural deviations on same side. Diagnosis— post meningo-encephalitic syndrome. At age of 6 months patient had an injury with sequelae lasting 6 months, which was diagnosed as meningitis. This case shows the four most conspicuous signs of organic brain disease: large discrepancy between Verbal and Performance in favor of the former, very low Blocks combined with even lower Object Assembly and very low Digit Symbol. While all of the test scores on the verbal part of the examination are average or above, the two lowest are Similarities and Arithmetic which are in line with the organic picture. The only exception is the Digit Span which is good for both forwards (8) and backwards (6).

Vocabulary.............	10
Information............	11
Comprehension.........	11
Arithmetic.............	6
Digits..................	9

Case O-2. Male, married, age 54, fireman. Entered hospital with complaints of headaches and forgetfulness. History of old skull fracture. Physical examination, including blood-Wassermann and flat plates were negative. While under

Similarities............ 7
  Verbal.............. 45*
Picture Arr............ 7
Picture Comp.......... 10
Block Design.......... 7
Object Ass............. 11
Digit Symbol.......... 4
  Performance......... 39

Verbal I.Q............. 103
Performance I.Q....... 103

  Digits forwards....... 7
  Digits backwards..... 4

Vocabulary............ 7
Information........... 8
Comprehension........ 9
Arithmetic............ 7
Digits................. 6
Similarities............ 9
Verbal................ 39
Picture Arr............ 6
Picture Comp.......... 1
Block Design........... 1
Object Assembly....... 2
Digit Symbol........... 5
  Performance......... 15

Verbal I.Q............. 91
Performance I.Q........ 50

Digits Forwards........ 6
Digits Backwards....... 3

Comprehension......... 10
Arithmetic............. 10

observation referred by Neurological service for psychometric. On Bellevue Adult patient attained a rating of average intelligence with subtest score distribution as indicated in summary at left. The distribution shows the following organic signs: Arithmetic—low, Similarities—poor, Blocks—poor, Digit Symbol—very poor. Digit Span appears to be unimpaired, but actually average score of 9 was due primarily to subject's relatively good span for digits forward (7); backwards span was only 4 digits. A very low digit backwards in a person of otherwise normal intelligence is generally characteristic of organic brain disease. This patient, when his age is considered, seemingly manifests relatively little** deterioration but is of special interest because he shows many of the signs of organic brain disease; the one conspicuous exception is the relatively high Object Assembly score; but a good Object Assembly is occasionally found in organic cases who have not as yet deteriorated markedly.

Case O-3. White, male, adolescent, age 14. Brought to hospital because of marked change in personality. Had been normal boy until 6 months prior to admission. Illness first manifested by failure at school and increased irritability. Physical and neurological examination on admission essentially negative. Case presented to illustrate value of Scale in detecting possible organic brain conditions prior to manifestation of neurological symptoms. Psychometric organic signs are: Verbal much higher than Performance; very low scores on *both* Object Ass. and Block Design; large discrepancy between Digits Forwards and Digits Backwards. On the qualitative side, subject showed common organic manifestation of being able to reproduce designs if presented with a model of assembled blocks (see p. 92), after failing completely with the usual form of presentation.

Schizophrenia

Case S-1. Male, age 41, war veteran, 3 years college. Long history of inadequacy and mal-

* When Vocabulary is included, the Verbal score is obtained by taking 5/6 of total.
** Actually it is very considerable. See p. 67.

Information............ 15
Digits................. 14
Similarities............ 11
Verbal............... 60
Picture Arr............ 8
Picture Comp.......... 13
Block Deisgn........... 10
Object Ass............. 12
Digit Symbol.......... 4
Performance......... 47

Verbal I.Q.............. 116
Perform. I.Q........... 95

Information............ 10
Comprehension......... 6
Arithmetic............. 6
Digits................. 6
Similarities............ 1
Verbal............... 29
Picture Arr............ 4
Picture Comp.......... 10
Block Design.......... 1
Object Ass............. 2
Digit Symbol.......... 2
Performance......... 19

Verbal I.Q.............. 83
Perform. I.Q........... 71

Vocabulary............. 10
Information.. 10

adjustment. Has been at various mental hospitals and repeatedly diagnosed as paranoid praecox. Latest admission followed threats of violence to mother. Well preserved, no hallucinations or delusions elicited; but insists that mother and veterans hospitals are against him. Patient is of better than average intelligence. The schizophrenic signs in his psychometric are: Verbal much higher than Performance, low Picture Arrangement, very low Digit Symbol simultaneously with high Digit Span, large discrepancy between Information and general Comprehension in favor of the former. High intertest scatter within Performance group.

Case S-2. White, male, age 39, elevator operator. This patient shows marked deterioration, generally seen only in old cases but occasionally also in cases of relatively short duration. In his case, reported onset of disease was about six months prior to administration of test. First indication that something was radically wrong with patient occurred when he left his job with no apparent reason; said he was nervous and had no peace of mind. Later complained police were after him. On admission to hospital was bewildered, kept to himself but was passively cooperative. Although diagnosed as paranoid schizophrenic, general behaviour was that of a simple or mixed type. Psychometrically, he showed the following schizophrenic signs: Verbal higher than Performance, low Digit Symbol with much better Digit Span, low Object Assembly, zero scores on Similarities and Block Design, high Information. Most outstanding of all, very large intertest variability ranging from a score of zero to a score of ten. The very low scores on the Object Assembly and Digit Symbol together with zero score on the Block Design taken alone would suggest organic brain disease, but in that case we would also get a low Picture Completion and not an average score on this test. The inconsistency here is what definitely shows this case to be schizophrenic. Similarly, only a schizophrenic would give an average score on Information and a zero score on Similarities.

Case S-3. White, female, age 38. Admission following arrest for refusing to take shelter during

Comprehension.........	7
Arithmetic.............	9
Digits..................	11
Similarities.............	6
Verbal...............	43
Picture Arr.............	11
Picture Comp...........	10
Block Design...........	13
Object Assembly.......	6
Digit Symbol...........	13
Performance..........	53
Verbal I.Q..............	97
Performance I.Q........	113

blackout raid and committing commotion. History of previous commitment to State Hospital. On admission agitated, hallucinatory, seclusive, manneristic; threatens to kill doctor. Psychometrically of interest as a case of schizophrenia with Performance higher than Verbal: also as a case which though failing to show many of the listed signs, nevertheless reveals a test pattern which is definitely schizophrenic. The diagnostic signs present are a combined low Similarities and low Comprehension; Object Assembly much below Block Design; sum of Comprehension and Object Assembly much lower than sum of Information and Block Design; large intertest variability.

Adolescent Psychopaths

Comprehension.........	11
Arithmetic.............	6
Information............	10
Digits..................	6
Similarities.............	5
Verbal...............	38
Picture Arr.............	12
Picture Comp...........	10
Block Design...........	15
Object Ass..............	16
Digit Symbol...........	12
Performance..........	65
Verbal I.Q..............	90
Perform. I.Q............	123

Case P-1. White, male, age 15, 8th grade. Continuous history of stealing, incorrigibility and running away. Several admissions to Bellevue Hospital, the last one after suicidal attempt. While on wards persistently created disturbances, broke rules, fought with other boys and continuously tried to evade ordinary duties. Psychopathic patterning: Performance higher than Verbal, low Similarities, low Arithmetic, sum of Picture Arrangement plus Object Assembly greater than sum of scores on Blocks and Picture Completion.

Comprehension.........	8
Arithmetic.............	6
Information............	6
Digits..................	6
Similarities.............	6
Verbal...............	32
Picture Arr.............	10
Picture Comp...........	8
Block Design...........	7
Object Ass..............	11
Digit Symbol...........	9
Performance..........	45
Verbal I.Q..............	82

Case P-2. Male, age 16, schoolboy, 8th grade. Readmitted for observation from Correctional Institution where he was reported to have thrown acid into face of one boy and was suspected of pushing another into an open fire. History of outbursts, of violent temper and cruelty from early childhood. Would throw objects at least provocation and took pleasure in inflicting pain on others. Once pushed a boy, who he knew could not swim, off dock in hope of witnessing a drowning. Psychopathic patterning: Performance higher than Verbal, good Object Assembly, sum of scores on Object Assembly and Picture Arrangement greater than sum of scores on Block

Performance I.Q........ 92

Information............ 6
Comprehension......... 9
Arithmetic............ 7
Digit Span............ 10
Similarities............ 6
    Verbal............... 38
Picture Comp.......... 12
Picture Arr............ 13
Block Design.......... 11
Object Ass............. 13
Digit Symbol.......... 9
    Performance.......... 58

Verbal I.Q............. 90
Performance I.Q........ 115

Comprehension......... 14
Arithmetic............ 13
Information........... 14
Digit Span............ 10
Similarities........... 13
    Verbal............... 64
Picture Arr........... 10
Picture Comp.......... 14
Block Design.......... 15
Object. Ass............ 12
Digit Symbol.......... 9
    Performance.......... 60

Verbal I.Q............. 120
Performance I.Q........ 116

Comprehension......... 10
Arithmetic............ 6
Information........... 10
Digit Span............ 7
Similarities........... 7
    Verbal............... 40
Picture Arr........... 7

Design and Picture Completion. This subject does not show all the psychometric signs of the psychopath but the sum of Object Assembly plus Picture Arrangement is markedly higher than that of Picture Completion plus Block Design, and that in itself is almost pathognomic.

Case P-3. White, male, school-boy, age 14, 8th grade. Boy a behaviour problem since age of 3. Never responded to either cajoling or punishment. Brought to court for stealing, staying away from home days at a time and continued incorrigibility. Psychiatric diagnosis: Psychopathic personality. This subject shows almost all the psychometric signs for this diagnosis. Performance is higher than Verbal; sum of Picture Arrangement and Object Assembly is greater than sum of Picture Completion and Block Design. Information is low and Similarities low. Digit Symbol just at mean of all subtest scores but still lower than any of Performance. Highest Verbal score is on Digit Span. This is not typical of all psychopaths but rather characteristic of a certain group who have "good memory".

Neurotics

Case N-1. Male, age 25, college graduate, "Y" secretary. Complaints: easy fatigability, lack of concentration, sexual difficulty, and general symptoms associated with Neurasthenia. Has been under psychiatrist's care. Neurotic patterning: Verbal higher than Performance, high Comprehension and Information with relatively low Digit Span. Low Picture Arrangement and low Digit Symbol, Object Assembly less than Block Design. Negative sign: relatively good Arithmetic, but in this connection account must be taken of fact that subject is a college graduate with B.S. degree.

Case N-2. Female, age 15, school girl, High School—1st term. Difficulties began when subject entered high school. Commercial course, which subject has been failing, obviously unsuited to girl's ability. Main symptoms: gastric distress and vomiting, unhappiness at school. Physical examination essentially negative. Diag-

Picture Comp........... 9

Block Design........... 10

Object Assembly....... 7

Digit Symbol........... 8

   Performance......... 41

Verbal I.Q.............. 93

Performance I.Q....... 87

nosis: Conversion Hysteria. Neurotic patterning: poor Arithmetic and Digit Span with relatively good Information and Comprehension, low Picture Arrangement, Object Assembly less than Block Design. However, total Verbal and Performance scores are not markedly different. This is not uncommon in duller neurotics (especially of Hysterical type). Also to be taken into account is the fact that the subject comes from bilingual home. Low Similarities in this case only an indication of subject's limited intelligence.

We shall conclude our discussion of the diagnostic material elicitable from the Bellevue Scale by adding a few notes on what might be termed "qualitative indicators". These indicators are significant items which reveal themselves either in the form or in the content of the subject's responses. The perseverative, redundant quality of the schizophrenic's definitions on the Vocabulary test is an example. Another is the negativism which reflects itself in a subject's tendency to say or to do the opposite of what is requested. This is frequently brought out by the subject's responses to the Similarities test on which, instead of giving the asked for likenesses, he responds with gratuitous differences. The tendency to give differences when likenesses are called for, is also encountered in subjects of limited intellectual endowment (e.g., young children and mental defectives). But when given repeatedly by a person of above dull-normal or better intelligence it is almost always pathognomic of schizophrenia. The following, for example, are the responses to the Similarities test questions, made by schizophrenic patient (case S-2) who insisted upon giving differences even after repeated correction, and ended by making a zero score on the test:

   Orange-banana: orange is round, banana is long

   Coat-dress: a coat hangs over the dress

   Dog-lion: a lion is larger

   Wagon-bicycle: wagon has four wheels, bicycle has two wheels

   Daily paper-radio: you hear news on radio, read stories in newspaper

   Wood-alcohol: alcohol is white, wood is any color

and so on for all twelve test items.

Sometimes a patient merely persists with a stereotyped reply, "they are not alike". In such cases it is generally impossible to change his set, but even when one succeeds in so doing, the usual result is to elicit a difference instead of a likeness. For example, one patient after systematically answering "not alike" to the first four Similarities questions, altered his reply after much urging to the fifth question (Newspaper-radio) "one is for news, the other is for entertainment."

A common characteristic of schizophrenics and occasionally of certain types of psychopaths is the "spoiled" or contaminated response. The subject first gives a good or passing response, but then "spoils" it by an irrelevant or eccentric addition. Such responses are most frequently elicited by the Comprehension questions, occasionally, also, by the Similarities questions. Thus, *Why are shoes made of leather?*—"It fits (the foot) easily, it is an old custom." (schizophrenic) *Why does land in the city cost more than land in the country?*—"In the city land becomes more valuable because people need space while in the country acres are not so much in demand. In that way the law of supply and demand becomes counterbalances." (schizophrenic) *What is the thing to do if you find a letter, etc.?*—"Might mail it, but first I'd open it up to see if there was any money in it." *Suppose there wasn't any money in it?*—"Tear it up." (psychopath).

Sometimes abnormal trends are indicated by the question which a subject may ask. Thus, before answering the arithmetical problem, *If a man buys 6¢ worth of stamps and gives the clerk 10¢ how much should he get back?*, a schizophrenic wanted to know whether they were "2 or 3 cent stamps". At other times a casual question by the examiner will be equally effective in eliciting a telltale response. The following is a rather amusing example. *How far is it from New York to Paris? Patient:* "I don't know." *Examiner:* "Try to figure it out." *Patient:* "Well, it takes about a week to get from Paris to New York. There are seven days in a week and twenty four hours in a day; so multiply 24 by 7 and you get 161 which equals the hours in seven days or one week. Now there are twenty blocks in a mile; so multiply 161 by 20, and this gives you 3,220. The distance from Paris to New York is 3,220 miles." The arithmetic is not quite accurate but more important than the slight error in multiplication is the way in which the subject arrived at the almost correct answer. The response was made by a schizophrenic with manic features.

Part III

MANUAL OF INSTRUCTIONS
THE BELLEVUE INTELLIGENCE TESTS

THE BELLEVUE INTELLIGENCE TESTS

GENERAL INSTRUCTIONS

In administering the tests it is absolutely essential that the examiner follow directions as given. Until he has memorized the directions in their entirety, the examiner should read them from the manual. The examiner should not engage the subject in an interview while giving the tests; the only comments allowable are such as are needed to encourage the subject. Directions may be repeated as often as necessary but not explained. If the subject does badly on any given test, say, "*That was a little hard. Let us try another which is easier,*" and proceed with a test on which he is likely to succeed. The tests need not be given in the exact order listed; for adults a good test to start with is the *General Information:* with children it is well to begin with the *Object Assembly.*

The Bellevue Intelligence Examination consists of 11 tests, 6 of which are described as Verbal and 5 as Non-Verbal, or Performance. Whereever practicable it is desirable to give the Full Scale. This is particularly true in the case of adolescents where the examiner may wish to use the results for vocational guidance. There are three exceptions to the rule: First, cases where the subject suffers from some incapacitating physical handicap or defect (blindness, paralysis, etc.). In such instances, of course, only the Verbal part of the scale will be used. Second, illiterates and foreigners; with such subjects, only the Performance part of the scale may have to be used. We say *may* because our experience has shown that, even when subjects have a limited English vocabulary, they are not likely to be penalized to any great extent when given the Verbal tests. Third, individuals 50 years and older. In the case of older persons it is sometimes necessary to omit one or another of the tests in order to avoid penalizing these subjects for certain disabilities such as diminished vision or partial deafness. With such subjects a battery of 8 or 9 tests may be substituted for the Full Scale. When this is done one prorates for the omitted tests. But on such occasion omission of any test should be decided upon *before* the test is given, not afterwards. It is not permissible to drop out a test simply because a subject does badly on it. In any case, no rating should be given on a "Full" Scale examination consisting of less than 8 tests; in most cases at least 9 tests should be employed.   Our own experience has shown that one seldom has to omit more than one test.

DIRECTIONS FOR THE INDIVIDUAL TESTS

1. GENERAL INFORMATION

Directions: Read questions as stated and in order[1] given.   The first question "Who is President of the United States?" is used as a buffer and not scored.   Most of the questions are easily marked right (+) or wrong (−), but the examiner should familiarize himself with the right answers.   Ordinarily, it will be possible to score a response directly as plus or minus, but when the subject's answers are doubtful they should be written out.   It is always legitimate to say *"Explain more fully,"* but not to give leading questions.[2]

The questions with their correct answers are as follows:

(a) Who is the President of the U. S.?	(Franklin) Roosevelt[3]
1. Who was President before him?	(Herbert) Hoover[3]
2. What is a thermometer? (5)	(Instrument, thing, etc.) for measuring temperature.
3. What does rubber come from? (4)	Trees; sap of tree; rubber plant (if subject does not mean house variety)*
4. Where is London? (2)	England
5. How many pints make a quart? (3)	Two
6. How many weeks are there in a year? (6)	52
7. What is the capital of Italy? (7)	Rome
8. What is the capital of Japan? (16)	Tokyo
9. How tall is the average American woman? (9)	Any answer from 5′3″ to 5′6″ (inclusive)
10. Who invented the airplane? (10)	Wright Brothers (or Langley)
11. Where is Brazil? (12)	South America
12. How far is it from Paris to New York? (11)	2000 to 3500 miles (any figure within limits)

[1] The order of the questions is different from that given in the first and second editions.   The changes were made upon the basis of supplementary data communicated to the author and, more especially, of an item analysis made by Lt. Wm. D. Altus, AGD, U.S.A.   The new ranking corresponds more nearly to the difficulty of the items for adults, at the present time (1944).   The original order of the items is indicated by the numbers in parenthesis following each question.

[2] For example; If the subject answers "It beats" to the question "What does the heart do?" the examiner may not say "And what else?".

[3] The correct responses will naturally have to be altered with time.

* *Petroleum* and *alcohol* may also be credited plus.

13. What does the heart do? (17)	Pumps blood (through the body)
14. Who wrote Hamlet? (13)	Shakespeare
15. What is the population of the U. S.? (18)	100 to 150 million (any figure within limits)
16. When is Washington's birthday? (8)	February 22nd
17. Who discovered the North Pole? (14)	Peary
18. Where is Egypt? (20)	Africa
19. Who wrote Huckleberry Finn? (19)	Mark Twain (or Samuel Clemens)
20. What is the Vatican?	Home of the Pope or papal government
21. What is the Koran?	Mohammedan Bible
22. Who wrote Faust?	Goethe (or Gounod, if opera is specified)
23. What is an Habeas Corpus?	A writ requiring a person in custody to be brought before the court
	or
	A writ obtained by a person to demand of the court the reason for his detention and (if no sustaining charge is forthcoming) that he be freed
24. What is Ethnology?	The study of the origin of races
25. What is the Apocrypha?	Books of disputed authority in Old Testament
	or
	The reputedly unauthenticated or unacceptable versions of the Bible

Scoring: Each response is scored plus or minus. Ordinarily it will suffice to continue until 5 consecutive questions are successively failed. But unexpected successes are not uncommon and occasionally it may be necessary to disregard this rule and give the entire list. If, for some reason, the examiner suspects that a subject may be acquainted with the correct answer to any particular question, he should ask it, even though the item is below the 5 successive failure point. The total score is the sum of plus responses.

Maximum score: 25.

2. GENERAL COMPREHENSION

Directions: Be sure that the subject is attending when you give the questions. Very young and very old subjects sometimes find it difficult to remember the entire question from a single statement of it. It is, therefore, always permissible to repeat the question. In fact, it is a good practice to repeat the question, if no response is obtained after 10 or 15 seconds, but do not abbreviate or alter the wording. Record subject's responses verbatim. Sometimes it is necessary to encourage the subject. It is done with such remarks as, *"Yes," "Go ahead,"* etc. If response is not clear, add *"Please explain further."* Except for low grade individuals, ask all the questions.

QUESTIONS

1. What is the thing to do if you find an envelope in the street, that is sealed, and addressed and has a new stamp?
2. What should you do if while sitting in the movies (theatre) you were the first person to discover a fire (or see smoke and fire)?
3. Why should we keep away from bad company?
4. Why should people pay taxes?
5. Why are shoes made of leather?
6. Why does land in the city cost more than land in the country?
7. If you were lost in a forest (woods) in the daytime, how would you go about finding your way out?
8. Why are laws necessary?
9. Why does the state require people to get a license in order to be married?
10. Why are people who are born deaf usually unable to talk?

Two alternate questions are added in case a question is invalidated. It is not permissible to substitute the alternates for the above, merely because a subject has failed on a particular question.

Alternates:

Why should we save money?   (For questions 1–3.)
What should you do if a dear friend of yours asks you for something you haven't got?   (For questions 4–10.)

Scoring: Refer to Criteria sheets for answers. The responses are scored either 0, 1 or 2, depending upon the degree of generalization and the quality. In some cases the scoring is fairly obvious, but in others frequently difficult. The examiner should match his responses against the sample answers given on the scoring sheets. The samples are drawn from more than a thousand cases, but from time to time the examiner may find some unusual response which is not typified. In these cases he will have to use his own judgment. But it is not permissible for him to disagree with the credits allowed on the scoring sheets, because the norms are based on the credits as assigned. Total score is the sum of the credits on the 10 questions.

Maximum score: 20.

3. ARITHMETICAL REASONING

Directions: There are 10 problems, the first 8 of which are given orally and the last 2 handed to the subject on a printed card with the instructions, *"Now read this one aloud and do the problem mentally."* In the case of young children and subjects likely to be defective, it is well to begin with the first example, but with bright children and average adults it is better to begin with a problem which the examiner has reason to believe the subject will solve readily, but which is not "too easy". With the average adult one may begin with problem 3, allowing credit for the easier problems. Continue downward until three successive examples are failed. In presenting the first problem say, *"I want to see how good you are in arithmetic."* The wording of the questions may not be altered, but it is always permissible to repeat the problem. In fact, it is desirable to do so to make sure that the subject is not forgetting it in the process of trying to solve the example. The first five problems are solved almost immediately by subjects who know the correct answers, but liberal time is allowed (see time limits). If the subject does not answer within the time limit, proceed with the succeeding questions, saying, *"Now try this one."* (Record time in the case of the last two problems.)

The time limits are 15 seconds on questions 1, 2 and 3; 30 seconds on 4, 5 and 6; 60 seconds on 7 and 8; and 120 seconds on 9 and 10. Time credit is allowed only on the last two problems.

Scoring: Credit of 1 for each problem answered correctly within time limit; give additional credit of 1 for time on problems 9 and 10, if answer is given within 40″ and an additional credit of 2 if answer is given within 15″. (Timing to begin after subject has finished reading problems.)

Maximum score: 14.

PROBLEMS

Time		Answer
(15″)	1. How much is four dollars and five dollars?	9
(15″)	2. If a man buys six cents worth of stamps and gives the clerk ten cents, how much change should he get back?	4
(15″)	3. If a man buys eight cents worth of stamps and gives the clerk twenty-five cents, how much change should he get back?	17
(30″)	4. How many oranges can you buy for thirty-six cents if one orange costs four cents?	9
(30″)	5. How many hours will it take a man to walk twenty-four miles at the rate of three miles an hour?	8

(30″) 6. If a man buys seven two cent stamps and gives the clerk a
half dollar, how much change should he get back?   36
(60″) 7. If seven pounds of sugar cost twenty-five cents, how many
pounds can you get for a dollar?   28
(60″) 8. A man bought a second hand car for two-thirds of what it
cost new. He paid $400 for it. How much did it cost
new? $600
(120″) 9. If a train goes 150 yards in ten seconds, how many *feet* can
it go in one fifth of a second?   9*
(120″) 10. Eight men can finish a job in six days. How many men will
be needed to finish it in a half day?   96

4. Digits Forward and Backward

These are administered as separate tests, but the number of digits
correctly reproduced on each are added to give a total score.

(4a) Digits Forward: *Directions:* Use set of digits given below.
Say, "*I am going to say some numbers. Listen carefully, and when I
am through, say them right after me.*" If subject repeats series correctly,
mark plus and continue with the next higher series. If subject fails,
give second trial on series of equal length. Discontinue after subject
has failed on both trials of a given series. Score is highest number of
digits repeated without error on either of two trials. Thus, if subject
repeats correctly 5 digits forward, he gets a score of 5. Read digits at
rate of one per second.

(4b) Digits Backward: Say, "*Now I am going to say some more
numbers, but this time when I stop, I want you to say them backwards.
For example; if I say 7–1–9, you say* (Pause) *9–1–7.*" If subject gives
them correctly, say, "*That's right.*" If subject does not seem to understand, use another example. Always begin with the 3 digit series, con-
tinuing until subject fails both trials of the series. If subject fails the 3
digit series, it is permissible to give him the 2 digit series and allow him a
2 score if he is able to reverse them. Only use the 2 digit series when
there is failure on both of the 3 digit series. Score is the highest number
of digits correctly reversed.

The *total score* on tests is the sum of the number of digits repeated
forward and backward. Thus, if subject repeats 7 forward and 4
backward, his total score is 11.

Maximum score: 17.

---

* If subject answers, "3 yards," say, "*read it again*"; if answer is corrected to
9 feet, score plus.

DIGITS FORWARD

(3)	5, 8, 2	6, 9, 4
(4)	6, 4, 3, 9	7, 2, 8, 6
(5)	4, 2, 7, 3, 1	7, 5, 8, 3, 6
(6)	6, 1, 9, 4, 7, 3	3, 9, 2, 4, 8, 7
(7)	5, 9, 1, 7, 4, 2, 8	4, 1, 7, 9, 3, 8, 6
(8)	5, 8, 1, 9, 2, 6, 4, 7	3, 8, 2, 9, 5, 1, 7, 4
(9)	2, 7, 5, 8, 6, 2, 5, 8, 4	7, 1, 3, 9, 4, 2, 5, 6, 8

DIGITS BACKWARD

(2)	(2, 4)	(5, 8)
(3)	6, 2, 9	4, 1, 5
(4)	3, 2, 7, 9	4, 9, 6, 8
(5)	1, 5, 2, 8, 6	6, 1, 8, 4, 3
(6)	5, 3, 9, 4, 1, 8	7, 2, 4, 8, 5, 6
(7)	8, 1, 2, 9, 3, 6, 5	4, 7, 3, 9, 1, 2, 8
(8)	9, 4, 3, 7, 6, 2, 5, 8	7, 2, 8, 1, 9, 6, 5, 3

5. SIMILARITIES

Directions: Say, "*I am going to name two things which are the same or alike in certain ways and I want you to tell me in what way they are alike, For example:* "*In what way are an orange and banana the same?* (Pause). If subject answers with the reply "*They are fruits,*" say, "*that is right,*" and proceed with the list. If his response is "*They are not alike,*" the examiner adds, "*They are alike in some ways; tell me one way in which they are alike.*" If subject fails to answer within 10 to 15 seconds, expresses a difference or gives an inferior reply, the examiner says, "*Well, you might say you can eat them both, or that they both have skins, or that they are both fruits.*" Then proceed with the list as given. Continue until 4 successive pairs are completely failed. Record answers verbatim. The following is the list of *Similarities* to be read:

1.	Orange	Banana
2.	Coat	Dress
3.	Dog	Lion
4.	Wagon	Bicycle
5.	Daily paper	Radio
6.	Air	Water
7.	Wood	Alcohol
8.	Eye	Ear
9.	Egg	Seed
10.	Poem	Statue
11.	Praise	Punishment
12.	Fly	Tree

Now which one is it?

Scoring: Responses are scored either 0, 1 or 2, depending upon the degree and quality of the generalizations. Use criteria illustrations for evaluating the responses. The examiner matches his responses against the sample answers and scores accordingly. Sometimes the subject "spoils" an answer by an additional response. If the original response was scored 2, it reduces the score to 1. Spontaneous emendations are allowed. In such cases, the examiner asks, *"Now which one is it?"*

Total score on Tests is the sum of the partial credits on the 12 questions. *Maximum score: 24.*

6. PICTURE ARRANGEMENT

Directions: Present first sample series in mixed order as indicated on back of the card. Say, *"The pictures tell a story about a bird building its nest. As you see, they are in the wrong order, but if you put them in the right order—"like this"*—(the examiner starts rearranging the cards) *—"the pictures will tell a sensible story. Watch me. In the first picture the bird is building its nest, the next picture shows the eggs which the bird has laid, and the last picture shows the bird feeding its young which have been hatched."* (Pause). *"Now I have some other sets of pictures which I want you to arrange. In each case they are mixed up and what I want you to do is to put them in the right order so that they make the most sensible story. Try this set."* (E. presents set 1.)

PICTURE ARRANGEMENT

	Order of Presentation	Correct order	Time limit
Sample NEST	1, 2, 3		
1. HOUSE	1, 2, 3	P A T	1 minute
2. HOLD UP	1, 2, 3, 4	A B C D	1 minute
3. ELEVATOR	1, 2, 3, 4	L M N O	1 minute
4. FLIRT	1, 2, 3, 4, 5	J A N E T	2 minutes
5. TAXI	1, 2, 3, 4, 5, 6	S A M U E L	2 minutes
6. FISH	1, 2, 3, 4, 5, 6	E F G H I J	2 minutes

On the back of the pictures is indicated the order of arrangement for presentation, given by numerals 1, 2, 3, 4, etc., depending upon the number of cards. The correct order of rearrangement is indicated by code letters. There are time limits for each picture, and in the case of the last two, "FISH" and "TAXI," credit is given if they are completed within 40 seconds.

Record subject's actual arrangement by noting letters on back of successive cards, also note time required by subjects to complete the task. Some subjects after completing the arrangement pause to survey it, and it is sometimes difficult to ascertain whether they have or have not finished. In such cases it is well to suggest to the subject, *"Tell me when you are finished."*

TABLE 31

ACCURACY CREDITS FOR PICTURE ARRANGEMENT

Series	Order	Accuracy Credits	Time Credits
1. HOUSE	PAT	2	None
2. HOLD UP	ABCD	2	None
3. ELEVATOR	LMNO	2	None
4. FLIRT	JANET	3	None
	JNAET	3	None
	AJNET	2	None
5. FISH	EFGHIJ	3	As indicated in table
	EFHGIJ	2	As indicated in table
	EGFHIJ	1	None
	EFGIHJ	1	None
6. TAXI	SAMUEL	3	As indicated in table
	SAMEUL	2	As indicated in table
	SALEUM	1	None
	SALMEU	1	None
	SALMUE	1	None
	SALUEM	1	None

TABLE 32

Time bonus for "FISH" and "TAXI" (if accuracy scores are 2 or 3)

Time in Seconds	Bonus Credits
1–20	3
21–30	2
31–40	1
41 and over	0

Scoring: The first three series are scored either right or wrong. On the last three, partial credits are allowed for imperfect but nevertheless sensible arrangement. In the case of the last two series additional credits are given for satisfactory arrangements within various time limits. Use tables 31 and 32 for obtaining the different scores allowed. The final score on this test is the sum of partial credits received on the separate items.

Maximum credits: 21.

7. PICTURE COMPLETION

Directions: There are 15 cards in this Test, each of which has a part missing. The cards are presented to the subject in numerical order, and he is asked to name or indicate on each card the missing part. Prior to the presentation of the first card, the examiner says, "*I am going to show you some pictures in which there is a part missing. I*

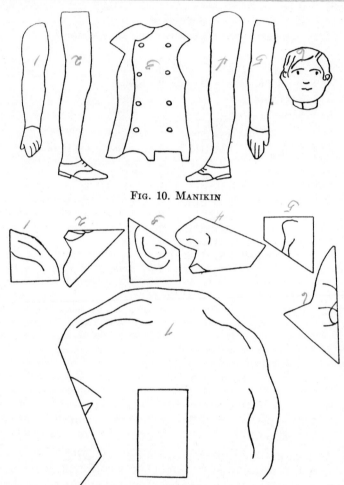

Fig. 10. Manikin

Fig. 11. Profile

want you to look at each picture carefully and tell me what it is. Now look at this picture" (presenting card No. I). "*What important part is missing?*" If correct answer is given, continue with succeeding pictures saying, "*Now what is missing in this one?*" If subject fails to detect omission, indicate to him, thus, "*You see, the nose is missing.*" If he fails on the second picture also, he is helped again, thus, "*You see here half of the mustache is missing.*" But beginning with the third picture no further help is given, the examiner merely repeating the formula *"Now what is missing in this picture?"* at each successive presentation. Sometimes the subject mentions an unessential missing part. The *first time* this occurs, the examiner may say, *"Yes, but what is the most important thing missing?"* The examiner may not repeat[3] this comment for the remaining presentations. Allow a maximum exposure of 15″ to 20″ per picture. If the subject does not indicate the missing part within this time, score as failure and continue with the succeeding picture. Except for very low grade individuals, present the entire series of pictures.

Scoring: The score is the number of pictures for which correct responses are given. In the case of picture 11 (the reflection of the arm in the mirror) if subject says, "leg is missing," say, *"Yes and what else?"* But if correct response is not still given, subject's response is scored as a failure.

Maximum score: 15.

PICTURE COMPLETION

	Picture	*Missing Part*
1.	Girl	Nose
2.	Man	Mustache
3.	Man	Ear
4.	Card	Diamond
5.	Crab	Leg
6.	Pig	Tail
7.	Boat	Stacks
8.	Door	Knob
9.	Watch	Hand
10.	Pitcher	Water
11.*	Mirror	Reflection of arm
12.	Man	Tie
13.	Bulb	Thread (or prong)
14.	Girl	Eyebrow
15.	Sun	Shadow of man

8. OBJECT ASSEMBLY

Directions: There are three different items on this test: a *Manikin,* a *Profile* and a *Hand.* Present these in order named, making sure that

---

[3] Except in case of card 11. See footnote below.
* If S. says "buttons" (on shirt), E. says "Yes and what else"; and if S. then gives correct response score plus.

in each case the pieces have been arranged beforehand as indicated on
the diagrams. (See figures 10, 11 and 12.)

(a) *Manikin:* Say, *"If these pieces are put together correctly they will
form something. Go ahead and put them together just as quickly as you
can."* Time limit, *2 minutes.*

(b) *Profile:* Say, *"Put this together as quickly as you can."* Time
limit, *3 minutes.* Record time in seconds.

(c) *Hand:* Say, *"Put this together as quickly as you can."* Time limit,
3 minutes. Record time in seconds.

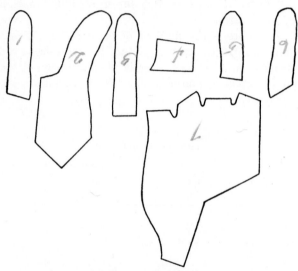

FIG. 12. HAND

Scoring: Part of this test (the Manikin) is scored for accuracy alone;
and part for both time and accuracy (the Profile and Hand). When
both accuracy and time are credited, the subject's score on the test
items is the arithmetical sum of his time and accuracy credits. The
scoring for each of the items is as follows:

(a) *Manikin:* Score 1 point for each piece properly placed and 1
point for neat fitting of all joints. Perfect performance = 6; all correct except that joints are not well fitted, score = 5; one reversal (of
either arms or legs) = 4; one reversal, and remaining pieces not properly fitted = 3; two reversals, that is, both of arms and legs = 2; head
only correctly in place = 1. No time bonus. Maximum score on
Manikin: *6.*

(b) *Profile: Accuracy credits:* 1 point for each piece in correct position, making a maximum of 6 credits.   Thus, nose, chin and eye pieces properly placed = 3; ear,[4] nose and skull pieces in position = 4; both ear pieces alone, correctly in place = 2.

Time credits: From 1 to 4 points, according to limits given in table 33. Time credits are allowed only if subject's accuracy score is 5 or 6.

Full score on Profile is the sum of accuracy and time credits.

(c) *Hand: Accuracy credits:* 1 point for each piece in correct position and if attached to palm, making a possible maximum for accuracy alone, 6.

Time credits: From 1 to 4 points according to limits given in table 33. Time credits are allowed only if subject's accuracy score is 5 or 6.

Full score on the Hand is the sum of accuracy and time credits.

Total score on (a) (b) and (c) is the sum of the partial scores on all items.   Maximum   score: *26*.

TABLE 33

TABLE OF TIME CREDITS

For *"Profile"* and *"Hand"*

Time in Seconds	Credits
19 and below	4
20–29	3
30–44	2
45–64	1
65 and over	0

9. BLOCK DESIGN

Directions: This requires a box of 16 cubes and 9 designs, two of which are samples.   Remove four cubes from the box and say: *"You see these blocks are painted different colors on the different sides.   One side is blue, one red, one white, one yellow, one red and white, one blue and yellow.   And all the blocks are exactly alike."*   The examiner next places Demonstration Card I in front of subject and says: *"Now I want you to make me a design with the blocks so that it will look like the drawing on this card."*   *"Notice that the drawing is all red; so, to make one just like it with these 4 blocks I would have to arrange them this way."*   (Illustrating.) *"Do you understand?"*   (Pause.)   *"Well, let's try another.   This one is more difficult."*   Examiner assembles blocks to make design shown on

---

[4] The ear is made up of 2 pieces; if inverted, but otherwise correctly fitted into proper space credit 1 point.

Card II, pausing to make clear to subject how two half designs can be put together to make one solid patch of color. When reasonably sure that subject understands, examiner presents card I and says—*"Now you take these 4 blocks and put them together so they'll make a design (picture) like the one you see on this card." "Go ahead."* When subject has finished with design, remark, *"That's pretty good."* Brush up the blocks, place second design before him saying, *"Now make me one like this."* Proceed with cards in order until design (5) is reached when examiner

TABLE 34

Card	Number of Blocks	Time Limit
Demonstration I and II	4	
Designs 1 to 4	4	75 seconds
Designs 5 and 6	9	150 seconds
Design 7	16	195 seconds

TABLE 35

TIME SCORES FOR BLOCK DESIGN (WHEN CORRECT)

Design 1-2-3 Time	Credits	Design 4 Time	Credits
1″-5″	3	1″-10″	3
6″-10″	2	11″-15″	2
11″-15″	1	16″-25″	1

Design 5 Time	Credits	Design 6 Time	Credits
1″-25″	3	1″-40″	3
26″-35″	2	41″-50″	2
36″-50″	1	51″-80″	1

Design 7 Time	Credits
1″-80″	3
81″-100″	2
101″-140″	1

takes 5 more blocks out and says, *"Now make me one like this, using 9 blocks."* When design (7) is reached examiner takes out the remaining 7 blocks and says, *"Now make me one like this using 16 blocks."* Continue presenting designs in numbered order until subject has failed three consecutive ones. Help or further demonstration on designs other than that given on Demonstration Cards (I & II) is not permissible. The maximum time allowed for completing the various designs is shown in table 34.

It is not uncommon for some subjects, particularly children, when making the first design either to rotate the pattern or to reverse color and background. When this happens say, "Is this right, does it look just like the design?", and pause for a while. Usually the subject will make a spontaneous correction or will do it if the instructions are repeated. Reversals and rotations appear to be associated with reading disability, but with many children they seem to be "normal" phenomena.

Scoring: The test is scored for both accuracy and time. Three (3) points are given for each design correctly reproduced within maximum time limits; and one (1), two (2), or three (3) additional points for success within certain times as indicated in table 35. To receive credit for time, the design must be reproduced just as shown on the card. Blocks do not have to fit perfectly together, but the design must be absolutely correct.

Maximum score: 42.

10. Digit Symbol

This test is taken from the Army Performance, but altered as to the directions and the time allowed. New time limit is $1\frac{1}{2}$ minutes.

Directions: "Look at these divided boxes or squares (pointing to key); *notice that each has a number on the upper part and a little mark on the lower part. Also, that with every number there is a different mark. Now, look here* (pointing to sample) *where the boxes have only numbers, and the squares underneath are empty. I want you to put in each of these squares* (pointing) *the little mark that should go there, like this."* (The examiner points alternately to key and to the digit.) *"Here is a 2, so you would put in this mark"* (writing in symbol). *"Here is a 1, so you put in this mark. This is a 3, therefore, you would put in this mark,"* etc. After doing *five* of the samples, pause and ask; *"Now what should I put here?"* (indicating the next empty square). If subject fails, examiner tells him and repeats question with next sample. After finishing the demonstration, examiner says; *"Now you begin here and fill as many squares as you can. Do one right after the other, without skipping."*

Scoring: Subject's score is the total number of symbols correctly entered. Precision and neatness are disregarded, but recorded symbols must be identifiable. For the symbol И, subjects sometimes use the letter *N*. Count such reversals as half right.

Maximum score: 67.

Vocabulary Test

Directions: Examiner says; *"I want to see about how many words you know. Listen carefully and tell me what these words mean. Apple— what does apple mean? Donkey—what does donkey mean?"* Then proceed with words in listed order, repeating at each presentation the formula *"What does ——— mean?"* With more intelligent subjects, the phrase *"What does —— mean?"* may be omitted after the third presentation. The following is the list and order[5] of words to be used:

VOCABULARY

1. Apple	12. Cedar	23. Vesper	34. Hara-kiri
2. Donkey	13. Tint	24. Belfry	35. Chattel
3. Join	14. Armory	25. Recede	36. Dilatory
4. Diamond	15. Fable	26. Affliction	37. Amanuensis
5. Nuisance	16. Brim	27. Pewter	38. Proselyte
6. Fur	17. Guillotine	28. Ballast	39. Moiety
7. Cushion	18. Plural	29. Catacomb	40. Aseptic
8. Shilling	19. Seclude	30. Spangle	41. Flout
9. Gamble	20. Nitroglycerine	31. Espionage	42. Traduce
10. Bacon	21. Stanza	32. Imminent	
11. Nail	22. Microscope	33. Mantis	

Scoring: Scoring of definitions should be made with the aid of criteria given below. The general rule is that any recognized meaning of the word is acceptable, elegance of language and precision being disregarded. With this rule observed, most of the words on our list can be scored without great difficulty. Occasionally, however, one is hard put to decide whether the subject does or does not know the meaning of a word. In such cases it is always permissible, and indeed imperative, to say: *"Please explain a little more."* While elegance of expression is disregarded, poverty of content is penalized to some extent. When a subject seems to know only vaguely what a word means his response is credited only as half right. Thus, ½ credit is given for such responses as "Apple" = "It grows on trees." "Diamond" = "A diamond ring." "Nuisance" = "A bad boy."

Except for very superior subjects, it will seldom be necessary to go through the entire list. The general rule is to continue down the list until 5[6] successive words have received 0 credit and to count the remaining ones as failures. A subject's final score is the sum of his partial (½) and full credits (+).

It is generally desirable for the examiner to take down the subject's responses verbatim. This not only permits rechecking the scoring, but, what is particularly important in mental cases, a qualitative evaluation of the subject's thought processes.

Maximum score: 42.

[5] The war and other factors have affected the difficulty of some of the words. Thus, 'nitroglycerine,' 'espionage' and 'hara-kiri' are much easier than originally estimated; on the other hand, 'seclude' seems to have been misplaced from the start and should be farther down the list. The original listing of the words, however, has not been altered, and the necessary changes in order of presentation are left to the examiner.

[6] See footnote 5.

RECORDING AND SCORING OF TESTS

The examiner will find the recording and scoring of tests greatly expedited if he uses the standard blank provided for this purpose. This blank consists of coded item outlines for the tests, with spaces at the right for responses and for time notations where the latter are required. Most of the subject's responses or notations may be entered directly in the space next to each item, but in the case of the *Vocabulary, Similarities* and the *Comprehension Tests* where verbatim recording is required, the subject's answers should be written out in full on the reverse side of the record blank. Where a time record is required, the time counted is that which elapses from the moment the examiner has finished his instructions, to the moment that the subject indicates that he has completed a test.

OBTAINING A SUBJECT'S WEIGHTED AND TOTAL SCORE

To obtain a subject's total weighted-score on any of the Bellevue Scales, proceed as follows: (1) Score the individual items of each test separately as indicated in the manual of directions. (2) Add the partial credits allowed for each item into a single score. These sums are the *raw scores* for each test. (3) Enter the raw scores attained by the subject on each test in the summary box of the record sheet in the column marked RS. (4) Look up the *weighted* scores for each raw score in the table of equivalent weighted scores (table 36). This is done by first locating in the table, the column of the particular test that is being considered, finding the row in which that score occurs and running one's finger to the extreme left or right of the column marked weighted score. The score thus found is entered in the column WT in the summary box on the line reserved for that test. It is these weighted scores which are used in obtaining M.A.'s, I.Q.'s, and other ratings. (5) The tests are divided into two groups, one *Verbal* and the other *Performance*. Sum the *Verbal* and *Performance* test scores separately, prorating when necessary. Then add the sub-totals together to give the *Full Scale* score.

The examiner should remember it is always the weighted or sigma scores that are used for the various ratings as given in our tables. The use of the I.Q. Tables is explained below. I.Q.'s may be obtained for Performance, Verbal or Full Scales, but ordinarily *only the Full Scale I.Q. should be used in defining a subject's general intelligence level.*

FINDING A SUBJECT'S I.Q.

METHOD OF DERIVATION

The I.Q.'s in the appended tables have been calculated by dividing, at each age, the sigma score of the individual by the mean sigma score for his age group, with the zero point at different ages so adjusted as to make the I.Q.'s of all ages strictly comparable.

I.Q.'S FOR THE FULL SCALE-ADULTS, AGES 16 TO 60

All I.Q.'s are obtained from total scores.   The examiner should note that while the Scale consists of 11 sub-tests, the I.Q. tables are based on

TABLE 36
Table of weighted scores

EQUIVALENT WEIGHTED SCORE	Information	Comprehension	Digit Span	Arithmetic	Similarities	Vocabulary	Picture Arrangement	Picture Completion	Block Design	Object Assembly	Digit Symbol	EQUIVALENT WEIGHTED SCORE
						RAW SCORE						
0		0	5	1		0		2		5–6	0–3	0
1	0	1		2	0	1–2	0	3	0	7	4–7	1
2	1	2	6		1–2	3–4	1	4	1–2	8	8–11	2
3	2–3	3	7	3	3	5–6	2–3	5	3–5	9	12–15	3
4	4–5	4	8	4	4	7–9	4	6	6–7	10–11	16–19	4
5	6	5–6			5–6	10–11	5		8–10	12	20–23	5
6	7–8	7	9	5	7	12–14	6	7	11–12	13	24–28	6
7	9	8	10	6	8	15–16	7–8	8	13–15	14–15	29–32	7
8	10–11	9			9–10	17–19	9	9	16–17	16	33–36	8
9	12	10	11	7	11	20–21	10	10	18–19	17	37–40	9
10	13–14	11	12	8	12	22–24	11	11	20–22	18	41–44	10
11	15–16	12–13	13		13–14	25–26	12–13		23–24	19	45–48	11
12	17	14		9	15	27–28	14	12	25–27	20–21	49–52	12
13	18–19	15	14	10	16	29–31	15	13	28–29	22	53–56	13
14	20	16	15		17–18		16–17	14	30–32	23	57–61	14
15	21–22	17		11	19		18	15	33–34	24	62–65	15
16	23	18	16	12	20		19		35–37		66–67	16
17	24	19	17	13	21–22		20 and over		38 and over			17
18	25	20		14	23–24							18

a weighted score of 10 tests for the Full Scale, and a total score of 5 tests for the Verbal and Performance parts respectively.   This requires an adjustment in the totals of the Verbal and Full Scale weighted scores. The additional test is the Vocabulary which originally was used as an alternate but is now recommended as a regular sub-test.   When the Vocabulary test is included, the Verbal part of the Scale is reduced to a 5-test base by taking 5/6 of the weighted Verbal score.   This amount is then added to the Performance sub-total to obtain the Full Scale score.   If for some reason any test has been omitted, the incomplete score is brought up to a ten test equivalent by prorating.   For example, if a subject has been given only 9 tests, the total score on which is 72, the examiner prorates by taking 10/9th of 72 and uses the resulting figure (80) as the subject's Full Scale score.   Having obtained the subject's total weighted score, the examiner turns to the table marked Full Scale.   Here he looks for the score total in that part of the table in which the subject's age group is listed.   He does this by running his finger across from the column in which the weighted scores appear to the column listing the subject's age.   The number given in this column is the subject's I.Q.   Thus, if a subject aged 27, makes a weighted score of 75 on the Full Scale, one finds the number 75 in the column marked Weighted Score (page 237), runs his finger across to the column marked Age 25 to 29 and notes the figure there given.   In this case it happens to be 86, and this accordingly is the subject's I.Q.

PERFORMANCE AND VERBAL I.Q.'S

These I.Q.'s are obtained in the same way as the Full Scale I.Q.'s except that the total weighted score represents the sum of 5 Performance or 5 Verbal Tests respectively.   The I.Q.'s for each scale are given separately.

I.Q.'S FOR CHILDREN, AGES 10–15

While the Bellevue Examination is intended primarily for the examination of adults and adolescents, it was standardized from the age of 7 upwards.   The I.Q. tables, however, have not been constructed for ages below 10, because it seemed unlikely that the tests would be used to any considerable extent below this age; at least, as organized at present.   Looking up I.Q.'s from ages 10–15 is done in the same way as in the case of adults, except that one must take into consideration the months as well as the years of the subject's chronological age.   For the age period 10 years 0 months to 14 years 6 months, the I.Q.'s have been calculated at successive three month intervals; from age 14 years 6 months to 15 years 6 months, only at every 6 month interval.   In obtaining a child's I.Q. one looks for it under the year-month interval most proximate to his actual chronological age.   Thus, if a child is 10 years and 4 months, one should look for it under the interval 10–3, if 13 years and 11 months, under the interval 14–0, etc.

INTERPRETATION AND MEANING OF I.Q.'S

The interpretation of an I.Q. or the mental classification assigned to it necessarily varies not only with the test used but also with the assumptions, statistical and otherwise, made by the classifier. If, however, the per cent of population included in each category is definitely

TABLE 37
Intelligence classifications

I.Q.	CLASSIFICATION	LIMITS IN TERMS OF P.E.	PER CENT INCLUDED
65 and below	Mental Defective	−3 P.E.* and over	2.2*
66–79	Borderline	−2 P.E. to −3 P.E.	6.7
80–90	Dull Normal	−1 P.E. to −2 P.E.	16.1
91–110	Average	−1 P.E. to +1 P.E.	50.0
111–119	Bright Normal	+1 P.E. to +2 P.E.	16.1
120–127	Superior	+2 P.E. to +3 P.E.	6.7
128 and over	Very Superior	+3 P.E. and over	2.2

* Setting −3 P.E. as the upper limit of the mentally defective group reduces the expected incidence of Mental Defectives in the total population to 2.2 per cent. We are not sure but that this figure is a little low, and that 3 per cent is a better estimate of the "probable" incidence for the country as a whole, and even for our own standardizing population. If it should turn out to be that 3 per cent does more nearly represent the "truer" figure, then the P.E. demarcation of the upper limit of mental deficiency would have to be set at − 2.8 P.E. from the mean. In that case the I.Q. limits in our table would have to be altered as follows: *Mental Defective:* I.Q. limits—68 and below *Borderline:* I.Q. limits—69–79.

indicated, it is possible to compare the relative standings of individuals whatever the basis used. The table of classifications that is offered here is based on the assumption that class limits are best defined statistically. Thus, Mental Defectives are those who (with respect to intelligence) fall in the lowest 3 per cent of the population; Borderline, those who fall in the next 7 per cent; Dull-Normals, the 15 per cent following; Average, those included in the middle 50 per cent of the population, etc., etc. These limits have been chosen for the reason explained in chapter 4.

While I.Q. limits given in the table will ordinarily determine the classification of the individual, there will arise from time to time cases which need special consideration. At borderline points the examiner will necessarily have to use his own judgment. Thus, while an I.Q. of 65 is given on our table as the upper limit of mental deficiency, it is possible that there will be cases attaining I.Q.'s of 69 or 70 whom the examiner will more justifiably want to class as defective. So also, will there be individuals who attain I.Q.'s of 64 or 65 on the Bellevue who might be better placed in the Borderline group. But the examiner may not deviate from these limits to any considerable extent or use another scheme of interpreting these same I.Q.'s, for example, that of Terman or Kuhlmann. If the examiner believes for some reason that an I.Q. obtained on the Bellevue scale does not adequately represent the intelligence level of the subject, as defined by the table, the only conclusion that he may legitimately draw is that in this case the tests are not suitable for measuring the subject's intelligence. He may accordingly either reject the results, or use them only in a qualitative way, but having accepted them he is not privileged to disregard the I.Q. interpretation as given.

CRITERIA FOR SCORING VARIOUS TESTS

GENERAL COMPREHENSION TEST

1. ENVELOPE.   General: Mail it.
   Samples of
   2 credits
   Put it in mail box
   Drop in nearest box
   (In rural regions also credit.)   Give to postman or bring to Post Office
   1 credit
   Run to post office and mail it
   Take it to the police or post office
   Give to the mail man (see above)
   If it is nearby I'd bring it to man to whom it is addressed, if far away,
      I'd put it in the mail box
   Take it to lost and found
   0 credit
   Take to owner
   Open it
   Take to person to whom it is addressed
   Send it back to whoever sent it
   Bring it back if you know the address

2. Theatre. General: Notify responsible person (prevent panic).
Samples of
   2 credits
      Keep quiet and notify the manager immediately
      Tell the manager about it
      Call it to the attention of one of the ushers
      Tell orchestra to play—and notify manager
      Quietly call the usher and have him give the general alarm
      Tell the man who shows you to your seat
   1 credit
      Give alarm quietly
      Ring the fire alarm
      Call the fire engines, or firemen
      Investigate if fire is real and, if so, notify usher
   0 credit
      Warn the other people
      Scream there is a fire
      Run out
      Walk to nearest exit
      Tell people there is a fire and to use the nearest exit
      Go for water
      Try to get friends out as quickly as possible

3. Bad Company. General: Influence.
Samples of
   2 credits
      They teach you to be bad
      So that you wouldn't be bad yourself
      Influence our behavior—our thoughts
      We degenerate ourselves
      Keep from being spoiled by them
      Usually follow in their footsteps
      Degrade us
      Affect our morals
      Become like them
   1 credit
      To keep your reputation
      Will get you into trouble
      Keep ourselves out of trouble
      Finally become criminal yourself
      Teaches you to be a crook
      Because if you hang around you have to be like them
      Because I don't want to be bad

0 credit
    'Cause they don't talk what good children should hear
    'Cause don't learn anything good
    They give trouble
    They are not good for anybody
    Not beneficial
    To live honest
    So we wouldn't be picked up

4. TAXES.   General: To support the government.
   Samples of
    2 credits
       To support government
       Upkeep of the community in which they live
       So government should keep going
       To pay government bills
       To run country (explained)
    1 credit
       For upkeep of institutions of all kinds
       To help with the war effort
       Pay police, firemen, public officials
       Pay for the army and navy and the things they need.
       To support schools and parks
       Support for public works
       So city can get things done
       Pay for public organizations of government
       For Home Relief and hospitals[7]
    0 credit
       For unemployed (poor people)[7]
       Because the President has to pay off people
       So that other people could make more money
       Have government do things that are expensive
       They have property protected; must pay for that
       Give relief (alone)[7]
       Higher taxes, better service
       Help city and city help you
       For the city

---

[7] N.B.: The answer, "for Home Relief," etc., is given no credit if stated as sole answer, but credited 1 if accompanied by mention of another governmental function, as "for Home Relief and hospitals." If subject mentions "Home Relief" alone, however, the Examiner may *not* say "and what else?" Similarly, 0 score is given for any other singly mentioned governmental function, e.g. "For police," or "For schools."

5. LEATHER (SHOES). General: Durable, flexible, comfortable, economical.
   2 credits if subject mentions *at least 3 different qualities*
   (1) *Durability:* Take a lot of wear, strong, wears well, lasts, durable, stands elements
   (2) *Flexibility:* Pliable, soft, molds well, shapes well, easy to wear, because of softness
   (3) *Comfort:* Not hard on feet, easy to wear, light, comfortable, porous
   (4) *Economic factor:* Good supply, have a lot of, easy to get, cheap, not too expensive
   1 credit if subject mentions *1 or 2 different qualities*
   0 credit if subject mentions *no essential quality*, thus;
   Most substantial product it can be made of
   Tradition
   To look dressed up
   Shock absorbers
   Most convenient
   Protect feet
   Can be fixed
   Leather does not burn
   Best wearing material (unexplained)

6. CITY LAND.   General: Greater demand.
   Samples of
   2 credits
   More demand for land in city
   Being used more, more people want the location
   More people want to buy it
   Supply and demand—more demand in crowded city
   Harder to get in the city (explained as demand)
   Many people after it (if explained satisfactorily)
   1 credit
   City has more people
   Limited amount of land
   Scarce in city
   Can profit more from land in city
   More conveniences, more stores and good transportation[8]
   Business possibilities
   Commercial reasons—one can erect buildings which would bring in more than in country

---

[8] A credit of 1 is given if 2 or more "conveniences" are mentioned. When only one is mentioned, no credit is allowed.

0 credit
  Buildings are larger in city, they cost more
  There are houses on land in city, house worth something
  Because hardly anyone wants to live in the country
  In city there are more things—taxes, congestion
  Because people have more chance to get work

7. FOREST.   General: Use of natural fact as means of finding direction.
   Samples of
   2 Credits
     By pointing hour hand of watch at sun and getting directions (ex-
       plained)[9]
     By noting what side moss grows on trees and getting my direction
       accordingly
   1 credit
     By the sun—(unexplained) Moss—(unexplained)
     Climb to top of tallest tree and try to locate landmark
     Follow a path
     Follow a stream
     Go in one direction—mark trees as I went
     Try to set a fire to cause a lot of smoke
     Look for landmarks for bearings
   0 credit
     Go back the way I came
     Ask somebody—or a policeman
     Walk until I get somewheres
     I would shout
     Look for my foot tracks
     Look at the sky and follow the open spaces
     Keep walking until I meet someone
     Wait for night to come and direct myself by the North Star

8. LAWS.   General: Social regulation.
   2 credits
     In order to regulate society
     To preserve life, liberty and keep people living together harmoniously
     For safeguarding lives and property of individuals
     To make human associations possible without friction
     Life so complex that laws are necessary to live amicably
     Where there is any group, there are rules necessary for the good of all

---

[9] It is important to make sure that the subject actually knows how the sun
would help in obtaining direction.   If there is any doubt, ask *"Just how would it
help you?"*

   1 credit
   Public good, public welfare
   Regulations to keep people in check, to make them respect other
      people's rights
   To govern people—to keep them in control
   Keep people from committing crimes
   Keep up the standards of civilization
   Otherwise people would act in confusion
   For an organized community, otherwise it would be chaos
   Insures fair play for all
   Protects the good people from the bad people
   To keep peace and order
   To protect the people
   To make people realize what is right and wrong
   Puts people in their place
   If there were no laws, people would do what they like
   0 credit
   Keep people from getting killed
   If it were not for the laws everyone would kill himself
   To make people obey—they make me obey
   To prevent accidents
   So that no one would get in trouble
   To keep up decency
   To keep us from making mistakes
   Otherwise would do wrong things
   So that people will do what is right
   Curb thieves

9. MARRIAGE.   General: As useful public record.
   Samples of
      2 credits
      Records (For)
      For traceable record
      As record to show they are legally married
      So that they could keep track of marriages
      1 credit
      Prevent bigamy (explained)
      For census purposes
      Proof that you're married in case of legal matters
      0 credit
      A formality
      To protect morals of community; to protect women and children
      So people will know they are married

Makes it legal
Gives offspring a name
Law demands it
Protect honor of womanhood
To keep self respect and not have a common law marriage
Otherwise people would be living like animals
If wife is in trouble she can go to court

10. DEAF—TALK. General: One must first hear spoken word before being
    able to repeat it.
Samples of
  2 credits
    Because you learn to talk by hearing
    If you can't hear language you can't learn to articulate sounds
    If you don't hear sounds they make, you don't know how to make the
        sounds afterwards
  1 credit
    Can't imagine what words are like
    Because he can't hear what is said
    Do not know how other people talk
    Can't talk because he can't hear[10]
  0 credit
    Can't hear themselves talk
    Ear and throat connected
    Along with deafness comes dumbness
    Something is wrong with their nerves
    Because they were born that way

Criteria for alternate questions

1. SAVE MONEY. General: To have something for "a rainy day," or for
   emergency or future use.
  2 credits
    For a rainy day
    So they'll have it when they'll need it
    In case of emergency
    In case of need in bad times
    Something to depend on—for security

---

[10] This answer cannot be taken at face value. Many subjects who give it
haven't the slightest idea of the connection. Examiner should then ask *"How
do you mean?"* If no satisfactory explanation is received, give zero credit. On
the other hand, if the subject improves his response by saying, "because you
can't learn," he is given full credit.

1 credit
In case of accidents
To have money to support father or mother, or for a funeral
To have something when you get too old to work
In case of sickness
You can never tell what happens
In case you lose your job
For college education
If they want to buy a house or a car
So they can have luxury (if explained`

0 credit
For their own interests
Save money for yourself
If they'll lose money they'll turn out to be beggars
If they spend it all they won't have money to buy food with
Use it for food to live on

2. Friend.   General: Try to procure it.

2 credits
Do my best to get it
I'd try to get it if it is possible
Borrow it
Tell him I don't have it and try to find someone who does

1 credit
Refer him to person who has it
Tell him I haven't it, suggest where he can get it
"Sorry haven't it."   Refer him to where he can get it

0 credit
Say "Sorry I haven't got it."
Explain I'd like to give it but haven't got it
Refuse him
If I didn't have it couldn't give it to him

CRITERIA FOR SIMILARITIES

General scoring:
2 credits for the most fundamental likeness
1 credit for any essential likeness
0 for failure to respond, giving a difference or mentioning some inconsequential similarity

1. Orange—Banana
Score 2   (Both) fruits
(Both) foods
Score 1   (Both) have peels
You eat both

Score 0
They both grow
Both contain vitamines
Both contain the same calories
They are both yellow
Both same color
Both same shape

2. COAT—DRESS

Score 2
(Both) garments
(Both) wearing apparel
(Both) articles of clothing

Score 1
You wear both
Cover the body
(Both) made from cloth
Keep you warm
Things to put on

Score 0
Both made of the same material
You put the coat on top of the dress
Both have buttons

3. DOG—LION

Score 2
(Both) animals
(Both) mammals

Score 1
(Both) have legs (or furs; eyes; tails, etc.)
(Both) belong to the same species

Score 0
Lion growls and dog barks

4. WAGON—BICYCLE

Score 2
(Both) vehicles
(Both) conveyances
(Both) means of transportation

Score 1
(Both) movable toys
You ride on them
They both have wheels
Can carry things around
Children play with them
They both roll—or both ride

Score 0
Can push both

5. DAILY PAPER—RADIO

Score 2
(Both) sources of information
Modes of communication
Can convey thoughts through them

Score 1
They give you the news

(Both) tell stories
(Both) means of amusement
(Both) teach you something
(Both) used for advertising
Score 0   You get music from the radio but not from the newspaper

6. AIR—WATER

Score 2   (Both) necessary for life
Have to have air to live and must have water to live
(Both) necessary for functioning of human body
Can't live without them
Score 1   (Both) elements
(Both) have oxygen
(Both) means of transportation
(Both) help us in living
You need both (explained)
(Both) are media for transmission of waves
Score 0   Nature's gifts
Oxygen is in the air and hydrogen is in the air and water is H_2O
For breathing, for fish, and human beings
Breathe the air and drink water
Water is a substance and air is a substance
Keeps on going; so does water keep on going
Both in clouds
Need both (unexplained)

7. WOOD—ALCOHOL

Score 2   (Both) organic substances
(Both) contain hydrogen and carbon (or have carbon in them)
Score 1   (Both) burn
(Both) used as fuel
(Both) used in the manufacturing of important materials
Score 0   Both useful
Alcohol comes from wood
Both knock you out

8. EYE—EAR

Score 2   (Both) sense organs (or senses)
(Both) receptors of stimuli
(Both) organs of perception
Score 1   Parts of the body
Parts of the head
You know from them
Get knowledge through them
Score 0   Hear with the ear and see with the eye

Both have an opening
Both can tell what you are saying—you read lips and ear
    hears what you say
You need both

9. Egg—Seed
    Score 2   (Both) embryonic substances
              (Both) beginnings of life
              (Both) reproduce what they come from
              Young comes from both
    Score 1   (Both) give life (incompletely explained)
              Means of reproduction (if not further explained)
              (Both) can create
              (Both) have shells
              Something grows from both
    Score 0   You can eat both of them
              Both have a yolk
              Both are round

10. Poem—Statue
    Score 2   (Both) works of art
              (Both) expression of artistic feeling
              (Both) are artistic creations
    Score 1   (Both) are beautiful things
              (Both) stir feelings
              (Both) symbolic
              (Both) are memorial, make you remember
              (Both) tell stories
              (Both) made by man
              Express an emotion or idea
    Score 0   Both lifeless
              A poem may describe a statue
              You read a poem and look at a statue
              People like them
              Lost a long time, if good

11. Praise—Punishment
    Score 2   (Both) means of influencing the behavior of others
              (Both) means of discipline
              (Both) methods of motivation
    Score 1   (Both) are forms of criticism
              Used on people to put them in a certain emotional state
              Means of getting things done

(Both) affect a person (if explained)
(Both) methods of training a child

12. FLY—TREE
    Score 2   (Both) have life
               (Both) living things
    Score 1   (Both) breathe
               (Both) created by nature
               (Both) grow
               (Both) need sunlight to live
               (Both) need food
    Score 0   Fly is small, tree is large
               Both useful to man
               Fly has wings and tree has leaves and branches
               Both outdoors all the time
               Both carry germs

CRITERIA FOR VOCABULARY TEST

1. APPLE.   Dictionary definition: *Edible fruit.*
   Samples of
   1 Credit
   Fruit
   Something to eat, like a peach or a pear
   ½ *Credit*
   Red and sweet
   It grows on trees

2. DONKEY.   Dictionary definition: *An ass, a long eared equine quadruped smaller than a horse.*
   1 Credit
   Animal
   Jackass
   Beast of burden
   Like a horse, only smaller
   Mule
   ½ *Credit*
   Has long ears
   Ride on him

3. JOIN.   Dictionary definition: *Set or bring together, to connect or to combine, To lie in contact, to become associated. To engage in together.*
   1 Credit
   To bring together
   Join a church or club

To register
To connect
To combine
To unite
To sign up
½ *Credit*
To contact

4. DIAMOND. Dictionary definition: *Gem of great brilliancy. Figure bounded by four equal straight sides and having two angles acute and two obtuse. Diamond-shaped spot on a playing card. (Baseball) Square space enclosed by the lines connecting bases.*
1 *Credit*
Gem
Precious stone
Diamond spot on card
Jewel
Something you get underground for a ring
Substance made of carbon
A baseball diamond
½ *Credit*
A (diamond) ring
It's valuable

5. NUISANCE. Dictionary definition: *That which annoys, vexes, or harms.*
1 *Credit*
A pest
Someone who bothers you
Pain in the neck
Person who gets in the way
½ *Credit*
A bad boy
Trouble

6. FUR. Dictionary definition: *Soft fine coat covering the skin of many mammals. Skins of fur-bearing animals, also apparel made from them. Any fuzzy covering.*
1 *Credit*
A skin
A coat of animal
What some animals have on top
Get from off an animal
Hair of animals
They make coats from them

½ *Credit*
  To keep warm
  People wear it
  Hairy stuff
  Clothes

7. CUSHION. Dictionary definition: *Place on a cushion. Flexible covering filled with elastic material or air. Any device to deaden jar.*
  1 Credit
  A soft seat
  A pillow
  A pad for a seat or sofa
  A shock absorber
  You sit on it
  You lie on it
  ½ *Credit*
  To make you comfortable

8. SHILLING. Dictionary definition: *A coin of Great Britain.* 24¢.
  1 Credit
  A foreign coin, (English) (Austrian) money
  It's worth 25 cents
  ½ *Credit*
  A penny
  A coin, money (unspecified)

9. GAMBLE. Dictionary definition: *Squander by gaming; to game; to risk or wager something of value upon a chance.*
  1 Credit
  Win or lose
  Take a chance
  To bet
  To speculate
  To gamble money
  To play cards or dice

10. BACON. Dictionary definition: *Salted, dried or smoked flesh of the hog.*
  1 Credit
  Meat from a pig
  (Type of) pork
  ½ *Credit*
  Meat
  Something you eat
  Food

0 Credit
   Ribs from an animal

11. NAIL. Dictionary definition: *Thin horny plate on end of finger or toe.*
      Slender piece of metal used for driving into wood.
      1 Credit
      Spike
      Brad
      To fix wood together
      A piece of metal to hold things together
      Hard skin at the end of the fingers or toes
      Fingernail
      ½ *Credit*
      Something to hammer
      Metal

12. CEDAR. Dictionary definition: *Tree of the pine family having fragrant wood.*
      1 Credit
      An evergreen
      A kind of wood
      A tree
      ½ *Credit*
      A cedar chest
      A kind of box

13. TINT. Dictionary definition: *Tinge, hue, a slight color.*
      1 Credit
      A dye
      A (blended) color
      To paint
      To brighten a faded fabric
      Add a bit of coloring
      0 Credit
      A texture

14. ARMORY. Dictionary definition: *Depository for arms; place for assembling*
      of troops.
      1 Credit
      Where they train to be soldiers
      Where soldiers and arms are kept
      Military building (explained)
      ½ *Credit*
      A soldier's club
      N. G. Headquarters

0 Credit
A training camp
People stay there
Fort

15 FABLE.   Dictionary definition: *Brief tale with moral, with persons, animals or inanimate things as speaker and actor.   Legend or myth; an invention, fabrication.*
1 Credit
A fairy tale
A short story with a moral
A myth
Fiction (story)
½ *Credit*
To tell a lie

16. BRIM.   Dictionary definition: *Margin, edge, border.   To fill or be filled to the brim.*
1 Credit
The edge of something (like a hat)
The rim
½ *Credit*
The end
0 Credit
Something wide
Surface

17 GUILLOTINE.   Dictionary definition: *To behead.   Instrument for beheading criminals in which a weighted knife is used.*
1 Credit
Form of execution (beheading) in France
Used to chop heads off
½ *Credit*
A knife

18. PLURAL.   Dictionary definition: *Containing more than one.*
1 Credit
More than one
Several
Not singular
½ *Credit*
Change "y" to "i" and add "es"
In grammar, number
Double of anything

0 Credit
Part of sentence
Part of a verb
Comparison

19. SECLUDE. Dictionary definition: *Remove and keep apart, as from society.*
1 Credit
Keep apart
To hide
To be alone, by yourself
To isolate
½ *Credit*
To separate
Out of the way
A quiet spot
Lonely
0 Credit
In a snug place

20. NITROGLYCERINE. Dictionary definition: *Light yellow oily explosive liquid made by treating glycerine with nitric acid.*
1 Credit
An explosive
A chemical
(a drug) used as heart stimulant
½ *Credit*
A medicine
Used in ammunition
0 Credit
A cleaning substance
A food
An acid

21. STANZA. Dictionary definition: *Group of rimed lines, forming one of series of divisions of a poem.*
1 Credit
Group of rimed lines
Part of a poem
Verse in a poem
Part of a song
There are so many stanzas in a poem
½ *Credit*
A line
A phrase

A few lines to make one thought
A paragraph
A poem

22. MICROSCOPE. Dictionary definition: *Instrument for assisting the eye to see minute objects.*

1 Credit
Used to magnify small objects
Instrument that makes small things look large

½ *Credit*
An instrument you see germs with
Something that enlarges

0 Credit
Something that brings things closer when you look through them
Something to look through

23. VESPER. Dictionary definition: *Pertaining to evening or to the service of Vesper prayers, or songs; bells that calls to Vespers.*

1 Credit
Church service
Hymn or evening prayer

½ *Credit*
Twilight

24. BELFRY. Dictionary definition: *Tower in which a bell is hung, or the part containing the bell.*

1 Credit
Bell tower in church
(Steeple) where bell is kept

½ *Credit*
Tower

0 Credit
A bell
The ringing of a bell

25. RECEDE. Dictionary definition: *To move, to tend or incline backward; to withdraw; to cede back.*

1 Credit
To go back
To withdraw

½ *Credit*
To quit

26. AFFLICTION. Dictionary definition: *Distress of body or mind or that which causes it; grief; calamity.*

½ *Credit*
Bug (unexplained)
0 *Credit*
A butterfly

34. HARAKIRI. Dictionary definition: *A Japanese method of committing suicide by ripping open the bowels.*
1 *Credit*
Japanese method of committing suicide
Disemboweling
½ *Credit*
Self-strangulation used by Japanese
Falling on a sword
0 *Credit*
Suicide in China

35. CHATTEL. Dictionary definition: *Article of personal property; a movable.*
1 *Credit*
Legal term for personal property
A possession
½ *Credit*
A horse
A slave
0 *Credit*
A (first) mortgage
Real property

36. DILATORY. Dictionary definition: *Tending to cause tardiness, slowness and delay.*
1 *Credit*
Postponing
Making for delay
Waits a long time before doing something
½ *Credit*
Slowness
Tardiness
Holding up
0 *Credit*
Dilate
Lazy

37. AMANUENSIS. Dictionary definition: *One who copies manuscript or takes dictation.*

1 Credit
A scribe
A secretary
0 Credit
A servant

38. PROSELYTE. Dictionary definition: *To win over to different religion or party; one thus won over.*
1 Credit
Convert
½ Credit
A man who changes his religion
It's a follower
0 Credit
A person connected with religion
A disciple

39. MOIETY. Dictionary definition: *Half, a small part.*
1 Credit
A half
A small portion
A lesser portion
½ Credit
A quantity

40. ASEPTIC. Dictionary definition: *Free from disease germs or tendency to putrefaction.*
1 Credit
Without germs
Sterile
½ Credit
Clean
0 Credit
Something against bacteria
Non-poisonous

41. FLOUT. Dictionary definition: *To scoff at; jeer.   A gibe; scoff.*
1 Credit
Sneer at
Ignore authority
½ Credit
Insult

0 Credit
To flaunt

42. TRADUCE.   Dictionary definition: *To misrepresent wilfully; defame; slander.*
    1 Credit
    Harm person's character
    Vilify
    ½ Credit
    To lower (in esteem)

BIBLIOGRAPHY

Studies with the Wechsler-Bellevue Scale

1. ANDERSON, E. E. ET AL.: Wilson College studies in psychology. I. A comparison of Wechsler-Bellevue, Binet and ACE at college level. *J. Psychol.*, 1942, **14:** 317 et seq.
2. BALINSKY, B.: An analysis of the mental factors of various age groups from 9–60. *Genet. Psychol. Monog.*, 1941, **23:** 191–234.
3. BALINSKY, B., ISRAEL, H., AND WECHSLER, D.: Relative effectiveness of the Stanford-Binet and Bellevue Scale, etc. *Amer. J. Orthopsychiat.*, 1939, **9:** 798–801.
4. BENTON, A. L., WEIDER, A., AND BLAUVELT, J.: Performance of adult patients on Bellevue and Revised Binet. *Psychiat. Quart.*, 1941, **15:** 802–806.
5. BRODY, M. B.: A survey of the results of intelligence tests in psychosis. *Brit. J. Med. Psych.*, 1942, **19:** 215–257.
6. BROWN, R. R., AND PARTINGTON, J. E.: The intelligence of the narcotic drug addict. *J. Genet. Psychol.*, 1942, **26:** 175.
7. BROWN, R. R., AND PARTINGTON, J. E.: A psychometric comparison of narcotic addicts with hospital attendants. *J. Genet. Psychol.*, 1942, **27:** 71.
8. FISHBEIN, S.: An evaluation of the Wechsler-Bellevue Intelligence tests... on the College Level. 1941. Master's Thesis, Temple University.
9. GOLDFARB, W.: An investigation of reaction time in older adults. *T. C. Contributions to Education, No. 831.* New York, 1941.
10. HALPERN, F.: Comparison of Revised Stanford with Bellevue Adult, etc. *Psychiat. Quart. Suppl.*, 1942, **16:** 206–211.
11. HAYES, S. P.: Alternative scales for the mental measurement of the visually handicapped. *Outlook for the Blind*, 1942, **36:** 225 et seq.
12. KNIGHT, R. P., GILL, M., LOZOFF, M., AND RAPAPORT, D.: Comparisons of clinical findings and psychological tests in three cases bearing on military selection of personnel. *Bull. Menninger Clinic*, 1943, **7:** 114–128.
13. LEWINSKI, R. J.: Performance of Naval Recruits on the Kent Oral Emergency Test and the verbal battery of the Wechsler-Bellevue Adult Inteltelligence Scale. *Amer. J. Opthopsychiat.*, 1943, **13:** 138–140.
14. LEWINSKI, R. J.: Intertest variability of subnormal Naval Recruits on the Bellevue Verbal Scale. *J. Abnorm. and Soc. Psychol.*, 1943, **38:** 540–44.
15. LEVI, J.: A psychometric pattern of the adolescent psychopathic personality. Doctoral Dissertation, New York University, N. Y., 1943.
16. MACHOVER, S.: Cultural and racial variations in patterns of intellect. *T. C. Contributions to Education, No. 875.* New York, 1943.

17. MARGARET, A.: Parallels in the behavior of schizophrenics, paretics and presenile non-psychotic patients. *J. Abnorm. and Soc. Psychol.*, 1942, **37:** 511–528.

18. MARGARET, A., AND WRIGHT, C.: Limitations in the use of test performances to detect mental disturbance. *J. Applied Psychol.*, 1943, **27:** 387–398.

19. MAIZLISH, I. L.: A comparison of Stanford-Binet & Bellevue with adult offenders. *Psych. Bull.*, 1942, **39:** 472.

20. MITCHELL, M. B.: Performance of mental hospital patients on the Wechsler-Bellevue and the Revised Stanford-Binet, Form L. *J. Educ. Psychol.*, 1942, 538–544.

21. RABIN, A. I.: Test score patterns in schizophrenic and nonpsychotic states. *J. Psychol.*, 1941, **12:** 91–100.

22. RABIN, A. I.: Differentiating psychometric patterns in schizophrenia and manic depressive psychosis. *J. Abn. and Soc. Psychol.*, 1942, **37:** 270–272.

23. RABIN, A. I.: Fluctuations in mental level of schizophrenic patients. *Psychiat. Quart.*, 1944, **18:** 78–92.

24. RABIN, A. I.: A short form of the Wechsler-Bellevue test. *J. Applied Psychol.*, 1943, **27:** 320–324.

25. REICHARD, S., AND SCHAFER, R.: The clinical significance of scatter on the Bellevue Scale. *Bull. Menninger Clinic*, 1943, **9:** 93–99.

26. TRIST, E. L.: Short tests of low grade intelligence. III. *Occup. Psych.*, London, 1941, **15:** 120.

27. WECHSLER, D.: Effects of alcohol on mental activity. *Quart. J. Stud. Alcohol*, 1942, **2:** 479.

28. WECHSLER, D., ISRAEL, H., AND BALINSKY, B.: A study of the subtests of the Bellevue Intelligence Scale in borderline and mental defective cases. *Amer. J. Ment. Def.*, 1941, **45:** 555–558.

29. WECHSLER, D., HALPERN, F., AND JAROS, E.: Psychometric study of insulin-treated schizophrenics. *Psychiat. Quart.*, 1940, **14:** 466.

30. WEIDER, A.: Effects of age on the Bellevue Scale in schizophrenic patients. *Psychiat. Quart.*, 1943, **17:** 337–346.

31. WEIDER, A., LEVI, J., AND RISCH, F.: Performance of problem children on the Wechsler-Bellevue Intelligence Scale and the Revised Stanford-Binet. *Psychiat. Quart.*, 1943, **17:** 695–701.

APPENDICES

SPECIAL STATISTICAL METHODS

A. METHOD USED TO CONVERT RAW SCORES INTO WEIGHTED (STANDARD) SCORES

1. Mean and S.D. of raw samplings obtained for each test.
2. New mean of 10 and S.D. of 3 assigned to each test.
3. Every raw score for each test equated against new weighted (standard) score, point by point, by following Hull's method:

$$X_2 = M_2 + \frac{\sigma_2}{\sigma_1}(X_1 - M_1)$$

Where, M_2 = assigned mean (10)
   σ_2 = assigned sigma (3)
   X_2 = new score to be found (weighted or standard score)
   M_1 = calculated mean
   σ_1 = calculated sigma
   X_1 = raw score

B. METHOD USED TO CALCULATE INTELLIGENCE QUOTIENTS

1. Mean and S.D. of *weighted* score distributions obtained for each age level.
2. All weighted scores for each level converted into "z" scores by usual formula ($z = \dfrac{X - M}{\sigma}$), where M's and σ's are the constants of the different age level distributions. Chartrs drawn up for each age level giving the weighted scores and their corresponding "z" scores.
3. "z" scores for the different age distributions equated against P.E. limits such that the score $.6745\sigma$ (1 P.E.) below the mean would in all age levels give an I.Q. of 90. This was carried through as follows:
   (a) For each age level locate the weighted score at $.6745\sigma$ below the mean of the group.
   (b) Calculate zero point for each age level by the formula

$$\frac{Y + z'}{Y} = \text{I.Q.}$$

   (where Y = zero point, $z' = -.6745$ and I.Q.$' = .90$).
   Obviously when I.Q.$'$ is set at 90 the zero point then will be equal to 6.745.
   (c) With the zero point at 6.745, get I.Q. for every weighted score in

each age level by (1) looking up charts containing "z" scores and their corrsponding weighted scores and then (2) solving the formula:

$$I.Q._a = \frac{6.745 + z_a}{6.745}$$

where I.Q.: = I.Q. for particular weighted score at any age and z: = "z" score for particular weighted score at any age.

. EQUATIONS FOR PREDICTING MEAN BELLEVUE TEST SCORES FOR ANY AGE—25 AND OVER

1. From equation obtained by method of least squares.

$$y = .746x + 81.63$$

Where y = mean (most representative) score at any age and x = difference between 47.5 and the chronological age (A) at which score is desired.

Illustration: Required mean score for age 57.5.

$$y = .746 (47.5 - 57.5) + 81.63 = 74.2$$

2. From regression equation of the two variables, age on test score.

$$y = .735x + 85.77$$

where y = mean (most representative) score at any age, and x = difference between 40 and the chronological age (A) at which score is desired.

Illustration: Required mean score at age 70.

$$y = .735 (40 - 70) + 85.77 = 63.7$$

N.B.: Equation (1) seems to give better values, but the dlcrepancies in score obtained by the two methods are very slight (seldom more than 1 or 2 points).

Conversely, one may use the above equations to calculate the age for which any given score is the mean. The case which is of particular interest is the age beyond which no further decline is possible. For our adult scale this age turns out to be approximtely 150 years. This value may be obtained from either equation. Thus from equation (1):

$$4 = .746 (47.5 - A) + 81.63$$

Setting y = 4 (lowest possible score).
Whence A = 151.5.

APPENDIX 2

EFFICIENCY QUOTIENTS

An individual's Efficiency Quotient is his mental ability score (on the Full Bellevue Adult Scale) when compared with the score of the average individual 20 to 24 years of age. We have chosen the age 20 to 24 as a standard of comparison because it may be regarded as our maximal age group. It is the age at which education for most adults is pretty much complete, and after which, again for most individuals, intelligence test scores begin to fall off. To get an E.Q. one obtains a subject's test score in the usual way, but instead of looking

TABLE 38
Efficiency Quotients (E.Q.)
Full Scale

WEIGHTED SCORE	E.Q.	WEIGHTED SCORE	E.Q.	WEIGHTED SCORE	E.Q.	WEIGHTED SCORE	E.Q.
5	34	35	56	65	77	95	98
6	35	36	56	66	77	96	99
7	35	37	57	67	78	97	99
8	36	38	57	68	79	98	100
9	37	39	58	69	79	99	101
10	37	40	59	70	80	100	101
11	38	41	59	71	81	101	102
12	39	42	60	72	81	102	103
13	40	43	61	73	82	103	104
14	40	44	62	74	83	104	104
15	41	45	62	75	84	105	105
16	42	46	63	76	84	106	106
17	42	47	64	77	85	107	106
18	43	48	64	78	86	108	107
19	44	49	65	79	86	109	108
20	44	50	66	80	87	110	109
21	45	51	67	81	88	111	109
22	46	52	67	82	89	112	110
23	47	53	68	83	89	113	111
24	47	54	69	84	90	114	111
25	48	55	69	85	91	115	112
26	49	56	70	86	92	120	116
27	49	57	71	87	92	125	119
28	50	58	72	88	93	130	123
29	51	59	72	89	94	135	126
30	52	60	73	90	94	140	130
31	52	61	74	91	95	145	133
32	53	62	74	92	96	150	137
33	54	63	75	93	96	155	141
34	55	64	76	94	97	160	144

up its positional rating under the subject's own age, one looks for it under the indices given for the age group 20–24. For the convenience of the reader these indices are now given apart and in more compact form. (See table 38.)

MEANS AND STANDARD DEVIATIONS OF SUBTESTS
TABLE 39
Verbal Subtests

AGE	N	INFORMATION		COMPRHENSION		ARITHMETIC		DIGIT SPAN		SIMILARITIES	
		Mean	S.D.	Mean	S.D.	Mean	S.D.	Mean	S.D.	Mean	S.D.
7	50	2.5	1.11	2.5	1.54	1.2	.97	5.2	2.52	3.0	1.08
8	50	2.9	1.56	3.8	1.94	1.9	1.94	5.7	2.16	3.6	1.55
9	50	3.9	2.01	4.9	1.85	3.6	2.31	6.8	2.5	5.0	1.66
10	60	5.7	2.38	6.5	1.97	5.3	2.7	7.4	2.14	6.7	2.06
11	60	7.6	3.24	7.5	2.34	7.1	3.35	8.5	2.61	7.7	2.49
12	60	9.8	2.89	8.6	2.59	8.1	2.71	7.9	2.33	8.8	2.13
13	70	9.9	3.13	9.0	2.80	8.8	2.44	9.1	2.00	9.3	2.00
14	70	10.5	2.82	9.6	2.72	9.0	2.78	8.6	2.36	9.6	2.16
15	100	10.6	2.61	9.8	2.93	8.9	2.54	9.0	2.63	9.6	2.13
16	100	10.4	2.75	10.0	2.98	9.1	2.72	8.8	2.63	9.8	2.19
17–19	100	10.5	2.88	9.9	3.07	8.5	2.67	9.3	2.74	9.5	2.25
20–24	120	10.4	2.86	10.0	2.76	9.8	2.60	10.1	2.96	10.2	2.06
25–29	125	10.1	2.98	10.7	3.10	9.7	2.91	9.9	3.13	10.0	2.40
30–34	110	9.8	3.12	9.7	3.15	9.2	3.31	8.95	3.41	9.5	2.76
35–39	100	9.8	3.37	9.8	3.18	9.1	3.08	8.7	3.12	9.4	2.67
40–44	75	10.1	3.70	10.0	3.32	8.9	3.84	9.0	2.92	9.7	2.67
45–49	60	9.5	3.21	9.5	3.33	9.2	2.94	7.8	2.52	9.3	2.90
50–54	45	9.6	4.08	9.5	3.00	8.3	2.85	7.7	3.11	8.8	2.94
55–59	36	9.5	3.86	8.8	2.87	6.9	4.18	7.5	3.23	7.9	3.38

MEANS AND STANDARD DEVIATIONS OF SUBTESTS
TABLE 40
Performance Subtests

AGE	N	PICTURE ARRANGEMENT		PICTURE COMPLETION		BLOCK DESIGN		OBJECT ASSEMBLY		DIGIT SYMBOL	
		Mean	S.D.	Mean	S.D.	Mean	S.D.	Mean	S.D.	Mean	S.D.
7	50	4.8	2.48	3.0	2.47	3.8	2.14	3.8	3.26	3.6	1.23
8	50	5.9	2.64	3.8	2.31	4.0	1.98	4.3	3.22	4.4	1.31
9	50	6.9	2.88	4.3	2.46	5.2	2.64	5.4	3.35	5.4	1.78
10	60	8.4	2.63	6.4	2.74	6.9	2.84	7.5	2.99	6.6	1.81
11	60	9.0	2.68	6.6	3.21	7.4	2.42	8.8	2.63	8.0	1.93
12	60	9.2	2.91	7.3	3.08	9.1	2.48	9.6	2.96	9.2	2.58
13	70	9.3	2.87	8.7	3.08	10.1	2.88	10.2	3.25	10.1	2.17
14	70	10.2	3.00	9.5	2.78	10.7	2.94	10.0	2.96	10.4	2.14
15	100	10.8	3.10	9.6	2.95	10.7	3.18	9.8	3.45	10.6	2.42
16	100	10.8	2.97	10.0	2.79	10.9	3.18	10.0	3.40	10.7	2.17
17–19	100	10.8	3.10	9.5	2.75	11.0	2.88	10.7	3.36	11.1	2.43
20–24	120	10.5	2.83	10.3	2.86	10.7	2.89	10.4	2.93	10.7	2.79
25–29	125	10.2	3.17	9.8	2.97	10.3	2.98	9.7	2.74	10.4	3.23
30–34	110	9.2	3.28	9.6	3.30	9.7	3.30	9.7	2.86	9.2	3.31
35–39	100	8.7	3.42	9.0	3.39	9.0	3.61	8.7	3.39	9.2	3.17
40–44	75	7.9	3.14	9.0	3.05	8.5	2.90	8.9	3.42	8.1	3.26
45–49	60	7.7	3.21	8.2	2.80	7.9	3.17	8.8	3.39	7.2	2.61
50–54	45	7.3	2.94	7.9	3.13	8.0	2.91	8.7	3.02	6.8	3.20
55–59	36	6.6	2.93	7.4	3.41	6.7	3.55	8.1	3.14	5.9	2.85

APPENDIX 3

CORRELATIONS

TABLE 41

Intertest correlations—each test with every other test—standard scores

Ages 20–34, 355 cases

	COMPRE-HENSION	INFOR-MATION	DIGIT SPAN	ARITHMETIC	PICTURE ARRANGE-MENT	PICTURE COMPLE-TION	BLOCK DESIGNS	OBJECT ASSEMBLY	DIGIT SYMBOL
Information	.668 ±.0198								
Digit Span	.444 ±.0287	.484 ±.0274							
Arithmetic	.517 ±.0262	.596 ±.0231	.443 ±.0288						
Picture Arrangement	.391 ±.0303	.384 ±.0305	.264 ±.0333	.366 ±.0309					
Picture Completion	.456 ±.0283	.465 ±.0283	.297 ±.0326	.403 ±.0299	.389 ±.0304				
Block Designs	.465 ±.0280	.488 ±.0273	.399 ±.0301	.514 ±.0263	.484 ±.0274	.566 ±.0255			
Object Assembly	.286 ±.0328	.224 ±.0339	.155 ±.0349	.233 ±.0338	.272 ±.0331	.439 ±.0288	.536 ±.0255		
Digit Symbol	.478 ±.0276	.561 ±.0245	.539 ±.0254	.429 ±.0292	.444 ±.0287	.400 ±.0300	.538 ±.0254	.319 ±.0322	
Similarities	.721 ±.0264	.679 ±.0297	.379 ±.0472	.600 ±.0352	.488 ±.04197	.456 ±.0436	.537 ±.0392	.306 ±.0499	.508 ±.0409

Note: All similarities intercorrelations based on data of 150 cases, ages 15–49. The remainder of the intercorrelations are based on the adult samplings of ages 20–34—355 cases.

TABLE 42

Interest correlations—each test with every other test—standard scores

Ages 35–49, 235 cases

	INFORMATION	COMPREHENSION	ARITHMETIC	DIGIT SPAN	PICTURE ARRANGEMENT	PICTURE COMPLETION	OBJECT ASSEMBLY	BLOCK DESIGNS
Comprehension	.705 ±.022							
Arithmetic	.594 ±.029	.534 ±.031						
Digit Span	.438 ±.036	.372 ±.034	.470 ±.034					
Picture Arrangement	.477 ±.034	.451 ±.035	.459 ±.035	.341 ±.039				
Picture Completion	.492 ±.034	.465 ±.035	.420 ±.036	.288 ±.040	.482 ±.034			
Object Assembly	.416 ±.036	.357 ±.038	.352 ±.039	.274 ±.041	.359 ±.038	.467 ±.034		
Block Designs	.597 ±.028	.516 ±.032	.519 ±.032	.416 ±.036	.365 ±.038	.534 ±.031	.506 ±.033	
Digit Symbol	.563 ±.030	.516 ±.032	.552 ±.031	.523 .032	.516 ±.032	.433 ±.036	.377 ±.038	.613 ±.028

TABLE 43

Correlations—each test vs. total minus the test (standard scores)

Ages 20–34, 355 cases

TEST	r	P.E.	ETA	BLAKEMAN'S CRITERION	
Information	.667	±.0198	.669	1.03	Linear
Comprehension	.661	±.0201	.668	3.30	Linear
Digit Span	.509	±.0265	.531	8.12	Linear
Arithmetic	.625	±.0218	.626	.639	Linear
Picture Arrangement	.514	±.0263	.548	12.89	Non-linear
Picture Completion	.605	±.0226	.619	6.11	Linear
Object Assembly	.409	±.0297	.435	7.63	Linear
Block Design	.714	±.0175	.721	3.58	Linear
Digit Symbol	.673	±.0195	.696	11.15	Linear
Similarities	.727	±.0260	.764	8.25	Linear

Note: Similarities correlation based on data of 150 cases, ages 15–49.

TABLE 44

Correlation—each test vs. total minus the test (standard scores)

Ages 35–49, 235 cases

TEST	r	P.E.	ETA	BLAKEMAN'S CRITERION	
Information...................	.705	±.0221	.724	6.380	Linear
Comprehension..............	.682	±.0237	.690	2.585	Linear
Digit Span.................	.517	±.0322	.530	3.290	Linear
Arithmetic.................	.671	±.0242	.679	2.600	Linear
Picture Arrangement........	.625	±.0269	.640	4.465	Linear
Picture Completion.........	.604	±.0279	.622	5.190	Linear
Object Assembly............	.508	±.0326	.562	13.560	Non-linear
Block Design...............	.727	±.0207	.763	12.880	Non-linear
Digit Symbol...............	.697	±.0226	.697	.000	Linear

APPENDIX 4

OBTAINING I.Q.'S FOR AGES BEYOND THOSE GIVEN IN TABLES

Although some 150 individuals between the ages of 60–80 were examined as part of our standardization, the number of subjects per 5 year interval for ages beyond 60, were generally too small to permit reliable calculation of I.Q.'s for all scores, on the basis of the data at hand. However, I.Q.'s for individuals between 60–80 may be extrapolated without serious error by the use of some simple multipliers which take care of the age factor. The multipliers have been obtained by plotting the successive I.Q. differences from ages 35 years and upwards, at different score levels, and then determining the rate change* in I.Q. per year. Evaluation of these changes give the following formulations:

Full Scale

a. When the subject attains a *weighted score below 60*, subtract 57.5 from the subject's age and multiply the age difference by 0.4; add this product to the I.Q. assigned to the weighted score made by the subject under age column 55–59 (Full scale I.Q. tables). The sum is the subject's corrected I.Q.

b. For subjects attaining *weighted scores above 60*, multiply the age difference by 0.3 and proceed as before.

Verbal Score

a. For subjects attaining *weighted scores below 40*, subtract 57.5 from the subject's age and multiply the age difference by 0.3. Add this product to the I.Q. assigned to the weighted score by the subject under age column 55–59 (Verbal I.Q. tables). The sum is the subject's corrected I.Q.

* The regression of I.Q. on age for any given score, beyond age 35, is practically a straight line.

b. For *weighted scores 40 and above,* multply the age difference by 0.2 and proceed as before.

Performance Scale

a. For *weighted scores below 25,* subtract 47.5 from the subject's age and multiply the age difference by 0.6. Add this product to the I.Q. assigned to the score made by the subject under age column 45–49 on the performance scale (Performance I.Q. tables). The sum is the subject's corrected I.Q.

b. For *weighted scores between 25–49* multiply age difference by 0.5 and proceed as before.

c. For *weighted scores between 50–69* multiply the age difference by 0.4.

d. For *weighted scores of 70 and over,* multiply the age difference by 0.3.

Examples:

1. *Subject age 68,* attaining *Full Scale* score of *85.* Subtract 57.5 from 68 (68 − 57.5 = 10.5). Since subject's score is above 60, multiply difference by 0.3 (0.3 × 10.5 = 3.2). Now look up subject's score (85) under age column 55–59 of Full Scale I.Q. table; the figure there given is 106. Adding 3.2 to 106 one gets 109.2 (or to nearest unit, 109), which is the subject's I.Q. corrected for age.

2. *Subject age 72,* attaining score of *34 on Performance Scale.* Subtract 47.5 from 72 (72 − 47.5 = 24.5). Since subject's score falls between 25 and 49, multply difference by 0.5 (0.5 × 24.5 = 12.3). Now look up subject's score (34) under age column 45–49 of Performance I.Q. tables; the figure there given is 97. Adding 12.3 to 97, one gets 109,which is the subject Performance I.Q. corrected for age.

APPENDIX 5

TABLE OF APPROXIMATE C.A. (ADULT M.A.) DENOMINATORS FOR BINET SCALES TO ALLOW FOR AGE FACTOR

TABLE 45

LIFE AGE	DENOMINATOR
20–24	15.5
25–29	15.0
30–34	14.5
35–39	14.0
40–44	13.5
45–49	13.0
50–54	12.5
55–59	12.0

N.B.: This table holds only for I.Q.'s about the mean. It is merely intended to indicate the approximate corrections required for the Binet Scales, in order to allow for the age factor.

APPENDIX 6

EQUIVALENTS OF WECHSLER-BELLVUE AND STANFORD I.Q. RATINGS IN TERMS OF COMPARABLE P.E. (AND PER-CENTILE) LIMITS

TABLE 46

| INCLUDED | | CLASSIFICATION* | BELLEVEUE* ADULT | OLD STANFORD TOTAL† | NEW STANFORD† | |
P.E.	Per-cent				8-12	14-18
−3 &	2.2	Mental defective	67–below	73–below	70–below	68–below
−2 to −3	6.7	Borderline	79–68	81–74	79–71	79–69
−1 to −2	16.1	Dull normal	90–79	91–82	91–80	91–81
1 to −1	50.0	Average	110–91	108–92	115–92	115–92
+1 to +2	16.1	High average to superior	119–111	109–17	116–125	116–126
+2 to +3	6.7	Superior	120–127	118–127	126–137	127–136
+3 &	2.2	Very superior	128–over	128–over	138–over	137–over

* See text, page 190.

† Conversions based on Merrill percentile distributions for Old and Revised Stanford. *Jour. Educa. Psychol.*, 1938, **29**: 641–651.

TABLE 47

Table of weighted scores

EQUIVALENT WEIGHTED SCORE	Information	Comprehension	Digit Span	Arithmetic	Similarites	Vocabulary	Picture Arrangement	Picture Completion	Block Design	Object Assembly	Digit Symbol	EQUIVALENT WEIGHTED SCORE
						RAW SCORE						
0		0	5	1		0		2		5-6	0-3	0
1	0	1		2	0	1-2	0	3	0	7	4-7	1
2	1	2	6		1-2	3-4	1	4	1-2	8	8-11	2
3	2-3	3	7	3	3	5-6	2-3	5	3-5	9	12-15	3
4	4-5	4	8	4	4	7-9	4	6	6-7	10-11	16-19	4
5	6	5-6			5-6	10-11	5		8-10	12	20-23	5
6	7-8	7	9	5	7	12-14	6	7	11-12	13	24-28	6
7	9	8	10	6	8	15-16	7-8	8	13-15	14-15	29-32	7
8	10-11	9			9-10	17-19	9	9	16-17	16	33-36	8
9	12	10	11	7	11	20-21	10	10	18-19	17	37-40	9
10	13-14	11	12	8	12	22-24	11	11	20-22	18	41-44	10
11	15-16	12-13	13		13-14	25-26	12-13		23-24	19	45-48	11
12	17	14		9	15	27-28	14	12	25-27	20-21	49-52	12
13	18-19	15	14	10	16	29-31	15	13	28-29	22	53-56	13
14	20	16	15		17-18	32-35	16-17	14	30-32	23	57-61	14
15	21-22	17		11	19	35-36	18	15	33-34	24	62-65	15
16	23	18	16	12	20	37-38	19		35-37	25	66-67	16
17	24	19	17	13	21-22	39-40	20 and		38 and	26		17
18	25	20		14	23-24	41-42	over		over			18

INTELLIGENCE QUOTIENTS TABLES

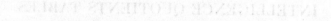

INTELLIGENCE QUOTIENTS—AGES 10—0 TO 10—11

FULL SCALE

WEIGHTED SCORE	10—0 I.Q.	10—3 I.Q.	10—6 I.Q.	10—9 I.Q.	WEIGHTED SCORE	10—0 I.Q.	10—3 I.Q.	10—6 I.Q.	10—9 I.Q.
5	54	51	49	47	65	108	105	102	99
6	55	52	50	48	66	109	106	103	100
7	56	53	51	49	67	110	107	104	101
8	57	54	52	50	68	111	108	105	102
9	58	55	53	51	69	112	109	106	103
10	59	56	54	52	70	113	110	107	104
11	59	56	54	52	71	114	111	108	105
12	60	57	55	53	72	115	112	109	106
13	61	58	56	54	73	116	113	110	107
14	62	59	57	55	74	117	113	110	107
15	63	60	58	56	75	118	114	111	108
16	64	61	59	57	76	118	115	112	109
17	65	62	60	58	77	119	116	113	110
18	66	63	61	50	78	120	117	114	111
19	67	64	62	60	79	121	118	115	112
20	67	64	62	60	80	122	119	116	112
21	68	65	63	61	81	123	120	117	114
22	69	66	64	62	82	124	120	117	114
23	70	67	65	63	83	125	121	118	115
24	71	68	66	64	84	126	122	119	116
25	72	69	67	65	85	127	123	120	117
26	73	70	68	66	86	128	124	121	118
27	74	71	69	66	87	129	125	112	119
28	75	72	70	67	88	130	126	123	120
29	76	73	70	68	89	131	127	124	121
30	77	74	71	69	90	131	128	125	122
31	78	75	72	70	91	132	129	126	123
32	79	76	73	71	92	133	129	126	123
33	79	76	74	72	93	134	130	127	124
34	80	77	75	72	94	135	131	128	125
35	81	78	76	73	95	136	132	129	126
36	82	79	77	74	96	137	133	130	127
37	83	80	77	75	97	138	134	131	128
38	84	81	78	76	98	139	135	132	129
39	85	82	79	77	99	140	136	133	130
40	86	83	80	78	100	140	137	133	130
41	87	84	81	78	101	141	137	134	131
42	88	85	82	79	102	142	138	135	132
43	89	86	83	80	103	143	139	136	133
44	90	87	84	81	104	144	140	137	134
45	91	88	85	82	105	145	141	138	135
46	92	89	86	83	106	146	142	139	136
47	92	89	86	83	107	147	143	140	137
48	93	90	87	84	106	148	144	141	138
49	94	91	88	85	109	149	145	142	139
50	95	92	89	86	110	149	145	142	139
51	96	93	90	87	111	150	146	143	140
52	97	94	91	88	112	151	147	144	141
53	98	95	92	89	113	152	148	145	142
54	99	96	93	90	114	153	149	146	143
55	100	97	94	91	115	154	150	147	144
56	100	97	94	91	120	158	154	151	148
57	101	98	95	92	125	163	159	156	153
58	102	99	96	93	130	168	164	160	157
59	103	100	97	94	135	172	168	165	162
60	104	101	98	95	140	177	173	169	166
61	105	102	99	96	145	181	177	173	170
62	106	103	100	97	150	186	182	178	175
63	107	104	101	98	155	190	186	182	179
64	108	105	102	99	160	195	191	187	184

INTELLIGENCE QUOTIENTS—AGES 11—0 TO 11—11

FULL SCALE

WEIGHTED SCORE	11—0 I.Q.	11—3 I.Q.	11—6 I.Q.	11—9 I.Q.	WEIGHTED SCORE	11—0 I.Q.	11—3 I.Q.	11—6 I.Q.	11—9 I.Q.
5	45	43	42	40	65	97	95	93	91
6	46	44	43	41	66	98	96	94	92
7	47	45	43	41	67	99	97	95	93
8	48	46	44	42	68	100	98	96	94
9	49	47	45	43	69	101	98	96	94
10	50	48	46	44	70	102	99	97	95
11	50	48	47	45	71	103	100	98	96
12	51	49	47	45	72	104	101	99	97
13	52	50	48	46	73	105	102	100	98
14	53	51	49	47	74	105	103	101	99
15	54	52	50	48	75	106	104	102	100
16	55	53	51	49	76	107	104	102	100
17	56	54	52	50	77	108	105	103	101
18	57	55	53	51	78	109	106	104	102
19	58	56	54	52	69	110	107	105	103
20	58	56	54	52	80	111	108	106	104
21	59	57	55	53	81	112	109	107	105
22	60	58	56	54	82	112	110	108	106
23	61	59	57	55	83	113	110	108	106
24	62	60	58	56	84	114	111	109	107
25	63	61	59	57	85	115	112	110	108
26	64	62	60	58	86	116	113	111	109
27	64	62	60	58	87	117	114	112	110
28	65	63	61	59	88	118	115	113	110
29	66	64	62	60	89	119	116	114	111
30	67	65	63	61	90	120	117	115	112
31	68	66	64	62	91	121	118	115	113
32	69	67	65	63	92	121	118	116	114
33	70	68	66	64	93	122	119	117	114
34	70	68	66	64	94	123	120	118	115
35	71	69	67	65	95	124	121	119	116
36	72	70	68	66	96	125	122	120	117
37	73	71	69	67	97	125	122	120	118
38	74	72	70	68	98	126	123	121	119
39	75	73	71	69	99	127	124	122	120
40	76	74	72	70	100	128	125	123	120
41	76	74	72	70	101	129	126	124	121
42	77	75	73	71	102	130	127	125	122
43	78	76	74	72	103	131	128	126	123
44	79	77	75	73	104	131	128	126	124
45	80	78	76	74	105	132	129	127	125
46	81	79	77	75	106	133	130	128	125
47	81	79	77	75	107	134	131	129	126
48	82	80	78	76	108	135	132	130	127
49	83	81	79	77	109	136	133	131	128
50	84	82	80	78	110	137	134	132	129
51	85	83	81	79	111	137	134	132	130
52	86	84	82	80	112	138	135	133	130
53	87	85	83	81	113	139	136	134	131
54	88	86	84	82	114	140	137	135	132
55	89	86	84	82	115	141	138	136	133
56	89	87	85	83	120	145	142	140	137
57	90	88	86	84	125	150	147	145	142
58	91	89	87	85	130	154	151	149	146
59	92	90	88	86	135	159	156	153	150
60	93	91	89	87	140	163	160	157	154
61	94	92	90	88	145	167	164	162	159
62	95	92	90	88	150	172	169	166	163
63	96	93	91	89	155	176	173	170	167
64	97	94	92	90	160	181	178	175	172

INTELLIGENCE QUOTIENTS—AGES 12—0 TO 12—11

FULL SCALE

WEIGHTED SCORE	12—0 I.Q.	12—3 I.Q.	12—6 I.Q.	12—9 I.Q.	WEIGHTED SCORE	12—0 I.Q.	12—3 I.Q.	12—6 I.Q.	12—9 I.Q.
5	38	36	35	33	65	89	87	85	83
6	39	37	36	34	66	90	88	86	84
7	40	38	37	35	67	91	89	87	85
8	41	39	38	36	68	92	90	88	86
9	42	40	39	37	69	92	90	89	87
10	42	40	39	37	70	93	91	89	87
11	43	41	40	38	71	94	92	90	88
12	44	42	41	39	72	95	93	91	89
13	45	43	42	40	73	96	94	92	90
14	46	44	43	41	74	97	95	93	91
15	47	45	44	42	75	98	96	94	92
16	48	46	45	43	76	98	96	95	93
17	48	46	45	43	77	99	97	95	93
18	49	47	46	44	78	100	98	96	94
19	50	48	47	45	79	101	99	97	95
20	51	49	48	46	80	102	100	98	96
21	52	50	49	47	81	103	101	99	97
22	53	51	50	48	82	104	102	100	98
23	53	51	50	48	83	104	102	100	98
24	54	52	51	49	84	105	103	101	99
25	55	53	52	50	85	106	104	102	100
26	56	54	53	51	86	107	105	103	101
27	57	55	54	52	87	108	106	104	102
28	57	55	54	52	88	108	106	104	102
29	58	56	55	53	89	109	107	105	103
30	59	57	56	54	90	110	108	106	104
31	60	58	57	55	91	111	109	107	105
32	61	59	58	56	92	112	110	108	106
33	62	60	59	57	93	112	110	108	106
34	63	61	60	58	94	113	111	109	107
35	63	61	60	58	95	114	112	110	108
36	64	62	61	59	96	115	113	111	109
37	65	63	62	60	97	116	114	112	110
38	66	64	63	61	98	117	115	113	111
39	67	65	64	62	99	118	116	114	112
40	68	66	65	63	100	118	116	114	112
41	68	66	65	63	101	119	117	115	113
42	69	67	66	64	102	120	118	116	114
43	70	68	67	65	103	121	119	117	115
44	71	69	68	66	104	122	120	118	116
45	72	70	69	67	105	123	121	119	117
46	73	71	69	67	106	123	121	119	117
47	73	71	70	68	107	124	122	120	118
48	74	72	71	69	108	125	123	121	119
49	75	73	72	70	109	126	124	122	120
50	76	74	73	71	110	127	125	123	121
51	77	75	74	72	111	128	126	124	122
52	78	76	74	72	112	128	126	124	122
53	79	77	75	73	113	129	127	125	123
54	80	78	76	74	114	130	128	126	124
55	80	78	77	75	115	131	129	127	125
56	81	79	78	76	120	135	133	131	129
57	82	80	79	77	125	140	137	135	133
58	83	81	80	78	130	144	141	139	137
59	84	82	80	78	135	148	146	144	142
60	85	83	81	79	140	152	150	148	146
61	86	84	82	80	145	157	154	152	150
62	86	84	83	81	150	161	158	156	154
63	87	85	84	82	155	165	162	160	158
64	88	86	85	83	160	170	167	165	163

INTELLIGENCE QUOTIENTS—AGES 13—0 TO 13—11
FULL SCALE

WEIGHTED SCORE	13—0 I.Q.	13—3 I.Q.	13—6 I.Q.	13—9 I.Q.	WEIGHTED SCORE	13—0 I.Q.	13—3 I.Q.	13—6 I.Q.	13—9 I.Q.
5	32	31	30	29	65	82	81	80	79
6	33	32	31	30	66	83	81	80	79
7	34	33	32	31	67	84	82	81	80
8	35	34	33	32	68	85	83	82	81
9	36	34	33	32	69	86	84	83	82
10	36	35	34	33	70	86	85	84	83
11	37	36	35	34	71	87	86	85	84
12	38	37	36	35	72	88	86	85	84
13	39	38	37	36	73	89	87	86	85
14	40	39	38	37	74	90	88	87	86
15	41	39	38	37	75	91	89	88	87
16	42	40	39	38	76	92	90	89	88
17	42	41	40	39	77	92	90	89	88
18	43	42	41	40	78	93	91	90	89
19	44	43	42	41	79	94	92	91	90
20	45	44	43	42	80	95	93	92	91
21	46	44	43	42	81	96	94	93	92
22	47	45	44	43	82	97	95	94	93
23	47	46	45	44	83	97	95	94	93
24	48	47	46	45	84	98	96	95	94
25	49	48	47	46	85	99	97	96	95
26	50	49	48	47	86	100	98	97	96
27	51	49	48	47	87	101	99	98	97
28	51	50	49	48	88	101	99	98	97
29	52	51	50	49	89	102	100	99	98
30	53	52	51	50	90	103	101	100	99
31	54	53	52	51	91	104	102	101	100
32	55	53	52	51	92	105	103	102	101
33	56	54	53	52	93	105	104	103	102
34	57	55	54	53	94	106	104	103	102
35	57	56	55	54	95	107	105	104	103
36	58	57	56	55	96	108	106	105	104
37	59	58	57	56	97	109	107	106	105
38	60	58	57	56	98	110	108	107	106
39	61	59	58	57	99	110	108	107	106
40	62	60	59	58	100	111	109	108	107
41	62	61	60	59	101	112	110	109	108
42	63	62	61	60	102	113	111	110	109
43	64	62	61	60	103	114	112	111	110
44	65	63	62	61	104	115	113	112	110
45	66	64	63	62	105	115	113	112	111
46	66	65	64	63	106	116	114	113	112
47	67	66	65	64	107	117	115	114	113
48	68	67	66	65	108	118	116	115	114
49	69	67	66	65	109	119	117	116	115
50	70	68	67	66	110	119	117	116	115
51	71	69	68	67	111	120	118	117	116
52	71	70	69	68	112	121	119	118	117
53	72	71	70	69	113	122	120	119	118
54	73	71	70	69	114	123	121	120	119
55	74	72	71	70	115	124	122	121	120
56	75	73	72	71	120	128	126	125	124
57	76	74	73	72	125	132	130	129	128
58	77	75	74	73	130	136	134	133	132
59	77	76	75	74	135	140	138	137	136
60	78	76	75	74	140	144	142	141	140
61	79	77	76	75	145	148	146	145	144
62	80	78	77	76	150	152	150	149	148
63	81	79	78	77	155	156	154	153	152
64	82	80	79	78	160	161	159	158	157

INTELLIGENCE QUOTIENTS—AGES 14—0 TO 14—11
FULL SCALE

WEIGHTED SCORES	14—0 I.Q.	14—3 I.Q.	14—6 I.Q.	WEIGHTED SCORES	14—0 I.Q.	14—3 I.Q.	14—6 I.Q.
5	29	28	28	65	78	77	77
6	30	29	29	66	79	78	78
7	31	30	30	67	80	79	79
8	32	31	31	68	80	79	79
9	32	32	32	69	81	80	80
10	33	32	32	70	82	81	81
11	34	33	33	71	83	82	82
12	35	34	34	72	84	83	83
13	36	35	35	73	85	84	84
14	37	36	36	74	85	84	84
15	37	37	37	75	86	85	85
16	38	37	37	76	87	86	86
17	39	38	38	77	88	87	87
18	40	39	39	78	89	88	88
19	41	40	40	79	89	88	88
20	42	41	41	80	90	89	89
21	42	41	41	81	91	90	90
22	43	42	42	82	92	91	91
23	44	43	43	83	93	92	92
24	45	44	44	84	93	92	92
25	46	45	45	85	94	93	93
26	46	45	45	86	95	94	94
27	47	46	46	87	96	95	95
28	48	47	47	88	96	95	95
29	49	48	48	89	97	96	96
30	50	49	49	90	98	97	97
31	50	49	49	91	99	98	98
32	51	50	50	92	100	99	99
33	52	51	51	93	101	100	100
34	53	52	52	94	101	100	100
35	54	53	53	95	102	101	101
36	55	54	53	96	103	102	102
37	55	54	54	97	104	103	103
38	56	55	55	98	105	104	104
39	57	56	56	99	105	104	104
40	58	57	57	100	106	105	105
41	59	58	58	101	107	106	106
42	59	58	58	102	108	107	107
43	60	59	59	103	109	108	108
44	61	60	60	104	109	108	108
45	62	61	61	105	(101)	109	109
46	63	62	62	106	111	110	110
57	63	62	62	107	112	111	111
48	64	63	63	108	113	112	112
49	65	64	64	109	114	113	112
50	66	65	65	110	114	113	113
51	67	66	66	111	115	114	114
52	67	66	66	112	116	115	115
53	68	67	67	113	117	116	116
54	69	68	68	114	118	117	117
55	70	69	69	115	119	118	118
56	71	70	70	120	123	122	122
57	71	70	70	125	127	126	126
58	72	71	71	130	131	130	130
59	73	72	72	135	135	134	134
60	74	73	73	140	139	138	138
61	75	74	74	145	143	142	142
62	75	74	74	150	147	146	146
63	76	75	75	155	151	150	150
64	77	76	76	160	156	155	154

INTELLIGENCE QUOTIENTS—AGES 15 TO 19

FULL SCALE

WEIGHTED SCORE	15 I.Q.	16 I.Q.	17-19 I.Q.	WEIGHTED SCORE	15 I.Q.	16 I.Q.	17-19 I.Q.
5	29	28	29	65	76	76	75
6	30	29	30	66	77	76	76
7	31	30	31	67	78	77	77
8	31	31	32	68	79	78	77
9	32	32	32	69	80	79	78
10	33	32	33	70	80	79	79
11	34	33	34	71	81	80	80
12	35	34	35	72	82	81	80
13	35	35	35	73	83	82	81
14	36	35	36	74	83	83	82
15	37	36	37	75	84	83	83
16	38	37	38	76	85	84	83
17	39	38	39	77	86	85	84
18	39	39	39	78	87	86	85
19	40	39	40	79	87	86	86
20	41	40	41	80	88	87	86
21	42	41	42	81	89	88	87
22	43	42	42	82	90	89	88
23	43	43	43	83	90	90	89
24	44	43	44	84	91	90	90
25	45	44	45	85	92	91	90
26	46	45	45	86	93	92	91
27	46	46	46	87	94	93	92
28	47	46	47	88	94	94	93
29	48	47	48	89	95	94	93
30	49	48	48	90	96	95	94
31	50	49	49	91	97	96	95
32	50	50	50	92	98	97	96
33	51	50	51	93	98	97	96
34	52	51	51	94	99	98	97
35	53	52	52	95	100	99	98
36	53	53	53	96	101	100	99
37	54	53	54	97	102	101	99
38	55	54	55	98	102	101	100
39	56	55	55	99	103	102	101
40	57	56	56	100	104	103	102
41	57	57	57	101	105	104	102
42	58	57	57	102	105	105	103
43	59	58	58	103	106	105	104
44	60	59	59	104	107	106	105
45	61	60	60	105	108	107	106
46	61	61	61	106	109	108	106
47	62	61	61	107	109	109	107
48	63	62	62	108	110	109	108
49	64	63	63	109	111	110	109
50	65	64	64	110	112	111	109
51	65	64	64	111	113	112	110
52	66	65	65	112	113	112	111
53	67	66	66	113	114	113	112
54	68	67	67	114	115	114	112
55	68	68	67	115	116	115	113
56	69	68	68	120	120	119	117
57	70	69	69	125	124	123	121
58	71	70	70	130	128	127	125
59	72	71	70	135	132	130	128
60	72	72	71	140	135	135	132
61	73	72	72	145	139	138	136
62	74	73	73	150	143	142	140
63	75	74	73	155	147	146	144
64	76	75	74	160	151	150	147

INTELLIGENCE QUOTIENTS—AGES 20 TO 39

FULL SCALE

WEIGHTED SCORE	20–24 I.Q.	25–29 I.Q.	30–34 I.Q.	35–39 I.Q.	WEIGHTED SCORE	20–24 I.Q.	25–49 I.Q.	30–34 I.Q.	35–39 I.Q.
5	34	39	43	47	65	77	80	83	86
6	35	40	44	48	66	77	80	83	87
7	35	40	44	49	67	78	81	84	87
8	36	41	45	49	68	79	82	84	88
9	37	42	46	50	69	79	82	85	89
10	37	42	46	50	70	80	83	86	89
11	38	43	47	51	71	81	84	86	90
12	39	44	47	52	72	81	84	87	90
13	40	44	48	52	73	82	85	88	91
14	40	45	49	53	74	83	86	88	92
15	41	46	50	54	75	84	86	89	92
16	42	46	50	54	76	84	87	90	93
17	42	47	51	55	77	85	88	90	94
18	43	48	51	56	78	86	88	91	94
19	44	48	52	56	79	86	89	92	95
20	44	49	53	57	80	87	90	92	96
21	45	50	53	57	81	88	90	93	96
22	46	50	54	58	82	89	91	94	97
23	47	51	55	59	83	89	92	94	97
24	47	52	56	59	84	90	93	95	98
25	48	52	56	60	85	91	93	96	99
26	49	53	57	61	86	92	94	96	99
27	49	54	57	61	87	92	94	97	100
28	50	54	58	62	88	93	95	98	101
29	51	55	59	62	89	94	96	98	101
30	52	56	59	63	90	94	96	99	102
31	52	57	60	64	91	95	97	100	103
32	53	57	61	64	92	96	98	100	103
33	54	58	61	65	93	96	99	101	104
34	55	58	62	66	94	97	99	102	104
35	55	59	63	66	95	98	100	102	105
36	56	60	63	67	96	99	101	103	105
37	57	61	64	68	97	99	101	104	106
38	57	61	65	68	98	100	102	104	106
39	58	62	65	69	99	101	103	105	107
40	59	63	66	69	100	101	103	106	108
41	59	63	67	70	101	102	104	106	108
42	60	64	67	71	102	103	105	107	109
43	61	65	68	71	103	104	105	108	110
44	62	65	69	72	104	104	106	108	110
45	62	66	69	73	105	105	107	109	111
46	63	67	70	73	106	106	107	110	111
47	64	67	71	74	107	106	108	110	112
48	64	68	71	75	108	107	109	111	113
49	65	69	72	75	109	108	110	111	113
50	66	69	73	76	110	109	110	112	114
51	67	70	73	77	111	109	111	113	115
52	67	71	74	78	112	110	112	114	115
53	68	71	74	78	113	111	112	114	116
54	69	72	75	79	114	111	113	115	117
55	69	73	76	80	115	112	114	115	117
56	70	74	77	80	120	116	117	119	120
57	71	74	77	81	125	119	120	122	124
58	72	75	78	82	130	123	124	125	127
59	72	76	79	82	135	126	127	129	130
60	73	76	79	83	140	130	130	132	133
61	74	77	80	83	145	133	134	135	136
62	74	78	80	84	150	137	137	139	139
63	75	78	81	85	155	141	141	142	143
64	76	79	82	85	160	144	144	145	146

INTELLIGENCE QUOTIENTS—AGES 40 TO 59
FULL SCALE

WEIGHTED SCORE	40-44 I.Q.	45-49 I.Q.	50-54 I.Q.	55-59 I.Q.	WEIGHTED SCORE	40-44 I.Q.	45-49 I.Q	50-54 I.Q.	55-59 I.Q.
5	50	53	55	58	65	88	90	93	94
6	51	54	56	58	66	88	91	93	95
7	51	54	56	59	67	89	91	94	95
8	52	55	57	60	68	90	92	94	96
9	53	55	58	60	69	90	92	95	96
10	53	56	58	61	70	91	93	95	97
11	54	57	59	61	71	91	94	96	98
12	55	57	59	62	72	92	94	96	98
13	55	58	60	63	73	93	95	97	99
14	56	59	61	63	74	93	96	97	100
15	57	59	61	64	75	94	96	98	100
16	57	60	62	64	76	94	97	99	101
17	58	60	62	65	77	95	97	99	101
18	58	61	63	66	78	96	98	100	102
19	59	62	64	66	79	96	99	101	102
20	60	62	64	67	80	97	99	101	103
21	60	63	65	67	81	98	100	102	104
22	61	63	66	68	82	98	100	103	104
23	61	64	66	69	83	99	101	103	105
24	62	65	67	69	84	100	102	104	106
25	63	65	68	70	85	100	102	104	106
26	63	66	68	70	86	101	103	105	107
27	64	67	69	71	87	101	104	105	107
28	65	67	69	72	88	102	104	106	108
29	65	68	70	72	89	103	105	107	109
30	66	68	71	73	90	103	105	107	109
31	67	69	71	73	91	104	106	108	110
32	67	70	72	74	92	104	107	109	110
33	68	70	72	75	93	105	107	109	111
34	68	71	73	75	94	106	108	110	112
35	69	71	74	76	95	106	108	110	112
36	70	72	74	77	96	107	109	111	113
37	70	73	75	77	97	108	110	112	113
38	71	73	75	78	98	108	110	112	114
39	71	74	76	78	99	109	111	113	115
40	72	75	77	79	100	110	112	114	115
41	73	75	77	80	101	110	112	114	116
42	73	76	78	80	102	111	113	115	116
43	74	76	78	81	103	111	113	115	117
44	75	77	79	81	104	112	114	116	118
45	75	78	80	82	105	113	114	117	118
46	76	78	80	82	106	113	115	117	119
47	76	79	81	83	107	114	116	118	119
48	77	79	82	84	108	114	116	118	120
49	78	80	82	84	109	115	117	119	121
50	78	81	83	85	110	116	118	120	121
51	79	81	83	86	111	116	118	120	122
52	80	82	84	86	112	117	119	121	122
53	80	83	85	87	113	118	119	122	123
54	81	83	85	87	114	118	120	122	124
55	81	84	86	88	115	119	121	123	124
56	82	84	86	89	120	122	124	126	127
57	83	85	87	89	125	125	127	129	130
58	83	86	88	90	130	128	130	132	133
59	84	86	89	90	135	131	133	135	136
60	85	87	90	91	140	134	136	138	139
61	85	87	90	92	145	137	139	141	142
62	86	88	91	92	150	141	142	144	145
63	86	89	91	93	155	144	145	147	148
64	87	89	92	93	160	147	148	150	152

INTELLIGENCE QUOTIENTS—AGES 10—0 TO 10—11
VERBAL SCALE

WEIGHTED SCORES	10—0 I.Q.	10—3 I.Q.	10—6 I.Q.	10—9 I.Q.	WEIGHTED SCORES	10—0 I.Q.	10—3 I.Q.	10—6 I.Q.	10—9 I.Q.
5	65	62	60	58	45	131	127	124	121
6	67	64	62	60	46	132	128	125	122
7	68	65	63	61	47	134	130	127	124
8	70	67	65	63	48	136	132	129	126
9	72	69	67	65	49	138	134	130	127
10	74	71	68	66	50	139	135	132	129
11	75	72	70	68	51	141	137	133	130
12	77	74	71	69	52	143	139	135	132
13	79	76	73	71	53	144	140	137	134
14	80	77	75	73	54	146	142	138	135
15	82	79	76	74	55	148	144	140	137
16	84	81	78	76	56	149	145	141	138
17	85	82	79	77	57	151	147	143	140
18	87	84	81	79	58	153	149	145	141
19	89	86	83	80	59	154	150	146	143
20	90	87	84	82	60	156	152	148	144
21	92	89	86	83	61	157	153	149	146
22	93	90	87	85	62	159	155	151	147
23	95	92	89	86	63	160	156	152	149
24	96	93	90	88	64	162	158	154	150
25	98	95	92	89	65	164	160	156	152
26	100	97	94	91	66	165	161	157	153
27	101	98	95	92	67	167	163	159	155
28	103	100	97	94	68	169	164	160	156
29	105	101	98	95	69	170	166	162	158
30	106	103	100	97	70	172	168	164	160
31	108	105	102	99	71	174	169	165	161
32	110	106	103	100	72	175	171	167	163
33	111	108	105	102	73	177	172	168	164
34	113	109	106	103	74	179	174	170	166
35	115	111	108	105	75	180	176	172	168
36	117	113	110	107	76	182	177	173	169
37	118	114	111	108	77	184	179	175	171
38	120	116	113	110	78	185	180	176	172
39	121	117	114	111	79	187	182	178	174
40	123	119	116	113	80	188	183	179	175
41	124	120	117	114	81	190	185	181	177
42	126	122	119	116	82	192	187	183	178
43	128	124	121	118	83	193	188	184	180
44	129	125	122	119	84	195	190	186	182

INTELLIGENCE QUOTIENTS—AGES 11—0 TO 11—11

VERBAL SCALE

WEIGHTED SCORES	11—0 I.Q.	11—3 I.Q.	11—6 I.Q.	11—9 I.Q.	WEIGHTED SCORES	11—0 I.Q.	11—3 I.Q.	11—6 I.Q.	11—9 I.Q.
5	56	54	53	51	45	118	115	113	111
6	58	56	55	53	46	119	116	114	112
7	59	57	56	54	47	121	118	116	114
8	61	59	58	56	48	123	120	117	115
9	63	61	59	57	49	·124	121	119	117
10	64	62	61	59	50	126	123	120	118
11	66	64	62	60	51	127	124	122	120
12	67	65	64	62	52	129	126	123	121
13	69	67	65	63	53	131	128	125	123
14	71	69	67	65	54	132	129	126	124
15	72	70	68	66	55	134	131	128	126
16	74	72	70	68	56	135	132	129	127
17	75	73	71	69	57	137	134	131	129
18	77	75	73	71	58	138	135	132	130
19	78	76	74	72	59	140	137	134	132
20	80	78	76	74	60	141	138	135	133
21	81	79	77	75	61	143	140	137	135
22	83	81	79	77	62	144	141	138	136
23	84	82	80	78	63	146	143	140	138
24	86	84	82	80	64	147	144	141	139
25	87	85	83	81	65	149	146	143	141
26	89	87	85	83	66	150	147	144	142
27	90	88	86	84	67	152	149	146	144
28	92	89	87	85	68	153	150	147	145
29	93	91	89	87	69	155	152	149	147
30	95	92	90	88	70	157	153	150	148
31	97	94	92	90	71	158	154	151	149
32	98	96	94	92	72	160	156	153	151
33	100	97	95	93	73	161	158	155	153
34	101	98	96	94	74	163	159	156	154
35	103	100	98	96	75	165	161	158	156
36	104	101	99	97	76	166	162	159	157
37	106	103	101	99	77	167	163	160	158
38	107	104	102	100	78	169	165	162	160
39	109	106	104	102	79	170	166	163	161
40	110	107	105	103	80	172	168	165	163
41	112	109	107	105	81	173	169	166	164
42	113	110	108	106	82	174	171	168	166
43	115	112	110	108	83	176	172	169	167
44	116	113	111	109	84	178	174	171	169

INTELLIGENCE QUOTIENTS—AGES 12—0 TO 12—11

VERBAL SCALE

WEIGHTED SCORES	12—0 I.Q.	12—3 I.Q.	12—6 I.Q.	12—9 I.Q.	WEIGHTED SCORES	12—0 I.Q.	12—3 I.Q.	12—6 I.Q.	12—9 I.Q.
5	50	48	47	46	45	109	107	106	105
6	51	49	48	47	46	110	108	107	106
7	53	51	50	49	47	112	110	109	108
8	54	52	51	50	48	113	111	110	109
9	56	54	53	52	49	115	113	112	111
10	57	55	54	53	50	116	114	113	112
11	59	57	56	55	51	118	116	115	114
12	61	59	57	56	52	119	117	116	115
13	62	60	59	58	53	121	119	118	117
14	63	61	60	59	54	122	120	119	118
15	65	63	62	61	55	124	122	121	120
16	66	64	63	62	56	125	123	122	121
17	68	66	65	64	57	127	125	124	122
18	69	67	66	65	58	128	126	125	124
19	71	69	68	67	59	130	128	127	125
20	72	70	69	68	60	131	129	128	127
21	74	72	71	70	61	133	131	130	128
22	75	73	72	71	62	134	132	131	130
23	77	75	74	73	63	136	134	133	131
24	78	76	75	74	64	137	135	134	133
25	80	78	77	76	65	139	137	136	134
26	81	79	78	77	66	140	138	137	136
27	82	80	79	78	67	142	140	139	137
28	84	82	81	80	68	143	141	140	138
29	85	83	82	81	69	145	143	142	140
30	87	85	84	83	70	146	144	143	141
31	88	86	85	84	71	148	146	145	143
32	90	88	87	86	72	149	147	146	144
33	91	89	88	87	73	151	149	148	146
34	93	91	90	89	74	152	150	149	147
35	94	92	91	90	75	154	152	150	149
36	96	94	93	92	76	155	153	152	150
37	97	95	94	93	77	156	154	153	151
38	99	97	96	95	78	158	156	155	153
39	100	98	97	96	79	159	157	156	154
40	102	100	99	98	80	161	159	158	156
41	103	101	100	99	81	162	160	159	157
42	105	103	102	101	82	164	162	161	159
43	106	104	103	102	83	165	163	162	160
44	108	106	105	104	84	167	165	164	162

INTELLIGENCE QUOTIENTS—AGES 13—0 TO 13—11

VERBAL SCALE

WEIGHTED SCORES	13—0 I.Q.	13—3 I.Q.	13—6 I.Q.	13—9 I.Q.	WEIGHTED SCORES	13—0 I.Q.	13—3 I.Q.	13—6 I.Q.	13—9 I.Q.
5	45	44	44	43	45	104	103	102	101
6	47	46	46	45	46	105	104	104	103
7	48	47	47	46	47	107	106	105	104
8	50	49	49	48	48	108	107	106	105
9	51	50	50	49	49	110	109	108	107
10	53	52	52	51	50	111	110	109	108
11	54	53	53	52	51	113	112	111	110
12	55	54	54	53	52	114	113	112	111
13	57	56	56	55	53	116	115	114	113
14	58	57	57	56	54	117	116	115	114
15	60	59	59	58	55	119	118	117	116
16	61	60	60	59	56	120	119	118	117
17	63	62	62	61	57	121	120	119	118
18	64	63	63	62	58	123	122	121	120
19	66	65	65	64	59	124	123	122	121
20	67	66	66	65	60	126	125	124	123
21	69	68	67	66	61	127	126	125	124
22	70	69	69	68	62	129	128	127	126
23	72	71	70	69	63	130	129	128	127
24	73	72	72	71	64	132	131	130	129
25	75	74	73	72	65	133	132	131	130
26	76	75	75	74	66	135	134	133	132
27	77	76	76	75	67	136	135	134	133
28	79	78	78	77	68	137	136	135	134
29	80	79	79	78	69	139	138	137	136
30	82	81	81	80	70	140	139	138	137
31	83	82	82	81	71	142	141	140	139
32	85	84	83	82	72	143	142	141	140
33	86	85	85	84	73	145	144	143	142
34	88	87	86	85	74	146	145	144	143
35	89	88	88	87	75	148	147	146	145
36	91	90	89	88	76	149	148	147	146
37	92	91	91	90	77	150	149	148	147
38	94	93	92	91	78	152	151	150	149
39	95	94	94	93	79	153	152	151	150
40	97	96	95	94	80	155	154	153	152
41	98	97	96	95	81	156	155	154	153
42	100	99	98	97	82	158	157	156	155
43	101	100	99	98	83	159	158	157	156
44	103	102	101	100	84	161	160	159	158

INTELLIGENCE QUOTIENTS—AGES 14—0 TO 14—11
VERBAL SCALE

WEIGHTED SCORES	14—0 I.Q.	14—3 I.Q.	14—6 I.Q.	WEIGHTED SCORES	14—0 I.Q.	14—3 I.Q.	14—6 I.Q.
5	43	43	43	45	101	100	100
6	45	44	44	46	103	102	102
7	46	46	46	47	104	103	103
8	48	47	47	48	105	104	104
9	49	48	48	49	107	106	106
10	51	50	50	50	108	107	107
11	52	51	51	51	110	109	109
12	53	53	53	52	111	110	110
13	55	54	54	53	113	112	112
14	56	56	56	54	114	113	113
15	58	57	57	55	115	114	114
16	59	58	58	56	117	116	116
17	61	60	60	57	118	117	117
18	62	61	61	58	120	119	119
19	64	63	63	59	121	120	120
20	65	64	64	60	123	122	122
21	66	66	66	61	124	123	123
22	68	67	67	62	125	124	124
23	69	68	68	63	127	126	126
24	71	70	70	64	128	127	127
25	72	71	71	65	130	129	129
26	74	73	73	66	131	130	130
27	75	74	74	67	133	132	132
28	77	76	76	68	134	133	133
29	78	77	77	69	136	135	135
30	80	79	79	70	137	136	136
31	81	80	80	71	138	137	137
32	82	81	81	72	140	139	139
33	84	83	83	73	141	140	140
34	85	84	84	74	143	142	142
35	87	86	86	75	144	143	143
36	88	87	87	76	146	145	145
37	90	89	89	77	147	146	146
38	91	90	90	78	148	147	147
39	92	91	91	79	150	149	149
40	94	93	93	80	151	150	150
41	95	94	94	81	153	152	152
42	97	96	96	82	154	153	153
43	98	97	97	83	156	155	155
44	100	99	99	84	157	156	156

INTELLIGENCE QUOTIENTS—AGES 15 TO 19

VERBAL SCALE

WEIGHTED SCORES	15 I.Q.	16 I.Q.	17–19 I.Q.	WEIGHTED SCORES	15 I.Q.	16 I.Q.	17–19 I.Q.
5	45	46	47	45	99	98	98
6	46	47	48	46	101	100	99
7	48	48	49	47	102	101	100
8	49	49	50	48	104	102	101
9	51	51	52	49	105	104	103
10	52	52	53	50	106	105	104
11	53	53	54	51	108	106	105
12	55	55	55	52	109	108	107
13	56	56	57	53	110	109	108
14	57	57	58	54	112	110	109
15	59	59	59	55	113	112	110
16	60	60	61	56	114	113	112
17	61	61	62	57	116	114	113
18	63	63	63	58	117	116	114
19	64	64	64	59	118	117	116
20	65	65	66	60	120	118	117
21	67	67	67	61	121	119	118
22	68	68	68	62	122	121	119
23	69	69	70	63	124	122	121
24	71	71	71	64	125	123	122
25	72	72	72	65	126	125	123
26	74	73	73	66	128	126	125
27	75	75	75	67	129	127	126
28	76	76	76	68.	131	129	127
29	78	77	77	69	132	130	128
30	79	79	79	70	133	131	130
31	80	80	80	71	135	133	131
32	82	81	81	72	136	134	132
33	83	83	82	73	137	135	134
34	84	84	84	74	139	137	135
35	86	85	85	75	140	138	136
36	87	86	86	76	141	139	137
37	89	88	88	77	143	141	139
38	90	89	89	78	144	142	140
39	91	90	90	79	145	143	141
40	93	92	91	80	147	144	143
41	94	93	93	81	148	146	144
42	95	94	94	82	149	147	145
43	97	96	95	83	151	148	146
44	98	97	96	84	152	150	148

INTELLIGENCE QUOTIENTS—AGES 20 TO 39

VERBAL SCALE

WEIGHTED SCORES	20–24 I.Q.	25–29 I.Q.	30–34 I.Q.	35–39 I.Q.	WEIGHTED SCORES	20–24 I.Q.	25–29 I.Q.	30–34 I.Q.	35–39 I.Q.
5	47	50	51	54	45	97	98	98	99
6	49	51	52	55	46	99	99	99	101
7	50	53	53	56	47	100	100	101	102
8	51	54	54	57	48	101	101	102	103
9	52	55	56	58	49	103	102	103	104
10	54	56	57	60	50	104	104	104	105
11	55	57	58	61	51	105	105	105	106
12	56	59	59	62	52	106	106	107	107
13	57	60	60	63	53	107	107	108	109
14	59	61	62	64	54	109	108	109	110
15	60	62	63	65	55	110	110	110	111
16	61	63	64	66	56	111	111	111	112
17	62	64	65	68	57	112	112	112	113
18	64	66	66	69	58	113	113	114	114
19	65	67	67	70	59	144	114	115	115
20	66	68	69	71	60	115	115	116	116
21	67	69	70	72	61	117	117	117	118
22	69	70	71	73	62	118	118	118	119
23	70	71	72	74	63	119	119	120	120
24	71	73	73	76	64	120	120	121	121
25	72	74	75	77	65	121	121	122	122
26	74	75	76	78	66	122	123	123	123
27	75	76	77	79	67	124	124	124	124
28	76	78	78	80	68	125	125	126	126
29	77	79	79	81	69	126	126	127	127
30	79	80	80	82	70	127	127	128	128
31	80	81	82	83	71	129	129	129	129
32	81	82	83	85	72	130	130	130	130
33	82	83	84	86	73	131	131	131	131
34	84	85	85	87	74	132	132	133	133
35	85	86	86	88	75	133	133	134	134
36	86	87	88	89	76	134	134	135	135
37	87	88	89	90	77	135	136	136	136
38	89	89	90	91	78	137	137	137	137
39	90	90	91	93	79	138	138	139	140
40	91	92	92	94	80	139	139	140	141
41	93	93	93	95	81	140	140	141	143
42	94	94	95	96	82	142	142	142	144
43	95	95	96	97	83	143	143	143	145
44	96	96	97	98	84	144	144	145	146

INTELLIGENCE QUOTIENTS—AGES 40 TO 59
VERBAL SCALE

WEIGHTED SCORES	40-44 I.Q.	45-49 I.Q.	50-54 I.Q.	55-59 I.Q.	WEIGHTED SCORES	40-44 I.Q.	45-49 I.Q.	50-54 I.Q.	55-59 I.Q.
5	56	58	61	63	45	101	102	103	104
6	57	59	62	64	46	102	103	104	105
7	58	61	63	65	47	103	104	105	106
8	59	62	64	66	48	104	105	106	107
9	60	63	65	67	49	105	106	107	108
10	62	64	66	68	50	106	107	108	109
11	63	65	67	69	51	107	108	109	110
12	64	66	68	70	52	108	109	110	111
13	65	67	69	71	53	109	110	111	112
14	66	68	70	72	54	111	111	112	113
15	67	69	71	73	55	112	113	114	114
16	68	70	72	74	56	113	114	115	115
17	69	71	73	75	57	114	115	116	116
18	70	72	74	76	58	115	116	117	117
19	72	74	75	77	59	116	117	118	118
20	73	75	76	79	60	117	118	119	119
21	74	76	78	80	61	118	119	120	120
22	75	77	79	81	62	120	120	121	121
23	76	78	80	82	63	121	121	122	122
24	77	79	81	83	64	122	122	123	123
25	78	80	82	84	65	123	123	124	124
26	79	81	83	85	66	124	124	125	125
27	80	82	84	86	67	125	125	126	126
28	82	83	85	87	68	126	127	127	127
29	83	84	86	88	69	127	128	128	129
30	84	85	87	89	70	128	129	130	130
31	85	86	88	90	71	129	130	131	131
32	86	87	89	91	72	130	131	132	132
33	87	89	90	92	73	132	132	133	133
34	88	90	91	93	74	133	133	134	134
35	89	91	92	94	75	134	134	135	135
36	91	92	93	95	76	135	135	136	136
37	92	93	95	96	77	136	136	137	137
38	93	94	96	97	78	137	137	138	138
39	94	95	97	98	79	138	138	139	139
40	95	96	98	99	80	140	139	140	140
41	96	97	99	100	81	141	141	141	141
42	97	98	100	101	82	142	142	142	142
43	98	99	101	102	83	143	143	143	143
44	99	101	102	103	84	144	144	144	144

INTELLIGENCE QUOTIENTS—AGES 10—0 TO 10—11
PERFORMANCE SCALE

WEIGHTED SCORES	10—0 I.Q.	10—3 I.Q.	10—6 I.Q.	10—9 I.Q.	WEIGHTED SCORES	10—0 I.Q.	10—3 I.Q.	10—6 I.Q.	10—9 I.Q.
5	63	61	59	57	45	125	123	121	118
6	65	63	61	59	46	127	124	122	119
7	66	64	62	60	47	129	126	124	121
8	68	66	64	62	48	130	127	125	123
9	69	67	65	63	49	132	129	127	124
10	71	69	67	65	50	133	130	128	125
11	72	70	68	66	51	135	132	130	127
12	74	72	70	68	52	136	133	131	128
13	75	73	71	69	53	138	135	133	130
14	77	75	73	71	54	140	137	135	132
15	79	77	75	73	55	141	138	136	133
16	80	78	76	74	56	143	140	138	135
17	81	79	77	75	57	144	141	139	136
18	83	81	79	77	58	146	143	141	138
19	85	83	81	79	59	148	145	143	140
20	86	84	82	80	60	149	146	144	141
21	88	86	84	82	61	150	147	145	142
22	89	87	85	83	62	152	149	147	144
23	91	89	87	85	63	153	150	148	145
24	92	90	88	86	64	155	152	150	147
25	94	92	90	88	65	156	153	151	148
26	95	93	91	89	66	158	155	153	150
27	97	95	93	91	67	160	157	155	152
28	99	97	95	92	68	161	158	156	153
29	100	98	96	94	69	163	160	158	155
30	102	100	98	95	70	164	161	159	156
31	103	101	99	97	71	165	163	161	158
32	105	103	101	98	72	167	164	162	159
33	107	104	102	100	73	169	166	164	161
34	108	106	104	101	74	171	168	165	162
35	110	107	105	103	75	172	169	167	164
36	111	109	107	104	76	174	171	168	165
37	113	110	108	106	77	175	172	170	167
38	114	112	110	107	78	177	174	171	168
39	116	113	111	109	79	179	176	173	170
40	118	115	113	110	80	180	177	175	172
41	119	117	115	112	81	182	179	176	173
42	121	118	116	113	82	183	180	178	175
43	122	120	118	115	83	185	181	179	176
44	124	121	119	116	84	186	183	181	178

INTELLIGENCE QUOTIENTS—AGES 11—0 TO 11—11

PERFORMANCE SCALE

WEIGHTED SCORES	11—0 I.Q.	11—3 I.Q.	11—6 I.Q.	11—9 I.Q.	WEIGHTED SCORES	11—0 I.Q.	11—3 I.Q.	11—6 I.Q.	11—9 I.Q.
5	55	53	52	50	45	116	114	112	110
6	57	55	54	52	46	117	115	113	111
7	58	56	55	53	47	119	117	115	113
8	60	58	57	55	48	120	118	116	114
9	61	59	58	56	49	122	120	118	116
10	63	61	60	58	50	123	121	119	117
11	64	62	61	59	51	125	123	121	119
12	66	64	62	60	52	126	124	122	120
13	67	65	64	62	53	128	126	124	122
14	69	67	66	64	54	130	127	125	123
15	71	69	67	65	55	131	129	127	125
16	72	70	69	67	56	133	130	128	126
17	73	71	70	68	57	134	132	130	128
18	75	73	72	70	58	136	133	131	129
19	77	75	73	71	59	138	135	133	131
20	78	76	74	72	60	139	136	134	132
21	80	78	76	74	61	140	138	136	134
22	81	79	77	75	62	142	139	137	135
23	83	81	79	77	63	143	141	139	137
24	84	82	81	79	64	145	142	140	138
25	86	84	82	80	65	146	144	142	140
26	87	85	83	81	66	148	145	143	141
27	89	87	85	83	67	150	147	145	143
28	90	88	86	84	68	151	148	146	144
29	92	90	88	86	69	153	150	148	146
30	93	91	89	87	70	154	151	149	147
31	95	93	91	89	71	155	152	150	148
32	96	94	92	90	72	157	154	152	150
33	98	96	94	92	73	159	156	154	152
34	99	97	95	93	74	160	157	155	153
35	101	99	97	95	75	161	158	156	154
36	102	100	98	96	76	163	160	158	156
37	104	102	100	98	77	164	161	159	157
38	105	103	101	99	78	166	163	161	159
39	107	105	103	101	79	167	164	162	160
40	108	106	104	102	80	169	166	164	162
41	110	108	106	104	81	170	167	165	163
42	111	109	107	105	82	172	169	167	165
43	113	111	109	107	83	173	170	168	166
44	114	112	110	108	84	175	172	170	168

INTELLIGENCE QUOTIENTS—AGES 12—0 TO 12—11

PERFORMANCE SCALE

WEIGHTED SCORE	12—0 I.Q.	12—3 I.Q.	12—6 I.Q.	12—9 I.Q.	WEIGHTED SCORE	12—0 I.Q.	12—3 I.Q.	12—6 I.Q.	12—9 I.Q.
5	48	46	44	42	45	108	106	104	102
6	50	48	46	44	46	109	107	105	103
7	51	49	47	45	47	111	109	107	105
8	53	51	49	47	48	112	110	108	106
9	54	52	50	48	49	114	112	110	108
10	56	54	52	50	50	115	113	111	109
11	57	55	53	51	51	117	115	113	111
12	58	56	55	53	52	118	116	114	112
13	60	58	56	54	53	120	118	116	114
14	62	60	58	56	54	121	119	117	115
15	63	61	59	57	55	123	121	119	117
16	65	63	61	59	56	124	122	120	118
17	66	64	62	60	57	126	124	122	120
18	68	66	64	62	58	127	125	123	121
19	69	67	65	63	59	129	127	125	123
20	70	68	67	65	60	130	128	126	124
21	72	70	68	66	61	132	130	128	126
22	73	71	70	68	62	133	131	129	127
23	75	73	71	69	63	135	133	131	129
24	77	75	73	71	64	136	134	132	130
25	78	76	74	72	65	138	136	134	132
26	79	77	76	74	66	139	137	135	133
27	81	79	77	75	67	141	139	137	135
28	82	80	79	77	68	142	140	138	136
29	84	82	80	78	69	144	142	140	138
30	85	83	82	80	70	145	143	141	139
31	87	85	83	81	71	146	144	143	141
32	88	86	85	83	72	148	146	144	142
33	90	88	86	84	73	150	148	146	144
34	91	89	87	85	74	151	149	147	145
35	93	91	89	87	75	153	151	149	147
36	94	92	90	88	76	154	152	150	148
37	96	94	92	90	77	155	153	151	149
38	97	95	94	92	78	157	155	153	151
39	99	97	95	93	79	159	157	155	153
40	100	98	96	94	80	160	158	156	154
41	102	100	98	96	81	161	159	158	156
42	103	101	99	97	82	163	161	159	157
43	105	103	101	99	83	164	162	160	158
44	106	104	102	100	84	166	164	162	160

INTELLIGENCE QUOTIENTS—AGES 13—0 TO 13—11

PERFORMANCE SCALE

WEIGHTED SCORE	13—0 I.Q.	13—3 I.Q.	13—6 I.Q.	13—9 I.Q.	WEIGHTED SCORE	13—0 I.Q.	13—3 I.Q.	13—6 I.Q.	13—9 I.Q.
5	41	40	39	38	45	101	99	98	97
6	43	41	40	39	46	102	101	100	99
7	44	43	42	41	47	104	102	101	100
8	46	44	43	42	48	105	104	103	102
9	47	45	44	43	49	107	105	104	103
10	49	47	46	45	50	108	107	106	105
11	50	48	47	46	51	110	108	107	106
12	52	50	49	48	52	111	110	109	108
13	53	51	50	49	53	113	111	110	109
14	55	53	52	51	54	114	113	112	111
15	56	54	53	52	55	116	114	113	112
16	58	56	55	54	56	117	116	115	114
17	59	57	56	55	57	119	117	116	115
18	61	59	58	57	58	120	119	118	117
19	62	60	59	58	59	122	120	119	118
20	64	62	61	59	60	123	122	121	120
21	65	63	62	61	61	125	123	122	121
22	67	65	64	63	62	126	125	124	123
23	68	67	65	64	63	128	127	125	124
24	70	68	67	66	64	129	128	127	126
25	71	69	68	67	65	131	129	128	127
26	73	71	70	69	66	132	131	130	129
27	74	72	71	70	67	134	132	131	130
28	76	74	73	72	68	135	134	133	132
29	77	75	74	73	69	137	135	134	133
30	79	77	76	75	70	138	137	136	135
31	80	78	77	76	71	140	138	137	136
32	82	80	79	78	72	141	140	139	138
33	83	81	80	79	73	143	141	140	139
34	84	83	82	81	74	144	143	142	141
35	86	84	83	82	75	146	144	143	142
36	87	86	85	84	76	147	146	145	144
37	89	87	86	85	77	148	147	146	145
38	91	89	88	87	78	150	149	148	147
39	92	90	89	88	79	152	150	149	148
40	93	92	91	90	80	153	151	150	149
41	95	93	92	91	81	155	153	152	151
42	96	95	94	93	82	156	154	153	152
43	98	96	95	94	83	157	156	155	154
44	99	98	97	96	84	159	157	156	155

INTELLIGENCE QUOTIENTS—AGES 14—0 TO 14—11

PERFORMANCE SCALE

WEIGHTED SCORE	14—0 I.Q.	14—3 I.Q.	14—6 I.Q.	WEIGHTED SCORE	14—0 I.Q.	14—3 I.Q.	14—6 I.Q.
5	37	36	35	45	96	95	95
6	38	37	37	46	98	97	97
7	40	39	38	47	99	98	98
8	41	40	40	48	101	100	100
9	42	41	41	49	102	101	101
10	44	43	43	50	104	103	103
11	45	44	44	51	105	104	104
12	47	46	46	52	107	106	106
13	48	47	47	53	108	107	107
14	50	49	49	54	110	109	109
15	51	50	50	55	111	110	110
16	53	52	52	56	113	112	112
17	54	53	53	57	114	113	113
18	56	55	55	58	116	115	115
19	57	56	56	59	117	116	116
20	59	58	58	60	119	118	117
21	60	59	59	61	120	119	119
22	62	61	61	62	122	121	120
23	63	62	62	63	123	122	122
24	65	64	64	64	125	124	123
25	66	65	65	65	126	125	125
26	68	67	67	66	128	127	126
27	69	68	68	67	129	128	128
28	71	70	70	68	132	131	131
29	72	71	71	69	133	132	132
30	74	73	73	70	135	134	134
31	75	74	74	71	136	135	135
32	77	76	76	72	138	137	137
33	78	77	77	73	139	138	138
34	80	79	79	74	141	140	140
35	81	80	80	75	142	141	141
36	83	82	82	76	144	143	143
37	84	83	83	77	145	144	144
38	86	85	85	78	147	146	146
39	87	86	86	79	148	147	147
40	89	88	88	80	149	149	149
41	90	89	89	81	151	150	150
42	92	91	91	82	152	152	152
43	93	92	92	83	154	153	153
44	95	94	94	84	155	155	155

INTELLIGENCE QUOTIENTS—AGES 15 TO 19

PERFORMANCE SCALE

WEIGHTED SCORE	15 I.Q.	16 I.Q.	17–19 I.Q.	WEIGHTED SCORE	15 I.Q.	16 I.Q.	17–19 I.Q.
5	34	˙34	34	45	93	92	91
6	36	36	36	46	95	93	92
7	37	37	37	47	96	95	94
8	39	39	39	48	98	96	95
9	40	40	40	49	99	98	96
10	42	42	41	50	101	99	98
11	43	43	43	51	102	100	99
12	45	44	44	52	104	102	101
13	46	46	46	53	105	103	102
14	48	47	47	54	107	105	104
15	49	49	48	55	108	106	105
16	50	50	50	56	110	108	106
17	52	52	51	57	111	109	108
18	53	53	53	58	113	110	109
19	55	54	54	59	114	112	111
20	56	56	56	60	116	113	112
21	58	57	57	61	117	115	113
22	59	59	58	62	119	116	115
23	61	60	60	63	120	118	116
24	62	62	61	64	122	119	118
25	64	63	63	65	123	120	119
26	65	65	64	66	124	122	121
27	67	66	65	67	126	123	122
28	68	67	67	68	127	125	123
29	70	69	68	69	129	126	125
30	71	70	70	70	130	128	126
31	73	72	71	71	132	129	128
32	74	73	72	72	133	131	129
33	76	75	74	73	135	132	130
34	77	76	75	74	136	133	132
35	79	77	77	75	138	135	133
36	80	79	78	76	139	136	135
37	82	80	80	77	141	138	136
38	83	82	81	78	142	139	137
39	85	83	82	79	144	141	139
40	86	85	84	80	145	142	140
41	87	86	85	81	147	143	142
42	89	87	87	82	148	145	143
43	90	89	88	83	150	146	145
44	92	90	89	84	151	148	146

INTELLIGENCE QUOTIENTS—AGES 20 TO 34

PERFORMANCE SCALE

WEIGHTED SCORE	20-24 I.Q.	25-29 I.Q.	30-34 I.Q.	WEIGHTED SCORE	20-24 I.Q.	25-29 I.Q.	30-34 I.Q.
5	37	42	48	45	92	96	99
6	39	44	49	46	93	97	101
7	40	45	51	47	95	98	102
8	41	46	52	48	96	100	103
9	43	48	53	49	97	101	104
10	44	49	55	50	99	102	106
11	46	50	56	51	100	104	107
12	47	52	57	52	102	105	108
13	48	53	58	53	103	106	110
14	50	54	60	54	104	108	111
15	51	56	61	55	106	109	112
16	52	57	62	56	107	110	114
17	54	58	64	57	109	112	115
18	55	60	65	58	110	113	116
19	56	61	66	59	111	114	117
20	58	62	67	60	113	116	119
21	59	64	69	61	114	117	120
22	61	65	70	62	115	118	121
23	62	66	71	63	117	120	122
24	63	68	73	64	118	121	124
25	65	69	74	65	119	122	125
26	66	70	75	66	121	124	126
27	67	72	76	67	122	125	127
28	69	73	78	68	124	126	129
29	70	74	79	69	125	128	130
30	72	76	80	70	126	129	131
31	73	77	81	71	128	130	133
32	74	78	83	72	129	132	134
33	76	80	84	73	130	133	135
34	77	81	85	74	132	134	137
35	78	82	87	75	133	136	138
36	80	84	88	76	135	137	139
37	81	85	89	77	136	138	140
38	83	86	90	78	137	140	142
39	84	88	92	79	139	141	143
40	85	89	93	80	140	142	144
41	87	90	94	81	141	144	145
42	88	92	96	82	143	145	147
43	89	93	97	83	144	146	148
44	91	94	98	84	146	148	149

INTELLIGENCE QUOTIENTS—AGES 35 TO 49

PERFORMANCE SCALE

WEIGHTED SCORES	35—39 I.Q.	40—44 I.Q.	45—49 I.Q.	WEIGHTED SCORES	35—39 I.Q.	40—44 I.Q.	45—49 I.Q.
5	54	59	63	45	103	106	110
6	55	60	64	46	104	107	111
7	56	61	65	47	105	109	112
8	57	62	67	48	107	110	113
9	58	63	68	49	108	111	114
10	60	65	69	50	109	112	115
11	61	66	70	51	110	113	116
12	62	67	71	52	112	115	118
13	63	68	72	53	113	116	119
14	65	69	74	54	114	117	120
15	66	70	75	55	115	118	121
16	67	72	76	56	117	119	122
17	68	73	77	57	118	121	123
18	70	74	78	58	119	122	125
19	71	75	79	59	120	123	126
20	72	76	81	60	121	124	127
21	73	78	82	61	123	125	128
22	74	79	83	62	124	127	129
23	76	80	84	63	125	128	130
24	77	81	85	64	126	129	132
25	78	82	86	65	128	130	133
26	80	84	88	66	129	131	134
27	81	85	89	67	130	133	135
28	82	86	90	68	131	134	136
29	83	87	91	69	133	135	137
30	84	88	92	70	134	136	138
31	86	90	93	71	135	137	140
32	87	91	94	72	136	139	141
33	88	92	96	73	137	140	142
34	89	93	97	74	139	141	143
35	91	94	98	75	140	142	144
36	92	96	99	76	141	143	145
37	93	97	100	77	142	145	147
38	94	98	101	78	144	146	148
39	96	99	103	79	145	147	149
40	97	100	104	80	146	148	150
41	98	102	105	81	147	149	151
42	99	103	106	82	149	150	152
43	100	104	107	83	150	152	154
44	102	105	108	84	151	153	155

INDEX

Abilities, effect of mental disorders on, 146

Ability, different types of, 4, 5

Adult I.Q.'s, 28, 30, 189

Adult mental age, 15, 22, 30

Age, as factor in calculating adult I.Q.'s, 12, 28, 30, 31; as factor in mental deterioration, 56, 60; as factor in standardization, 103; in relation to brain weight, 59–61; in relation to decline of various mental functions, 56–61, 64; of maximum mental ability, 25, 56, 200; regression equation for, on test scores, 143; tables of mean test scores, 118–119, 222

Alcoholic psychosis, memory disturbances in, 67, 84

Alexander, W. P., 9, 10

Alpha Intelligence tests, 14, 16, 32, 33, 38, 53, 76, 78, 80, 81, 90, 108, 117, 127, 129, 140

Altus, Lt. W. D., AGD., U.S.A., 172

Aphasia, disturbance of Gestalt function in, 69

Arithmetic reasoning test, description of, 82; directions for, 175; scoring of, 175

Army Memoirs, 87

Army Performance tests, 14, 16, 88, 95

Arthur, G., 92, 126

Average intelligence, statistical limits of, 39–41, 190

Babcock, H., 63, 68

Balinsky, B., 130, 157

Bellevue Intelligence Scales, directions for administering, 171–213

Bellevue Psychiatric Hospital, 136

Bellevue Tests, basis of selection, 75–77; mean scores and S.D.'s of Full Scale, 122; of Performance Scale, 123; of Verbal Scale, 122; of subtests, 222; method of weighting, 117

Bender, L., 68, 69

Beta Intelligence tests, 14, 16, 33, 53, 76, 90, 95

Binet, A., contributions of, 6, 14, 19

Block design test, description of, 91–94; directions for, 183–185; scoring of, 185

Borderline intelligence, statistical limits of, 40, 190

Bown, M.D., 149

Brain weight, variations with age, 59, 61

Bright Normal, definition of, 41; statistical limits of, 41, 190

Burt, C., 25, 104

C.A., psychometric definition of, 23

Cattell, McK., 58

Clinical features of Bellevue Scale, 146–148

Coefficients of variation, of I.Q.'s at each age, 124; of weighted score, 121

Common factor, 5, 7

Comprehension test, description of, 80–81; directions for, 173–174; scoring of, 174

Conrad, H. S., 29, 59, 106

Cornell-Coxe Performance tests, 87–95

Correlations between Bellevue and other scales, 134; between Bellevue subtests and total scale, 224

Court of General Sessions, use of Bellevue Tests, 136

Criteria for scoring, for general comprehension test, 191–198; for similarities test, 198–202; for vocabulary test, 202–213

Criticisms of I.Q. discrepancies, 136–140

Curve of mental growth, 27

Curve of mental growth and decline, 29

DeCroly, 87

Dementia praecox, 152

255